ABNORMAL PSYCHOLOGY

*the text of this book is printed
on 100% recycled paper*

ABOUT THE AUTHORS

WALTER J. COVILLE received the degree of Doctor of Philosophy from Fordham University in 1942 and is a certified psychologist in the State of New York. He is a consultant to St. Vincent's Hospital of the City of New York, where he served as Director and Chief of Clinical Psychology for 18 years and had developed, in 1946, one of the first active departments of clinical psychology in a general hospital. A private clinical psychologist, specializing in personality assessment, Dr. Coville serves as consultant to seminaries, business, and industry in matters of executive selection. He is President-elect of the American Catholic Psychological Association. He has held the rank of Adjunct Associate Professor, Graduate School, Fordham University and is a Fellow of the divisions of Clinical and Consulting Psychology of the American Psychological Association. His publications include articles on human relations training and personality assessment.

TIMOTHY W. COSTELLO received his degree of Doctor of Philosophy at Fordham University in 1944 and is a certified psychologist in the State of New York. He is Professor of Psychology and Management in the Graduate School of Business Administration, New York University, and is educational director and Chief Psychologist of the Staten Island Mental Health Society. For the past fifteen years he has been concerned with the application of Clinical Psychology to management development and human relations programs for business and industry and has written articles concerning these topics. He is a member of the American Psychological Association.

The late FABIAN L. ROUKE completed his work for the degree of Doctor of Philosophy at Fordham University just prior to World War II. He was Professor of Psychology and Head of Department at Manhattan College, New York City. A certified psychologist in New York State, and an ABEPP Diplomate in Clinical Psychology, he served as consultant to industry on problems of morale and to police and other investigating agencies, as a lie detection expert. He helped found the Manhattan College Institute for Forensic Research and the Metropolitan Law Enforcement Conference, a group which brings together professional clinicians and those active in police work for education and discussion. He wrote numerous articles on lie detection and criminal motivation for textbooks and journals and was a Fellow of the Division of Clinical and Abnormal Psychology of the American Psychological Association.

COLLEGE OUTLINE SERIES

ABNORMAL PSYCHOLOGY

WALTER J. COVILLE
TIMOTHY W. COSTELLO
FABIAN L. ROUKE

BARNES & NOBLE BOOKS
A DIVISION OF HARPER & ROW, PUBLISHERS
New York, Evanston, San Francisco, London

Manufactured in the United States of America

PREFACE

This Outline presents a descriptive and interpretative summary of the field of abnormal behavior beginning with a discussion of the differences between the abnormal and the normal, tracing the history of man's efforts to understand deviations in behavior, and analyzing current theories which attempt to explain the development of personality and the causes of mental illness. After examining the various kinds of abnormal behavior in accordance with the most recent classification system of the American Psychiatric Association, this book describes diagnostic and therapeutic procedures and techniques used in the field of prevention. The Outline is not exclusively oriented toward any one school of thought, although the principal theoretical orientations are summarized objectively. This book may be used either in conjunction with a standard textbook or as a basic text to be supplemented by assigned outside readings in accordance with the preferences of the instructor.

In preparing this Outline, the authors had in mind its usefulness not only to the college student but also the general reader as well as practitioners in the fields of personnel, teaching, law, social service, religion, nursing and the medical specialties. They hope that for these groups it will provide a ready compendium of accurate and up-to-date factual material about human behavior. Particular care has been devoted to the index for this purpose.

For editorial assistance and constructive help in the organization of materials, the authors gratefully acknowledge their debt to Dr. Samuel Smith and to Mrs. Suzanne Della Corte of the Barnes and Noble staff, to Mr. George Cantzlaar, who smoothed their phrasing in many places, and who also prepared the index, and to Miss Dorothy Heslin, who typed the manuscripts.

TABLE OF CONTENTS

ABNORMAL PSYCHOLOGY

THE NATURE AND SCOPE
OF ABNORMAL BEHAVIOR

The newcomer to the study of abnormal psychology does not approach the subject totally unprepared. Indeed, he is likely to come too well prepared—"conditioned" would be more to the point—with scattered bits of information and misinformation, preconceived notions, and fixed emotional prejudices toward abnormal people. Perhaps he has witnessed examples of bizarre behavior in public places or even in his own home; or he may have overheard or participated in family discussions about a mentally ill relative or friend. At the very least he has had ample glimpses of abnormal personalities in news releases and feature articles; in radio, television, and stage productions; and in books and magazines. In some of these instances the sources have been reliable and the content valid, but more often authenticity has suffered because the intention was to divert or shock rather than to enlighten.

Such isolated encounters with the subject of this Outline are not conducive to an ordered appreciation of the factors operative in abnormal behavior. Lacking are two of the requirements essential to the scientific method: controlled data and trained, unprejudiced observation. A more significant point, however, is that considerable disagreement prevails as to what constitutes abnormality. It is therefore necessary at the outset to bring this concept into proper perspective. This will be done in the present chapter by (1) discussing the relation between normal and abnormal, (2) describing the science of abnormal psychology and related disciplines, (3) examining the scope of the social and medical problems that are generated by personality disorders, and (4) finally, discussing the classification of mental disorders.

THE NORMAL AND THE ABNORMAL

Considered from any point of view, the concept of normality-abnormality is a relative one. Departures from whatever norm one

1

may accept can be so slight as to cause no concern at all, or they can be so striking as to leave no doubt of their abnormal nature. There is, however, no strict dichotomy in which normal and abnormal will always be readily distinguishable. In any large group of persons studied we cannot say with assurance that "these are normal" unless the abnormalities are so extreme as to be obvious. Observe how this holds true from the principal points of view: the pathological, the statistical, and the cultural.

Pathological Point of View. Considered from the pathological point of view, abnormal behavior is the result of a diseased or disordered state evidenced by the presence of certain clinically recognized symptoms (for example, unfounded fears in the psychoneurotic, delusions or hallucinations in the psychotic, antisocial behavior in the person suffering from a sociopathic personality disturbance). Carried to its ultimate conclusion, this point of view would lead to the assumption that one who is possessed of a "normal" personality is without symptoms. Experience teaches otherwise, for it is the rare individual who is entirely symptom-free, especially under conditions of stress. Nevertheless, certain symptoms or syndromes (complexes of symptoms) are undeniable signs of a disordered personality, and persons exhibiting such symptoms can be regarded as abnormal.

Statistical Point of View. This is the graphic, mathematical approach to the question of what (or who) is normal or abnormal. The curve of *normal distribution* seen in the accompanying illustration (showing the results of a study of levels of intelligence in the

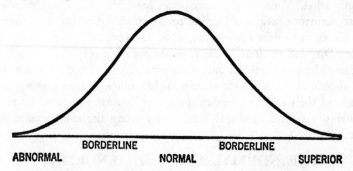

BORDERLINE   BORDERLINE
ABNORMAL   NORMAL   SUPERIOR

After James D. Page, *Abnormal Psychology* (New York: McGraw-Hill, 1947), p. 14.

general population) portrays the statistical concept of normality and abnormality. It will be noted that most of the subjects studied are clustered about the middle of the curve; from the statistical point of view, it would be held that these subjects are normal and that the fewer cases on either side of the middle of the curve are abnormal. By statistical convention the "normal range" embraces roughly the middle two-thirds of most groups studied.

This approach offers undoubted reliability and usefulness when one is measuring tangible factors such as weight and height. Psychological traits offer a much greater challenge. Statistical methods are used with success in the measurement of intelligence (see Chapter 16, Mental Deficiency), but the more complex characteristics of the total personality present serious problems, particularly in the areas of phenomena to be investigated and in their evaluation. The validity and applicability of findings in statistical studies of abnormal behavior and personality depend on the traits selected for measurement and the statistical criteria employed.

Cultural Point of View. From this vantage point, the behavior and attitudes of an individual are regarded as normal or abnormal according to the social (cultural) milieu in which he moves. The community is a hard taskmaster and tends to be impatient with departures from its established mores. Reasonable latitude may be allowed for individuality of expression, but radical digressions which create turmoil in the individual and those about him are usually held to be evidence of abnormal personality. Today, however, two factors influence this situation: First, in a world society in which culture patterns are ever crossing and mingling, it must be increasingly recognized that customs and attitudes felt to be normal in one cultural group may be called abnormal in another. Second, what was considered abnormal a generation or a century ago may be accepted in present-day society; in some areas of human relationships such change is slow, while in others it is meteoric. The impact of these two factors and of immediate community pressure on the personality of the individual cannot be ignored and must be made a part of any conclusion as to whether a person is normal or abnormal.

Criteria for a Normal Personality. A comprehensive description of a healthy and normally functioning individual is provided in a list of criteria published by Maslow and Mittelmann.* Somewhat modified by the present authors, this list of criteria follows.

1. Adequate feelings of security.

* See A. H. Maslow and B. Mittelmann, *Principles of Abnormal Psychology* (rev. ed.; New York: Harper, 1951), pp. 14–15.

2. Reasonable degree of self-evaluation (insight).

3. Realistic life goals.

4. Effective contact with reality.

5. Integration and consistency of personality.

6. Ability to learn from experience.

7. Adequate spontaneity.

8. Appropriate emotionality.

9. Ability to satisfy the requirements of the group, coupled with some degree of emancipation from the group (as expressed in individuality).

10. Adequate but unexaggerated bodily desires, with the ability to gratify them in an approved fashion.

The reader is cautioned to examine these criteria carefully, with the understanding that they all suggest relative standards. The normal person is not expected to be a paragon of excellence with regard to each of them. He may be somewhat deficient in one or more characteristics, but still enjoy good over-all mental health; that is to say, he will be considered normal. If, however, he is deficient in too many of these characteristics or woefully deficient in one or two, he will probably be considered abnormal.

ABNORMAL PSYCHOLOGY AND RELATED DISCIPLINES

In its efforts to master the problems of disordered personality and behavior, abnormal psychology comes into contact with and draws upon many other disciplines. Some of them are closely related to abnormal psychology in the professional or scientific plane. Others are more or less indirectly associated with it, depending on the nature of the particular problem that is being studied; these include religion, education, law, sociology, biometrics, and anthropology, to mention a few. Definitions of the more intimately related fields follow.

Abnormal psychology—the branch of psychology which concerns itself with the study of all forms of mental disorder or abnormality. It strives to define and classify the causes of personality and behavioral disturbances, with a view to establishing a basis for their treatment in individuals and for the resolution of the social problems which they generate.

Clinical psychology—the applied aspect of abnormal psychology, which includes diagnostic interviewing and testing, remedial work (as with speech disabilities), counseling, and the treatment known as psychotherapy.

Psychiatry—a branch of medicine specializing in the diagnosis, prevention, and treatment of mental and emotional disorders.

Psychoanalysis—a method of psychological interpretation of the personality; a specialized form of psychotherapy based on the Freudian conception of psychodynamics.

Neurology—a branch of medicine concerned with the diagnosis and treatment of disorders of the nervous system. Within neurology is the specialty of *neurosurgery*.

Psychiatric social work—a branch of social work concentrating on the social problems associated with psychiatric disorders. From its clinical application, recommendations are made for the management of the patient's social situation (e.g., his family relationships, work and career objectives, and marital problems) as part of the therapeutic program.

Mental hygiene—not a professional discipline, but a movement primarily dedicated to the prevention of psychological disturbances and the promotion of improved treatment facilities for persons suffering from mental illnesses.

SCOPE OF THE PROBLEM OF ABNORMAL BEHAVIOR

Abnormal behavior constitutes a major medical and social problem. In its most measurable aspect (institutional population) it commands serious attention. Each day in the United States nearly 700 persons are admitted to mental hospitals or to psychiatric services of general hospitals. Close to 800,000 hospital beds (about half the beds in hospitals of *all* types in this country) are occupied by patients suffering from mental disorders. Another 120,000 persons are under care in institutions for mental defectives. Still another 100,000 or more convalescent patients are carried on the books of mental hospitals while they are receiving treatment at follow-up clinics or being cared for under a foster home plan.

Hospital statistics, however, provide only one segment of the total picture of personality disturbance and abnormal behavior. Several other groups of persons contribute to the growth of this social and medical problem. One such group comprises 950,000 chronic alcoholics, 4,000,000 problem drinkers, and 50,000 drug addicts. Another includes an indeterminate number of psychopaths and criminals, not to mention 265,000 children seen in juvenile courts each year. Divorce statistics (one out of every four marriages) are indicative of the prevalence of maladjustment. Personality problems are surely evident in the 17,000 suicides yearly. In addition to the foregoing is the large number of individuals with personality or behavior disorders who are treated in outpatient mental hygiene clinics or by privately practising psychiatrists and clinical psychologists.

Psychosomatic Illness. With the increasing attention that is being accorded the psychosomatic approach to medicine has come the realization that, among a great many of the patients being treated for the general run of medical disorders, psychological factors play either a minor or a major role in the background of the illness. One director of a large general hospital has estimated that 75 per cent of the patients seen at his institution's outpatient department during one year were suffering from either purely psychoneurotic symptoms, psychoneurotic symptoms superimposed on somatic disease, or somatic symptoms superimposed on psychoneurotic disorder.

Lessons from Industry and the Military. In recent years, numerous studies of the effect of psychoneurotic disorder have been taken from industry and the military.

INDUSTRY. Studies of absenteeism in industry show that nearly two-thirds of industrial absences are due to illness that is principally or exclusively neurotic in nature. "Accident-prone" individuals aggravate problems of safety in industrial plants. The extent to which personality disorder affects the economy can be deduced from the estimate that about $1,750,000,000 in potential earnings is lost annually because of mental illness or maladjustment.

MILITARY. Fruitful sources of information on the scope of personality disorders are the statistics amassed in two world wars. Before Pearl Harbor nearly 50 per cent of all patients being cared for in veterans' hospitals suffered from neuropsychiatric disorders. Approximately 18 per cent of all men called up for service in World War II were rejected as being mentally or emotionally unqualified. Over one-third of the medical discharges during that war prior to V-E (Victory in Europe) day were neuropsychiatric cases.

Summary. The scope of the problem of abnormal behavior is summed up in two statistical predictions which are generally accepted in the mental health field:

1. Of every twenty persons now living, one will eventually be

admitted to a mental hospital and another will at some time during his life be at least temporarily incapacitated by some form of mental disorder, though not seriously enough to require hospitalization. This indicates that 10 per cent of the newborn will at some time in their lives experience either permanent or temporary, severe or mild, mental disorder.

2. In one of every five families there will be occasion within the year to call on the services of a psychiatrist, clinical psychologist, or mental hygiene clinic, if not indeed to make use of mental hospital facilities.

HOW THE PROBLEM IS BEING MET

It cannot be said with assurance that mental disorder is more prevalent today than it was, either at the turn of the century or a hundred years ago. Data are not available which would permit a reliable comparison. There can be little doubt, though, that mental abnormality as a medical and social problem has received increasing attention. As the stigma attached to mental disorder has subsided and the mental hospital has been gradually accepted as a substitute for the "upstairs back room" or the almshouse, the demand for public facilities has grown by leaps and bounds. Need has consistently outdistanced supply; as many new mental hospitals have been built and as more effective therapeutic techniques have been devised, the greater has become the load which the hospitals have had to carry.

There are now about six hundred mental hospitals in the United States. About half of them are public, the largest being state hospitals with resident patient populations ranging from a little over a thousand to more than eight thousand. There are specifically designated psychiatric services in roughly one hundred general hospitals. In 1957 there were over two thousand outpatient psychiatric facilities. In 1956 the cost of public facilities (federal and state) dedicated to the treatment of patients with mental illnesses was about four billions of dollars.

Nevertheless, three of every four state mental hospitals are seriously overcrowded. The average mental hospital is 55 per cent understaffed in physicians, 74 per cent in psychologists, 67 per cent in psychiatric social workers, 79 per cent in registered nurses, and 20 per cent in ward attendants. (This problem is discussed further in Chapter 20, Mental Hygiene.) Although substantial progress has been made, it is apparent that the major tasks of diagnosis, prevention, and treatment remain to be accomplished.

CLASSIFICATION OF MENTAL DISORDERS

The modern grouping of mental disorders in a systematic classification has its basis in the work of EMIL KRAEPELIN (1856–1926). He was among the earliest investigators to observe that certain symptoms of mental illness tended to appear in clusters. This suggested to him that the clusters of symptoms (syndromes) were manifestations of specific types of mental disease. On this slender circumstantial basis Kraepelin described various disease entities and from his findings worked out the first modern classification of mental disorders.

Evolution of Classification. Kraepelin's nosologic system was followed for several decades, but with the evolution of improved diagnostic techniques and more discriminating interpretations of personality problems significant changes took place. For example, with the passage of time (into the third and fourth decades of this century) a large accumulation of clinical experience forced a new interpretation of the mental disorder called dementia praecox ("insanity of youth")—so named because it was commonly observed to emerge in adolescence. However, as more accurate statistics were compiled, individuals showing the clinical picture of "dementia praecox" grew to comprise the largest single diagnostic bloc of patients in mental hospitals; it was soon apparent that the most frequent age of onset was not during adolescence. A more dynamic approach to this disease led to the descriptive term "schizophrenia," which means a splitting up or a fragmentation of mental life so that the individual is incapable of appropriate, integrated responses to external reality.

Classification in America. In America the Kraepelin classification system underwent several modifications at the centers devoted to the study of mental diseases. Therefore, each large teaching center had its own classification system based on the predilections of the center's leading investigators. Such diversified interpretation was bound to hamper communication and complicate research efforts in the field. In 1917 the first rudimentary nomenclature was set up by the American Psychiatric Association (then known as the American Medico-Psychological Association), and through the efforts of Dr. Thomas Salmon and the National Committee for Mental Hygiene the system was adopted in hospitals and research centers throughout the country.

It is interesting to note that the tendency was still strong to assume a cause-and-effect relationship between mental states and immediate environmental influences. The largest category of psychoneuroses at that time included a diagnosis of "shell shock," which many psychiatrists regarded as a definite misnomer because a large number of men so diagnosed never left training camp and never heard shellfire. In World War II the same condition was described as "combat fatigue." However, this syndrome, like that which may be seen in response to economic disaster, or in the course of a great debacle, is now more properly recognized as an aspect of transient situational personality disorder (see Chapter 6).

The "APA" Classification Today. A major revision in the APA (American Psychiatric Association) classification was made in 1934 and this remained in use through the early years of World War II. The system, designed primarily for civilian use, proved to be inadequate for the clinical description of mental breakdowns occurring under military stress. Relatively minor personality disturbances arising specifically in the military setting were classified under "psychopathic" personality; men were diagnosed as "psychoneurotics" who were merely responding with transient neurotic symptoms to excessive stress. It was estimated that 90 per cent of the cases treated by the military were not being properly classified. Under these circumstances the Navy in 1944 and the Army in 1945 established systems of classification which were more adaptable to their purposes. This only added to the already existing confusion and by 1950 there was general agreement on the need for a single psychiatric nomenclature. A proposed revision, developed through the joint efforts of the National Institute for Mental Health and the American Psychiatric Association, was circularized among a nationally representative group of medical practitioners in neurology, psychiatry, and psychoanalysis. The resultant classification was adopted in 1951 and a manual was published in 1952.

This new APA classification, which will be found as an Appendix of this book, separates all mental disorders into two major groups:

1. Those in which the disturbance in mental functioning is associated primarily with brain damage (that is, "organogenic").

2. Those in which adjustment difficulties are more general and brain damage is either not demonstrable or not relatively significant (that is, "psychogenic").

Groups of related psychiatric syndromes within these two general categories are designated "disorders"; where such disorders need to be further subdivided, they are termed "reactions."

In the foreword to its classification manual, the American Psychiatric Association suggests that the system takes into account the modern descriptive nature of all psychiatric diagnoses. Two virtues of the structure of the new classification are: (1) It makes possible the gathering of data for future clarification of thinking concerning etiology, pathology, prognosis, and treatment in the field of mental disorders. (2) In the future, when new concepts of diagnosis become crystallized and generally agreed upon, they may be fitted into the structure of this system without need to make any radical change in the over-all pattern.

Our next chapter reviews briefly the historical background of the problem of mental illness, and thus provides a perspective for evaluation of the contemporary situation.

2

HISTORY OF THE PROBLEM
OF ABNORMAL BEHAVIOR

The problem of mental disorder is probably as old as man. Recorded history reports a broad range of interpretations of abnormal behavior and methods for its alleviation or eradication, which have generally reflected the degree of enlightenment and the trends of religious, philosophical, and social beliefs and practices of the times. It is not surprising that earlier efforts to deal with the problem were fraught with difficulties and that the evolution of a science of abnormal psychology has been painfully slow. This has been the case for two reasons:

First, the very nature of the problems generated by abnormal behavior has made it a "thing apart," arousing fear, shame, and guilt in the families and communities of those afflicted. Hence, the management of the mentally disordered has been turned over to the state and the church, which have been the traditional guardians of both group and individual behavior. *Second,* the evolution of all the sciences has been slow and sporadic, many of the most important advances having been achieved only against great resistance. While this has been more typical of abnormal psychology than of other disciplines, the difference is only relative. In reviewing the historical account which follows, one should restrain the impulse to view with alarm or to criticize too severely; although it is true that in earlier times the abnormal person was misunderstood and often mistreated, the lot of the "normal" individual was not a much happier one.

PRIMITIVE PERIOD

Archaeological findings suggest that some types of mental illness must have been recognized as far back as the Stone Age. Primordial remains reveal that attempts were made to relieve brain pressure by chipping away an area of the skull. Though the procedure was similar to the operative technique now known as trephining, there is serious question as to whether it was based on any knowledge of brain pathology. It seems more likely that the operation was performed in the belief that in this way an avenue of escape was provided for "evil spirits." Our knowledge of primitive "psychiatry" does not go beyond speculations suggested by such primordial remains.

PRECLASSICAL PERIOD

Although, as the reader will discover, primitive superstitions persisted into and beyond the Classical period, history shows that attempts were being made before the golden ages of Greece and Rome to find a more rational approach to the understanding and treatment of the mentally disordered.

In the Orient. About 2600 B.C. in *China* some forms of faith healing, diversion of interest, and change of environment emerged as the chief methods for treating mental disorders. By 1140 B.C. institutions for the "insane" had been established there, and patients were being cared for until "recovery." In the writings of physicians in *India* around 600 B.C. are found detailed descriptions of some forms of mental disease and epilepsy, with recommendations for kindness in treatment.

In the Middle East. *Egyptian* and *Babylonian* manuscripts dating back to 5000 B.C. describe the behavior of the mentally disturbed as being due to influences of evil spirits. Aside from the practice of trephining, treatment was restricted almost exclusively to the ministrations of priests and magicians. Biblical sources indicate that the *Hebrews* conceived of mental illness as a punishment from God and that treatment was principally along lines of atonement to Him.

CLASSICAL PERIOD

As in all areas of scientific and social thought, in the era of classical Greece and Rome important strides were made toward a more reasonable and humane treatment of the mentally disordered, and the first glimmer of a medical approach to the problem appeared.

In Greece. Some of the more significant assumptions of Greek thought have been confirmed by modern research and much of the terminology of modern psychiatry (as indeed of medicine and science in general) is a legacy from this period. The humane, rational approach to mental illness that emerged during this era was due largely to the findings of the following men:

PYTHAGORAS (c. 500 B.C.). Before 500 B.C. priest-physicians combined suggestion, diet, massage, and recreation with their more regular prescriptions of incantations and sacrifices, but in all treatment the guiding motive was appeasement of good or evil spirits. However, Pythagoras was the first to teach a natural explanation for mental illness. He identified the brain as the center of intelligence and attributed mental disease to a disorder of the brain.

HIPPOCRATES (460–377 B.C.). The "Father of Medicine" held that brain disturbance is the cause of mental disorder. He emphasized that treatment should be physical in nature, urging the use of baths, special diets, bleeding, and drugs. Hippocrates taught the importance of heredity and of predisposition to mental illness. He related sensory and motor disturbances to head injuries. Anticipating modern psychiatry, he also realized that the analysis of dreams can be useful in understanding the patient's personality.

PLATO (429–347 B.C.). This Greek philosopher manifested keen insight into the human personality. He recognized the existence of individual differences in intelligence and in other psychological characteristics, and he asserted that man is motivated by "natural appetites." To Plato, mental disorder is partly moral, partly physical, and partly divine in origin. He described the patient-doctor relationship in the treatment pattern, believed that fantasy and dreams are substitute satisfactions for inhibited "passions," and introduced the concept of the criminal as a mentally disturbed person. Plato also pointed out the significance of cultural influences as factors in thinking and action.

ARISTOTLE (384–322 B.C.). Aristotle accepted a physiological basis for mental illness, as taught by Hippocrates. While he did consider the possibility of a psychological cause, he rejected it, and so strong was his influence on philosophical thought that for nearly two thousand years his point of view discouraged further exploration along these lines.

ALEXANDER THE GREAT (356–322 B.C.). Alexander established sanatoriums for the mentally ill, where occupation, entertainment, and exercise were provided—practices which were continued during the later Greek and Roman periods.

In Rome. The Romans, for the most part, continued to follow the teachings of the Greek physicians and philosophers in their treatment of mental illness. Greek physicians, the most outstanding of whom were Aesclepiades, Areateus, and Galen, settled in Rome, where they continued their studies and teachings.

AESCLEPIADES (c. 124–c. 40 B.C.). This Greek-born physician and philosopher was the first to differentiate between acute and chronic mental illness. He developed mechanical devices for the comfort and relaxation of mental patients; he opposed bleeding, restraints, and isolation in dungeons. Whereas his predecessors had considered both delusions and hallucinations under one heading ("phantasia"), Aesclepiades differentiated between the two.

ARETAEUS. (fl. 1st to 2nd centuries A.D.). Aretaeus was the first to suggest that mental illness is a psychological extension of normal personality traits. He believed that there existed a predisposition to certain forms of mental disorder. One of his original thoughts (placing the seat of mental disease in the brain *and* the abdomen) foreshadowed the psychosomatic approach to medicine.

GALEN (c. 130–c. 200 A.D.). Galen's contribution to medical science, though incalculably valuable in one respect, served to retard development in another. Like Hippocrates, who antedated him by seven centuries, he gathered and organized an enormous amount of data concerning mental and physical illness and conducted studies in the anatomy of the nervous system and its relation to human behavior. He recognized the duality of physical and psychic causation in mental illness, enumerating such varied factors as head injuries, alcoholism, fear, adolescence, menopausal changes, economic difficulties, and love affairs. On the other hand, like many others of his time, he permitted his concern with teleology to becloud his scientific conclusions. He felt impelled to assign specific divine or astrological influence to this or that organ of the body. Since his prestige was great, for centuries after his death progress was encumbered by controversies over the metaphysical aspects of his contributions and, thus, independent thinking in the medical sciences was delayed until well into the eighteenth century.

In Arabia. The last faint echo of the efforts of the classicists to conquer the problem of mental disorder was heard not in the West, but in Arabia, where AVICENNA (c. 980–1037 A.D.) and later his follower AVERRHOES (1126–1198 A.D.) maintained a scientific approach to the mentally ill and urged humane treatment. Elsewhere, as we shall see, a return to primitive notions prevailed.

MEDIEVAL PERIOD

With the dissolution of Graeco-Roman civilization, learning and scientific progress in Europe experienced a grave setback. Ancient superstitions and demonology were revived and contemporary theological thinking did little to discourage the "spiritistic" approach to the problem of mental illness. Exorcism was considered imperative; accordingly, incantations were regarded as a legitimate adjunct of medicine. Even the application of perfectly rational techniques had to be accompanied by the pronouncement of mystical phrases.

The best physicians of the time were given to the use of amulets. ALEXANDER of TRALLES (525–605 A.D.), for example, who stressed the importance of constitutional factors and related them to specific types of mental disorder, and who studied frontal lobe injuries and noted accompanying changes in behavior, treated colic by the application of a stone on which an image of Hercules overcoming the lion was carved.

The Dancing Mania. At intervals from the tenth to the fifteenth centuries the dancing mania, also referred to as "mass madness," in which large groups of people danced wildly until they dropped from exhaustion, was seen in Europe. In Italy the condition was called "tarantism" because the mania was thought to be due to the bite of the tarantula—a venomous ground spider. Elsewhere in western Europe the mania was called "St. Vitus's Dance." It is difficult to say whether these seemingly epidemic manifestations have been greatly exaggerated in the telling. It has been suggested that a large number of people may have been suffering from various forms of chorea. Fear of this unexplained disorder may have risen to a mass suggestibility and hysteria which mounted unchecked and which subsequently have been recorded as a single clinical entity.

Witchcraft: Belief in Demonology. The period from the fifteenth to the eighteenth centuries comprises a sorry chapter of history with respect to the fate of the mentally ill. Their afflictions were generally ascribed to possession by the devil; and treatment, consisting chiefly of attempts to "cast out the demon," was hardly distinguishable from punishment. The "Black Death" (bubonic plague) had ravaged Europe in the fourteenth century, and the resulting depression and fear rendered whole peoples highly susceptible to the ministrations of witchcraft. The humane, scientific approach to the mentally ill (for that matter, to all illness) was indeed at a low ebb.

Late in the fifteenth century the plight of abnormal people was intensified by the publication of *Malleus Maleficarum, The Hammer of Witches which destroyeth witches and their heresy as with a two-*

edged sword, by Henry Kraemer and James Sprenger, of the Order of Preachers. Their book, appearing in 1484 and fortified by an approving papal bull of Innocent VIII was to be the handbook of inquisitors for two hundred years. The bull authorized inquisitors to proceed according to the regulations of the Inquisition; ecclesiastical courts ferreted out persons thought to be "possessed of the Devil"; the unfortunates were then turned over to civil authorities to be tortured or executed. Sprenger and Kraemer met some early resistance from cooler heads in the church and community but soon won support from people already imbued with a fear of witchcraft; their crusade caught fire and thereafter spread throughout both Roman Catholic and Reformed centers in Europe. So firmly entrenched was the belief in witches that the persecution of witches broke out sporadically for the next three centuries. (In America the most notorious trials for witchcraft occurred in Salem, Massachusetts, in 1692.)

Institutional Care of the Mentally Ill. Emblematic of the kind of institutional care afforded the mentally ill during the late medieval-Renaissance periods was that seen at "Bedlam." (The name is a contraction of Bethlehem—as early as 1400 the monastery of St. Mary of Bethlehem in London began caring for lunatics; in 1547 the monastery was officially converted into a mental hospital.) Because of the inhumanity of the treatment there, "Bedlam" has become synonymous with anything that is cruel in the management of the mentally disturbed. But this era was not entirely without examples of tolerance and mercy. The shrine of St. Dymphna at Gheel in Belgium (established in the fifteenth century) not only lent solace to thousands of afflicted persons who visited there, but also grew gradually into a "colony" which was dedicated to the care of the mentally ill. Its work still goes on, and Gheel is regarded as the model for similar colony plans elsewhere.

RENAISSANCE PERIOD

Although the mentally disturbed became engulfed in the morass of superstition and inhumanity, in certain countries of Europe voices were raised in the cause of reason by enlightened men of religion, medicine, and philosophy. Their efforts during this period can well be described as "light in the darkness."

In Switzerland. PARACELSUS (THEOPHRASTUS VON HOHENHEIM, 1493–1541) rejected demonology, recognized psychological causes of mental illness, and proposed a theory of "bodily magnetism"—a forerunner of hypnosis. Like Hippocrates, he suggested the sexual nature of hysteria. However, like so many otherwise reasonable men of his time, he laid great store on astral influences, assigning to various planets control over specific organs of the body.

In Germany. HEINRICH CORNELIUS AGRIPPA (1486–1535) fought against the hypocrisy and bloodthirsty application of the edicts of the Inquisition. A scholar and later advocate of the city of Metz, Agrippa was persecuted and reviled for his views. He died in poverty. JOHANN WEYER (1515–1588) was a physician who studied under Agrippa. In 1563 he published a scientific analysis of witchcraft, repudiating demon causation in mental illness. His clinical descriptions of mental disorders were remarkably concise, uncluttered with opinions and theological illusions. Weyer is regarded by some as the "Father of Modern Psychiatry."

In England. REGINALD SCOT (1538–1599) published a scholarly, painstaking study entitled *The Discovery of Witchcraft: Proving That the Compacts and Contracts of Witches and Devils . . . Are But Erroneous Novelties and Imaginary Conceptions.* But James I ordered the book seized and burned, and he published a refutation of Scot's views.

In France. ST. VINCENT DE PAUL (1576–1660) urged a more humane approach to the mentally ill. St. Vincent emphasized the fact that mental disease differs in no way from bodily disease. In the hospital which he founded at St. Lazare, he put into practice what he held to be a basic Christian principle, namely, that we are as much obligated to care humanely for the mentally ill as for the physically ill.

EIGHTEENTH TO TWENTIETH CENTURIES

The transition from the demonological to the scientific approach to mental abnormality was not accomplished overnight. In France, for example, capital punishment for convicted "sorcerers" was not abolished until 1862. The first general trend toward specialized treatment of the mentally ill probably came in the wake of the social, political, economic, and scientific reforms that characterized the latter half of the eighteenth century.

In France. Shortly after the Revolution, PHILIPPE PINEL (1745–1826) removed the chains from the inmates at Bicêtre and provided pleasant, sanitary housing along with promenades and workshops. Later, at Salpêtrière, he introduced the practice of maintaining case histories of patients, record-keeping and the training of attendants. ESQUIROL (1772–1840) continued Pinel's work; through his efforts ten new mental hospitals were established in France.

In England. WILLIAM TUKE (1732–1822), a layman and a Quaker, interested the Society of Friends in establishing the York Retreat in 1796. Through his urging, special training was instituted for nurses working in this field. JOHN CONOLLY (1794–1866), founder of a small medical association which later became the British Medical Association, was mainly responsible for the wide acceptance of nonviolent measures in the treatment of the mentally ill.

In Germany. ANTON MULLER (1755–1827), working in a hospital for mental diseases, preached humane treatment of the insane and protested against brutal restraint of patients.

In Italy. VICENZO CHIARUGI (1759–1820) published his "Hundred Observations" on the mentally ill and demanded humanization of treatment of the deranged.

In Latin America. The first asylum for the "insane" in the Americas was San Hipolito, organized in 1566 or 1570 by BERNADINO ALVAREZ in Mexico City, but it is difficult to say whether it was really more than a place of confinement. Elsewhere in Latin America the earliest mental hospitals began to appear in the 1820's. As late as 1847, visitors to Mexico and Peru reported that "lunatics" were displayed for the amusement of the populace, who paid for the exhibition (as had been done at Bedlam three centuries earlier).

In the United States. In Philadelphia the Blockely Insane Asylum was opened in 1752. The only other institution for the mentally disturbed in the United States before the nineteenth century was the Eastern State Lunatic Asylum in Virginia, opened in 1773.

Humanitarian treatment of the mentally ill was encouraged by BENJAMIN RUSH (1745–1813), who is generally accepted as the "Father of American Psychiatry." Rush organized the first course in psychiatry and published the first systematic treatise on the subject in the United States. In the latter half of the nineteenth century, DOROTHEA LYNDE DIX (1802–1887) carried on a militant campaign for reform in the care of the mentally ill. She was responsible for a more enlightened attitude and improved programs in twenty states; in New York her efforts resulted in the State Care Act of 1889, which did away with confinement of the mentally disturbed in jails and almshouses. Her influence was felt also in Canada, Scotland, and England.

At Utica State Lunatic Asylum (now Utica State Hospital) an Association of Superintendents of American Institutions for the Insane was formed in 1846; the name was changed to American Medico-Psychological Association in the 1880's. It finally became the American Psychiatric Association of today. Its professional scientific publication, originally called the *American Journal of Insanity,* has been published continuously for over a hundred years.

In the early years of the twentieth century, CLIFFORD BEERS (1876–1943) described his experiences as a mental patient in the book *A Mind That Found Itself.* The wide distribution of this volume stimulated public interest in a movement to improve conditions in mental hospitals and gave rise to the formation of the National Committee for Mental Hygiene, in which Beers played an active role. That organization was later incorporated, along with other smaller groups, into the National Association for Mental Health.

In the Western World: National and International Efforts. The mental hygiene movement spread throughout the Western world. During the first half of the twentieth century a variety of national and international organizations were established to aid in the development of improved facilities for the mentally ill. In recent decades there has been a trend toward public acceptance of both humanitarian and scientific approaches to the problem of mental abnormality. This new attitude has been reflected in the activities of world organizations such as the World Health Organization, UNESCO, and the World Federation of Mental Health, as well as in those of innumerable national and local public and private agencies. (For a discussion of recent mental hygiene techniques and programs, see Chapter 20, Mental Hygiene.)

THE MODERN ERA: DEVELOPMENTS
IN PSYCHIATRIC THOUGHT

The development of psychiatric thought and the subsequent contributions to the understanding of mental abnormality during the eighteenth to twentieth centuries may be summarized under two headings: organic interpretations and psychological interpretations.

Organic Interpretations. The importance of brain pathology in the causation of mental illness was recognized by ALBRECHT VON HALLER (1708–1777), who sought corroboration of his beliefs through postmortem studies. In 1845 WILLIAM GRIESINGER (1817–1868) published his *Pathology and Therapy of Psychic Disorders,* in which he held that all mental disturbances must be based on brain pathology. The psychiatrist MOREL (1809–1873) attributed mental illness to hereditary neural weakness. VALENTIN MAGNAN (1835–1916) investigated mental illness occurring in relation to alcoholism, paralysis, and childbirth.

Perhaps the most influential figure in psychiatry in the latter nineteenth and early twentieth centuries was EMIL KRAEPELIN (see Chapter 1). In 1883 he published a textbook outlining mental illness in terms of organic pathology—in particular, the disordered functioning of the nervous system—a point of view which oriented his approach to the general problem of mental disturbances. He described and classified many types of disorders and provided a basis for descriptive psychiatry by drawing attention to clusters of symptoms. Kraepelin evolved a theoretical system which divided mental illness into two large categories: those due to endogenous factors (originating within the body) and those due to exogenous factors (originating outside the body). His classification remained substantially unchanged until a few years after World War I. Kraepelin made notable contributions to psychiatry, but his approach to mental illness was that of an experimentalist, and, consequently, he studied disease processes as entities in themselves rather than as the dynamic reactions of living individuals.

In 1897 RICHARD VON KRAFFT-EBING (1840–1902), a Viennese psychiatrist, disclosed experimental proof of the relationship of general paresis to syphilis. In 1907 ALZHEIMER established the presence of brain pathology in cerebral arteriosclerosis and senile psychoses. In 1917 JULIUS WAGNER-JAUREGG (1857–1940) inoculated nine paretic patients with malaria, with consequent alleviation of their condition. These and other discoveries during the early twentieth century lent strong support to the adherents of the organic approach to mental illness.

Psychological Interpretations. Despite the achievements of the organically oriented investigators in certain limited areas, very little progress was being made in treating mentally disordered patients. As early as the first decades of the eighteenth century vague and uncertain theories (e.g., mesmerism) had postulated psychological causation. This point of view, however, has had repercussions ever since. Outstanding contributors to a psychological interpretation have included Mesmer, Elliotson, Braid, Liébeault, Bernheim, and Charcot.

MESMERISM. The development of a psychological interpretation of mental illness can be traced from the early work of ANTON MESMER (1733–1815). Mesmer developed and applied a technique he called "animal magnetism." He attributed his cures to the control and alteration of "magnetic forces" which he believed to be the causes of mental disease. One English physician, JOHN ELLIOTSON (1791–1868), used mesmerism in surgery. Another, JAMES BRAID (1795–1861), studied the process and concluded that it was a purely psychological phenomenon whose chief characteristic was suggestion, and in 1841 he termed the process "hypnosis." LIÉBEAULT (1823–1904) and BERNHEIM (1840–1919), two French physicians practicing at Nancy, elaborated the influence of suggestion in inducing a hypnotic state. They concluded that both hypnosis and hysteria are due to suggestion. J. M. CHARCOT (1825–1893), a French neuropsychiatrist, disagreed with them, believing that hypnosis was dependent upon physiological processes as well as upon suggestion. He insisted that persons capable of being hypnotized are hysterical.

THE DEVELOPMENT OF PSYCHOANALYSIS. The foregoing observations laid the groundwork for the accomplishments of the psychologically oriented scientists—Janet, Breuer, Freud, and others.

PIERRE JANET (1859–1947) developed the first psychological theory explaining neurosis. Using hypnosis as his investigating technique, he did extensive research on hysteria, and his work did much to attract attention to the psychological point of view in mental illness.

In Vienna JOSEPH BREUER (1842–1925) in 1880 successfully treated hysteria with hypnosis and observed that the release of pent-up emotion resulted in the removal of symptoms. This discovery served as a point of departure for the development of psychoanalysis. However, in Vienna a colleague of his, SIGMUND FREUD (1856–1939), who was a physician and neurologist, was less successful with hypnosis and thus worked out the "cathartic" method in which free association and dream interpretation are used to uncover dynamic and unconscious material. Freud's technique and his theory are the cornerstones of the psychoanalytic school (see Chapter 3, Approaches to Personality).

The differences in the organic and psychological points of view that were present in the early history of abnormal psychology continue to form the backdrop of this field of scientific endeavor. The question of the relative importance of organic and psychological factors in the causation of mental illness remains unanswered.

3

APPROACHES TO PERSONALITY

Because the majority of current theories of personality development and structure are strongly influenced by the views of Sigmund Freud, the "father" of psychoanalysis, it is both convenient and logical to separate any presentation of this nature into two large divisions: psychoanalytic and nonpsychoanalytic theories. The present chapter, therefore, opens with remarks on the work of three non-Freudian contemporaries of Freud. There follow a delineation of Freud's concept of personality and a discussion of the views of other psychoanalysts. Some of Freud's earlier adherents (i.e., Adler, Jung, and Rank) deviated from his views to the point of opposition. Others, such as Fromm, Horney, and Sullivan, using Freud's findings as a point of departure, evolved theories of personality in which social and environmental factors are given greater importance. Finally, this chapter will discuss several present-day nonpsychoanalytic approaches, which include psychobiology (Meyer), the personality-and-learning theory, the constitutional theories (Kretschmer and Sheldon), and the existential approach (Binswanger, Von Gebsattel and Minkowski).

EARLY CONCEPTIONS

Three of Freud's contemporaries who left their imprint on our understanding of abnormal behavior were Pierre Janet, Morton Prince, and Ivan Pavlov.

Janet (1859–1947). The basic postulates offered by Janet were that there must exist a level of psychological *tension* for proper unification and integration of mental phenomena and that neurotic behavior develops as a result of an inadequate supply of the energy that creates this tension. Janet believed that the reduction in the energy level weakens the capacity of the individual to synthesize, and that, as a result, systems of ideas and feelings are dissociated from the total personality. The systems so dissociated then lead an insulated existence, beyond voluntary control and given expression in the form of such symptoms as somnambulism, tics, paralysis, and amnesia. Janet recognized two principal types of neurosis: psychasthenia and hysteria. Treatments, guided by the aforementioned "tension level" theory, consisted of helping the patient to reintegrate the dissociated elements. While Janet brought the psychological viewpoint to the fore, his theory was limited in being descriptive rather than dynamic.

Prince (1854–1929). The noteworthy contribution of Morton Prince was his detailed reporting of case histories describing multiple personalities. At first he used Janet's concept of dissociation to explain the development of such cases, but he later adopted a more dynamic orientation. Prince was one of the first to recognize the importance of association and conditioning in the causation of psychoneuroses. He employed hypnosis and automatic writing as treatment methods.

Pavlov (1849–1936). As an outgrowth of his studies in animal physiology, Pavlov evolved the concept of *conditioning* as a form of learning. His work served as a stimulus for the emergence of the behavioristic school of psychological thought. The core of Pavlov's theory of personality formation through conditioning lies in his attempts to explain sleep and hypnosis as being the result of a "spread of inhibitory influences" over the area of the cerebral cortex. Such investigations suggested to him that neurotic behavior analogous to that found in humans could be produced in animals by forcing a clash between excitatory and inhibitory responses. Pavlov produced the conflict by first conditioning the animal to respond positively to one stimulus and negatively to another, then gradually reducing the difference between the stimuli until it was impossible for the animal to discriminate between them. An animal forced to act in such a situation exhibited neurotic behavior.

The conflict between the neural excitation and inhibition was regarded by Pavlov as the precipitating factor in the development of neurosis. Constitutional factors, in particular the innate neural structure of the animal, were identified as the predisposing causes. According to Pavlov, *neurasthenia* (extreme fatigue) occurs in animals (and, by analogy, in human beings) in whose neural systems there is an exaggeration of the excitatory processes; *hysteria* (conversion of emotional stress into physical disability) arises when inhibitory processes predominate. Subsequent workers have used the methods of the conditioned response to produce *experimental neu-*

roses and to study the influence of electroshock and alcohol on the experimentally produced neurosis in the hope of drawing conclusions with regard to human behavior. Critics of such attempts point out that in the experimental neuroses the strife is produced by environmental factors and is severely limited by the experimental situation; the experimental neuroses, they say, are situational reactions rather than true neuroses. It has also been noted that the behavior observed in nonexperimental neuroses is more varied and complex than that found in experimental neuroses and, thus, they should not be regarded as identical.

PSYCHOANALYTIC APPROACHES

The psychoanalytic approach to the understanding of personality development received major attention through the teachings of Sigmund Freud. Early disciples of Freud (Adler, Jung, and Rank) soon developed divergent theories; later, other psychoanalysts (Fromm, Horney, Sullivan, Reik, members of the London School, and the Chicago Group) reinterpreted and modified some of Freud's findings. Still others (Abraham, Fenichel, Kardiner, and Stekel) advanced their own points of view.

Freudian Psychoanalysis. Sigmund Freud was born on May 6, 1856, at Freiburg, in the country then known as Austria-Hungary. He began as a research worker, later receiving an appointment as lecturer on nervous diseases at the University of Vienna. He commenced a private practice in neurology in 1886. Freud lived most of his life in Vienna, but escaped to London when the Nazis came into control. He died in 1939, having remained active through his writings almost to the day of his death.

Freud's Concept of Personality. The basic ideas in Freud's concept of personality formation and structure grew directly out of his experience in the treatment of neurotic patients. He recognized, for example, that many of the attitudes and feelings expressed by his patients could not come from consciousness and therefore must reside in the levels below consciousness. His further experiences in therapy convinced him that the unconscious was an important and dynamic determinant of behavior.

For convenience of presentation, the Freudian approach to personality is discussed here under the following categories: levels of mental activity; motivation; conflict; psychosexual development; structure of personality; and development of psychoneurosis.

LEVELS OF MENTAL ACTIVITY. In the therapeutic relationship, Freud observed that the verbal productions of many of his patients were illogical, not properly oriented as to time and place, and "out of character." It was obvious to him that this thought content could not come from consciousness but had to be derived from levels of mental activity below conscious awareness. He concluded that there are three levels of mental activity; the conscious, the preconscious (also called the "foreconscious"), and the unconscious. The *conscious,* obviously, is the overt thinking and acting level in which material is readily recalled and applied to the demands of the environment. The *preconscious* is made up of memories that can be recalled, though with some difficulty. Both conscious and preconscious material are consistent with and responsive to reality. The *unconscious,* however, is composed of attitudes, feelings, and ideas that are not subject to voluntary control, are brought to awareness only with the greatest difficulty (if at all), are not bound by laws of logic, and are not subject to the restrictions of time and place.

MOTIVATION. Freud believed that motivation springs from a general biological energy, which he subdivided into constructive and destructive urges. The development and differentiation of these basic urges are portrayed in the accompanying chart. The *constructive urges,* or life forces (eros) express themselves in ego drives and sex drives. The ego drives maintain the preservation of the self through satisfaction of nutritional needs; the sex (libido) drives express themselves in a wide variety of pleasurable and affectional activities. The *destructive urges* express themselves in hostile impulses directed toward the self as well as toward others. These impulses may take the form of aggression, hate, murder, or suicide.

According to Freud, these life and death urges create tensions which the individual experiences as unpleasant or distressing; most of the individual's meaningful behavior results from efforts to reduce these tensions. Such life and death urges are assumed to persist throughout life. Further, they tend to mingle and to become so complex that they are often both directed at the same love object. This fusion of the life and death urges is referred to as *ambivalence.* Ambivalent feelings toward parents, siblings, associates, and spouses are often observed clinically.

The motivation for man's activities, in the Freudian formulation, is guided by two other principles: the *pleasure principle* and the *reality principle.* In infancy the individual is motivated solely by pleasure, but in time the restrictions of life compel him to develop a sense of reality. Thus, there evolves the reality principle, which requires modification of the pleasure principle and gives rise to the checks and inhibitions which are placed on pleasure-seeking activities.

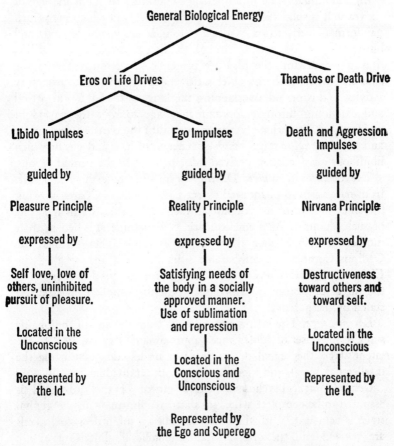

After James D. Page, *Abnormal Psychology* (New York: McGraw-Hill, 1947), p. 186.

CONFLICT. Life is a series of conflict situations, on the basis of which personality is formed. Some of the conflicts pointed out by Freud are those between pleasure-seeking and reality, love and hate, passivity and activity. Growth toward maturity is dependent on the individual's success in resolving these conflicts.

PSYCHOSEXUAL DEVELOPMENT. Three principal stages are described by Freud in his theory of the psychosexual development of the individual: the infantile stage (divided into three substages—the oral, the anal, and the phallic, a key feature of which is the Oedipus Complex), the latent stage, and the genital stage.

Infantile Stage. The infantile stage continues to about the age of six years. It is subdivided into (1) the *oral* stage, in which the principal form of satisfaction is drawn from sucking, swallowing, and biting (this period extends through the first eighteen months of life, during which time the pleasure principle predominates); (2) the *anal* stage, in which the chief satisfactions are related to excretory activities (this period, overlapping the latter part of the oral period and extending through approximately age four, is the period in which the reality principle begins to modify the pleasure principle); and (3) the *phallic* stage, between the ages of four and six, in which libidinous satisfaction is derived principally from the genital organs.

The Oedipus Complex. During the phallic stage there is a shift from narcissism to phantasied object satisfaction. The parents, being the chief sources of affectional satisfaction, become the first objects of such phantasy. As a consequence, boys become attached to their mothers and look upon their fathers as rivals. This is called the Oedipus Complex. A comparable situation for a girl is called the *Electra Complex.* The Oedipal strivings are repressed as a result of the threat of castration, which may be either implied or explicitly stated by the parents.

Latent Stage. The latent stage extends from the end of the phallic stage to the onset of adolescence (approximately age twelve). In the latent stage, the sexual drives lie more or less dormant while the intellectual, social, and moral growth of the individual continues.

Genital Stage. Psychosexual development of the individual is assumed to be complete when satisfactory adjustment in the genital stage is achieved. With the onset of puberty, infantile sexual needs are revived and the oral, anal, and phallic libidinous urges are regenerated. Initially, these urges are predominately narcissistic— that is, they are directed more to the individual's own satisfaction than to the giving of love to another. As the individual moves away from this narcissism, the first love-object is often someone of the same sex. This choice is not biologically determined but arises from the cultural setting, which emphasizes segregation of the sexes at this age. As development continues, the adolescent seeks heterosexual satisfactions which, however, are initially narcissistic and dominated by the pleasure principle.

STRUCTURE OF THE PERSONALITY. To explain personality structure Freud presented three components: the id, the ego, and the superego. The *id* is thought of as the main source of the biological energy that expresses itself in the life and death urges. The id is constantly demanding pleasure-seeking aggressive outlets and may be characterized as "the animal in man." It operates entirely at the unconscious level and is not governed by considerations of time, space, and logic. At birth the personality is completely id, but, as reality is encountered, the *ego* begins to develop. The ego is the "me" or "self" in which the individual differentiates himself from his surroundings and through which the integrating core of the personality is formed. The principal functions of the ego are: (1) to provide satisfaction for the nutritional and protective needs of the organism; (2) to adjust the id strivings to the demands of reality; (3) to repress impulses that are not acceptable to the superego; and (4) to co-ordinate and resolve the conflicting demands of the id and the superego. *Superego,* the third structural component of personality, develops as the ego internalizes social and cultural norms. Freud speaks of the id in terms of biological energy, of the ego and superego in terms of social and cultural development. The ego derives its energy from the id and its moral censorship from the superego.

THE DEVELOPMENT OF PSYCHONEUROSIS. Freud distinguished between true neuroses and psychoneuroses. *True neuroses,* he explained, arose from somatic or toxic conditions resulting from disturbances in the individual's sex life (such as complete abstinence or excessive indulgence); he believed *psychoneuroses* to be principally psychogenic in origin. In his theory of the development of psychoneurosis, Freud enunciated five different interpretations of the origin of neurotic behavior:

1. In his earliest writings, Freud stated that psychoneurosis originates as a result of trauma that is primarily sexual in nature.

2. Later, he explained psychoneurotic behavior on the basis of the unresolved Oedipus conflict.

3. Still later, he broadened his concept of the origin of psychoneurosis, assuming it to be the result of the conflict between the strivings of the id and the moral censorship of the superego.

4. Freud then included as precipitating factors the emotional reactions created by an early rejecting environment.

5. Finally, on the basis of this earlier work, he came to recognize that there was no single specific cause of psychoneurosis, ascribed neurotic behavior to a multiplicity of causes, and focused his attention on a description of neurotic reactions. From this evolved his concept of four neurotic reactions: *obsessive-compulsive neurosis, anxiety hysteria, conversion hysteria,* and *neurasthenia.*

Adlerian Approach. Alfred Adler (1870–1937) was one of Freud's early associates. He dissented from Freud's emphasis on the instinctual libido as the source of motivational energy and substituted as man's principal motive force a universal *will to power*. He also differed from Freud in denying the mechanism of repression, in refusing to accept a clear distinction between the conscious and the unconscious, and in substituting aggressive striving for sexual striving. Adler was the leader of the School of Individual Psychology, the major points of which follow:

INFERIORITY COMPLEX. The universal striving for superiority, as postulated by Adler, is essentially a compensation (or overcompensation) for feelings of inferiority which are traceable to the early life experiences of the individual. Awareness of organ inferiority is one source of the need to compensate. Practically all people are, in truth, inferior to some other individuals with respect to their physical characteristics (height, strength, beauty, etc.). The child perceives this inferiority and is aware that he is physically and intellectually weaker than the adults about him. His attempts at self-evaluation lead to feelings of inferiority, and he reacts to these feelings with a struggle for power, prestige, or status, as a compensation for his felt inadequacy.

The Adlerian theory of *penis envy* is based on the male child's realization of organic inferiority in the smallness of his penis and the female child's concern because she has no penis at all. In addition to organ inferiorities, Adler pointed to certain intrafamily situations which arouse inferiorities. Parental attitudes of pampering (leaving the child unprepared for later life's disappointments) and of rejection arouse feelings of inferiority. Order of birth is a factor, younger children comparing themselves unfavorably with older and more competent siblings. The importance of sex identification is also emphasized by Adler in his concept of "masculine protest" against assumed masculine superiority. The man fears his inability to live up to the masculine standard; the woman is concerned because she is not a male.

STYLE OF LIFE. Each person sets a goal early in life, often by the fifth year, to which all subsequent living will be subordinated. According to Adler, this goal establishes a "style of life" designed to buttress the individual against insecurity that may result from feelings of inadequacy. The style of life is used to help the individual to adjust to society, to his vocation, and to love. The direction the style of life will take is dependent on early environmental influences, family patterns, and the specific nature of the inferiority feeling. Style of life can lead to the development of talent and behavior that are effective and socially useful, but it can also lead to unhealthy overcompensation.

STRUCTURE OF PERSONALITY. Although Adler stressed a "unity of personality," and the need to understand the total personality, his theories are generally felt to lack the synthesis and completeness of Freud's. The two main goals of personality in the Adlerian School of Individual Psychology are: social adaptation and the attainment of power. For Adler, the personality develops out of the inevitable conflicts between these two goals. In seeking to explain personality, Adler shifted the emphasis from the basically sexual and unconscious conflict between the id and the ego to the more or less conscious conflict between the power strivings of the ego and the need to adapt to social living.

DEVELOPMENT OF NEUROSIS. Adler was the first to discard the sexual theory of neurosis. For Adler, every neurosis is an attempt to free oneself from a feeling of inferiority in order to gain a feeling of superiority. In the course of the attempt, however, the neurotic individual fears competitive activity and seeks protection from inferiority feelings in unhealthy defenses which lead neither to satisfactory social functioning nor to effective solution of his own life problems. Overwhelmed by the dread of possible failure, the neurotic seeks fictional or abnormal goals which give him easy but empty victories. He frequently isolates himself from the competitive struggle in society by taking refuge in illness and expresses his power striving in the small family circle by dominating others through his illness. Such factors, as well as physical defects or parental overprotection or rejection, predispose the individual to the neurotic pattern of behavior.

Jungian Approach. Carl Jung (1875–1961), another of the early associates of Freud, also found himself in disagreement on basic issues. He broke away to set up the school of Analytic Psychology.

His most significant contributions center around the following points:

LIBIDO THEORY. Jung's concept of the libido was not primarily sexual. He postulated a single great storehouse of undifferentiated life energy which, according to him, holds the motive forces for all of man's endeavors.

COLLECTIVE UNCONSCIOUS. In addition to repressed personal experiences, Jung maintained that the unconscious contains an *ancestral residue* which is the source of inherited racial habits and attitudes; these he called "archetypes." Jung claimed that the universality of some myths and folklore is evidence to prove this point.

PERSONALITY TYPES. The concept of *introversion-extroversion* was introduced by Jung. In extroverts the libido is directed outward; they react strongly to the world of objective reality. Introverts, on the other hand, with a libido turned inward toward subjective facts which only they themselves can observe, tend to withdraw from the world of fact to the world of fantasy. This direction of the libido toward external reality or toward the inner self is an inherent part of the individual's psychophysical constitution and determines his personality type. Psychopathology arises when a person follows his own type to an extreme, suppressing all other reactions, or when he suppresses his innate tendencies and adopts the life pattern of the other personality type.

WORD ASSOCIATION. Jung contributed an important tool for the clinician and the experimenter in his word association test. He had been working on this independently of Freud's development of free association. In Jung's test a list of one hundred words, chosen for their emotionally stimulating value, is prepared. The subject is told to respond with the first word that enters his mind after the stimulus word is presented. Variations in the pattern of response in time or in content may give clues to areas of significant conflict.

Rankian Approach. Otto Rank (1884–1939) was also one of the early members of the Freudian "inner circle." Reacting against some of the cardinal teachings of Freud, he evolved several widely variant theories.

BIRTH TRAUMA. In Rank's opinion, the birth process itself is the source of most of the anxiety experienced in later life, in terms of the threat of being separated from havens of security and love. His entire system of psychodynamics stems from the concept of this loss of protected passivity in the mother's womb.

IMPORTANCE OF WILL. Volition, or will, according to Rank, is the most vital force in the integration or disintegration of the personality. In conflict states, according to this theory, guilt arises from the inability of the will to make the right decision and to move toward integration and development. Rank perceived the neurotic as a dependent, emotionally immature individual whose potentialities for controlled, self-assertive problem solving have been inadequately developed.

DYNAMIC RELATIONSHIP THERAPY. The therapeutic setting devised by Rank deviated widely from that of Freud. Rank felt that it is the therapist's task to so plan the therapeutic sessions that the patient gradually assumes greater responsibility for solving his own problems and for freeing himself from the need of leaning on a parent figure for emotional support. Part of this procedure involves fixing a time limit on therapy so that the patient will know how long he has to rely on the therapist. In place of the interest in the past shown by Freud, Rank preferred to concentrate on the present experience of the patient as he reacted to the therapist.

Fromm's Approach. Erich Fromm (1900–   ) brought to his work in psychoanalysis a background of study in sociology and psychology, rather than in medicine. He stated that man is influenced by his social environment from the moment of birth and that therefore psychology could be meaningful only in an anthropological and philosophical frame of reference. His theory of personality is not a reaction against some of the basic Freudian concepts, but is rather a further development (through integration of knowledge derived from other disciplines) of these concepts.

INSTINCT. Fromm agreed with Freud in stressing the importance of motivation but disagreed that this motivation is mainly instinctual. He felt that over and above the satisfaction of organic needs, man's problems are connected with a striving for fame and power, for love, and for the realization of religious and humanistic ideals.

PSYCHOSEXUAL DEVELOPMENT. Fromm viewed the various stages of personality development not so much as successive phases of biological development but as products of the socializing process.

PERSONALITY TYPES. For Fromm, social adjustment is not the highest goal. The *productive person* is the only individual living a fully mature life. Fromm divides immature, nonproductive personalities into: (1) the *receiving type,* characterized by a basic attitude of expecting things to come to them through the generosity of others; (2) the *exploiting type,* who attempt to obtain everything by force or cunning; (3) the *hoarding type,* who have little faith in acquiring things from others and, thus, seek their security in keeping what they have; and (4) the *marketing type,* who are characterized by an attitude that their very personalities are a commodity to be sold, with the idea of gaining success by being adaptable.

Horney's Approach. Karen Horney (1885–1952), after fifteen years of orthodox psychoanalytic practice, turned away from the biologically oriented point of view of Freud to develop her own personality theory. She emphasized cultural and interpersonal experiences and identified basic anxiety as the cause of the neurosis.

BASIC ANXIETY. A central point in Horney's approach to personality is her concept of basic anxiety, which she described as a feeling of helplessness in a potentially hostile world. Basic anxiety develops out of the interplay between feelings of anxiety and hostility stirred up by rejecting parental attitudes. The feelings of hostility are aroused in the child by such parental attitudes as preference for other children, unjust reproaches, unpredictable changes from over-indulgence to scornful rejection, unfulfilled promises, lack of consideration for childhood feelings, and consistent interference in the child's activities. Such hostility as is aroused in the child cannot be expressed because of the child's precarious position of being completely dependent on the parent and because of his fear that overt acts might lead to even greater rejection. The anxiety precipitated by this insecure position, accentuated by the danger that his hostile impulses might be discovered, exposes him to increased sensitivity and to possible further rejection; this, in turn, engenders increased feelings of hostility. It is this vicious circle of mounting anxiety and hostility which provides a necessary condition for basic anxiety. If the earlier parental attitudes remain unmitigated by other, more favorable influences, the child projects his feelings of hostility onto the outside world and develops a *generalized anxiety,* acquiring an all-pervading feeling of loneliness and helplessness. This basic anxiety, according to Horney, is the cause of the neurosis. She suggests that the pathological anxiety may be prevented by providing the child with genuine warmth and affection so that he will develop the feelings of being wanted and loved.

TYPES OF INTERPERSONAL REACTIONS. Horney pointed out that in the attempt to work out a means of adjusting to the world of people three major approaches are available to the child: he can move toward, against, or away from people. Those who move *toward* people accept their own helplessness and seek out a compliant, dependent relationship, thus achieving a feeling of security and belongingness. The child who chooses to move *against* people assumes the hostility of all around him and is prepared to fight to win out over the others. The *withdrawing* child adopts the defense of detachment and aloofness and seeks satisfaction in his own private world.

Normal adjustment requires appropriate use of all three types of interpersonal relations. The neurotic, driven by his basic anxiety, comes to depend in an exaggerated, inappropriate way on one or another of these possible reactions. In adopting a one-sided approach he denies himself the very interpersonal satisfactions he is seeking. For example, excessive compliance denies the neurotic the opportunity for normal self-assertiveness; on the other hand, constant combativeness prevents him from achieving friendly, warm relationships.

NEUROTIC TRENDS. The living-out of any of these interpersonal reaction patterns leads to the development of neurotic trends which are protective devices against basic anxiety. Horney described several neurotic trends, as follows: (1) neurotic striving for power, a struggle for domination and prestige whereby the individual seeks to become so powerful that no one can hurt him; (2) neurotic striving for affection, an inordinate and indiscriminate expression of an otherwise normal drive; (3) neurotic submissiveness, in which the individual subordinates all his needs to those of others in the hope that by so submitting he will be protected from harm; and (4) neurotic withdrawal, a retreat from all contact with other persons in an attempt to avoid even the risk of danger (rejection). These neurotic trends, motivated by the basic anxiety, place the individual in conflict situations, which lead to a reestablishment of the anxiety in the manner of a vicious circle. In his attempt to resolve the conflict situation and so achieve a feeling of unity, the neurotic person creates a deceptive, *idealized image* which he believes to be himself or someone he ought to or could be.

CULTURAL FACTORS. Recognizing the relevance of cultural factors in evaluating behavior, Horney observed that many reactions which we look upon as being neurotic in our culture are considered quite normal in other cultures. In addition, she pointed out that many conflicts developed by the neurotic person mirror the contradictions of our society. In Horney's views, the Freudian concepts of id, ego, and superego are of much less significance than the contradictory cultural demands made on the individual.

Sullivan's Approach. Although Harry Stack Sullivan (1892–1949) had not, prior to his death, published a systematic exposition of his theory of personality, nevertheless, the impact of his thought on present-day psychiatry is appreciable. Sullivan defined psychiatry as "the science of interpersonal relationships." The keystone of his concept of personality development is summed up in the word *acculturation*. According to Sullivan, the human personality emerges out of the personal and social forces acting upon the individual from birth, and the final personality structure is the product of interaction with other human beings. In this respect, Sullivan is closer to Adolf Meyer (see following section) than he is to Freud.

Goals of Human Behavior. Motivation for human behavior is placed by Sullivan in (1) the person's efforts to satisfy essentially biological needs such as sleep, food, and sexual fulfillment, and (2) the pressure exerted by the culture on the individual to satisfy these needs in a socially approved fashion. The latter motive, named by Sullivan as the "security need," grows out of the process of acculturation, or socialization, which begins at birth for all individuals. The process of becoming a mature human being is synonymous with this acculturation process.

Empathy. An important means of handing down cultural values and of socializing the child is found in the empathic relationships between the infant and those who take care of him, particularly the mother. Long before verbal communication can be established, empathy makes possible emotional communication, which causes the infant to feel the tension or relaxation of those close to him. For example, feelings of tension in an anxious mother at feeding time can produce tension in the child and lead to feeding problems.

Tension and Anxiety. Achievement of satisfaction brings about a decrease in muscular tensions, and the further pursuit of these satisfactions is motivated by this release of tension. When the mother (or her substitute) begins to express prohibitions and disapprovals of need-satisfying behavior, this simple pattern is interfered with, and inhibitions and mounting muscular tensions develop. In addition, the mother's implied disapproval interferes with the child's security feelings and leads to feelings of anxiety, for which the muscular tensions are considered a necessary condition. However, anxiety is not identified with muscular tensions alone, but is said to be always related to interpersonal relations.

CONCEPT OF SELF. In the socialization process the child is exposed on countless occasions to evaluations made of him by others, particularly by the significant adults in his life. On the basis of these approvals and disapprovals, he develops a concept of self. In an attempt to avoid the feelings of discomfort produced by disapproval, the child emphasizes those aspects of self which are pleasing to the adult. On the other hand, aspects of his behavior which meet with disapproval tend to be "dissociated" and are not recognized by the child as part of himself. Behavior not of significance to adults is dealt with by the child through "selective inattention." Such material can be incorporated into the self-system later on; dissociated material cannot be easily incorporated.

THEORY OF PERSONALITY DEVELOPMENT. The process of acculturation provides the framework of Sullivan's concept of personality development. He divides growth, from birth to maturity, into six epochs: (1) infancy, in which empathic influences are dominant; (2) childhood, in which phase co-operation with peers becomes a possibility; (3) the juvenile epoch, in which the child, submerging his own interests, moves toward group solidarity; (4) preadolescence, in which the individual moves further toward a "fully social state" and begins to develop the capacity for intimacy; (5) adolescence, during which for the first time, the problems of sexuality as such become important; and (6) maturity, in which the individual develops the capacity for establishing durable situations of intimacy.

Reik's Approach. Theodore Reik (1880–   ), essentially a Freudian in theory, offered his own explanations of problems related to personality development.

EXTRASENSORY PERCEPTION. Reik stated that the unconscious is capable of receiving extrasensory stimuli. He explained this by postulating that the unconscious retains archaic remnants of sense modalities lost in the course of evolution.

NARCISSISM. According to Reik, narcissism is a later and secondary development and is not an instinctive state of the newborn baby.

ORIGIN OF NEUROSIS. For Reik, neurosis results when a loss of self-trust and self-confidence sets up anxieties and inhibitions in the individual.

EGO IDEAL. Reik set forth the "ego ideal." This, he said, is derived from ego drives and environment and is modeled after parents, teachers, and other figures of authority. It may be likened to a level of aspiration toward which we strive. The more nearly it is attained, the less is the degree of conflict and the better the adjustment.

The London School. Ernest Jones and Melanie Klein have been the principal contributors to the development of psychoanalysis in England.

ERNEST JONES (1879–1958). Jones, one of Freud's original inner circle, abandoned Freud's libido theory, gave more importance to anxiety, and as a result emphasized the methods by which a patient strives to escape danger or distress. Jones reduced the essential elements of psychoanalysis to: (1) the study of the patient's unconscious mental processes in order to reveal the determinants of his behavior; (2) the use of free association as a technique for exposing the determinants; and (3) the recognition of the phenomena of transference and resistance.

MELANIE KLEIN (1882–   ). Klein, working with children, equated play therapy with adult psychoanalysis. She believed that play activity closely resembles free association and that the therapist-child relationship develops into a true transference. Her method consists of directly relating to the child the meaning of his behavior.

The Chicago Group. The work of the Chicago Institute for Psychoanalysis has contributed greatly to more efficient use of the therapist's time through techniques for briefer analysis. FRANZ ALEXANDER (1891–   ) and THOMAS M. FRENCH (1892–   ) have been the principal spokesmen for this group. Although their greatest impact has been in the area of therapeutic technique, they have also contributed important studies on the libido theory, conflict, and the theory of neurosis.

LIBIDO THEORY. Members of the Chicago Group question the existence of a libido based on a biological instinct.

CONFLICT. The Chicago Group broadens the clinical view of conflict, holding that all conflict does not necessarily have its roots in infantile sexuality. Present problems of self-esteem, self-assertion, and the need for affection and love are considered to be important and are viewed as total personality reactions rather than as deviations of sexual strivings.

THEORY OF NEUROSIS. This group conceives of neurosis as being the result of an interrupted learning process, a series of stereotyped reactions to problems which the patient has not learned to solve in the past and is still unable to solve in the present.

Other Psychoanalysts. At least four other outstanding theorists in the Freudian tradition must be mentioned in any exposition of the psychoanalytic approach to personality. They are Abraham, Fenichel, Kardiner, and Stekel.

KARL ABRAHAM (1877–1925) was one of Freud's early associates. With Freud, he conducted studies on depression.

OTTO FENICHEL (1897–1946) was most widely known for his detailed writings on the psychoanalytic theory of the neurosis. He awarded a central place to anxiety and defenses against anxiety. Fenichel held that situational stresses which tend to reactivate childhood conflicts and threats are particularly potent in the production of neurotic reactions.

ABRAHAM KARDINER (1891–   ) has conducted research into the social origins of abnormal behavior. He has theorized that the basic personality traits are derived from such primary factors of society as family organization, subsistence economy, discipline system, and sex taboos. Thus, to the extent to which members of a particular culture are exposed to these common experiences, to that extent they will tend to develop certain basic similarities of personality.

WILHELM STEKEL (1868–1940) concerned himself with the techniques of psychoanalytic psychotherapy. He emphasized the role of the therapist as teacher, and his approach was one of persuasive reeducation.

Other significant names in the field of psychoanalysis are: FELIX DEUTSCH (1884–   ), SANDOR FERENCZI (1873–1933), JOHANN CARL FLÜGEL (1884–   ), EMILAN GUTHEIL (1899–   ), LAWRENCE S. KUBIE (1896–   ), the MENNINGERS (KARL, b. 1893 and WILLIAM, b. 1899), and PAUL SCHILDER (1886–1940).

NONPSYCHOANALYTICAL APPROACHES

Several important approaches to the understanding of personality formation and structure developed quite independently of the Freudian schools. In point of time, the first of these was the psychobiological school of ADOLF MEYER (1866–1950). Thereafter, a theory was postulated which was based mainly on the psychology of the learning process. Later, theories were formulated on a constitutional basis, in the body-type studies of Kretschmer and Sheldon. Finally, the ontological approach of the existential school has been developed.

Psychobiology. Adolf Meyer came to America as a neuropathologist. Through his clinicopathologic work, he felt impelled to draw certain conclusions, from which he evolved psychobiology, an approach to the understanding and treatment of mental illness. Meyer maintained that the inherited structures and tendencies, the life experiences, and the stresses of the environment all had to be evaluated and studied in order to trace and explain the genesis of a particular disorder.

Behavior, Meyer insisted, can be properly appreciated only by a study of the *total* personality, the *total* life history of the individual. In his opinion, the determinants of behavior are multiple and interactional, and all possible factors must be investigated and co-ordinated in any analysis of the developmental pattern of a mental illness.

In outlining his theory of the neurosis, Meyer emphasized unrealistic levels of aspiration and lack of self-acceptance as fundamental in the abnormal personality. People, he believed, become disturbed because they are unable to accept their own nature and the world as it is, and thus cannot shape their aims according to their assets. Failing in the achievement of their unrealistic goals, they develop feelings of inferiority, apprehensiveness, and other faulty emotional attitudes which lead to the use of neurotic defensive measures. These nonadjustive attitudes and responses gradually develop into habitual reaction patterns.

Personality-and-Learning Theory. In recent years an attempt has been made to make more extensive use of learning theory in the study of personality development. Psychological theories of learning have been synthesized with concepts developed in social anthropology and psychoanalysis. Prominent investigators along these lines have been Mowrer, Kluckhohn, Dollard, and Miller.

BASIC POSTULATES. Mowrer and Kluckhohn accept as basic assumptions for their dynamic theory of personality the following: [1]

1. *Behavior is functional.* Living organisms are propelled into action by stimulation or irritation and remain in action until the stimulation is reduced or eliminated. This process, described as adjustment, is distinguished by Mowrer and Kluckhohn from adaptation, which is behavior that keeps the organisms alive, healthy, and reproducing. Adaptation develops and changes inherited ways of

---

[1] After O. H. Mowrer and Clyde Kluckhohn, "Dynamic Theory of Personality," in J. McV. Hunt, ed., *Personality and the Behavior Disorders* (New York: Ronald, 1944), Vol. I, pp. 70–74.

behaving (instinct theory), whereas adjustment develops and changes habits (learning theory). Most adjustive acts are also adaptive, but need not be so.

2. *Behavior always includes conflict.* Mowrer and Kluckhohn accept the conflictual basis of behavior as suggested by psychoanalysis and reinforced by the findings of social anthropologists.

3. *Behavior must be understood in relation to the field in which it occurs.* Using as a point of departure the Gestalt concepts of field, or context, these authors point out that particular behavior produced by a given source of stimulation will be influenced by many different factors. Thus, they indicate that the individual's life history may be considered the field (or context) in which a particular adjustment occurs.

4. *All living organisms tend to preserve a state of internal consistency.* In explaining this postulate, Mowrer and Kluckhohn indicate that it is implied in the three preceding postulates, and they state: "Conflict is an ever-present feature of behavior, i.e., every act, however gainful, also entails some sacrifice or loss; no form of adjustment (stimulation reduction) can occur without some dis-adjustment (stimulation increase). But this fact is in no way inconsistent with the proposition that living organisms show a tendency to select those modes of adjustment which involve the least possible conflict, i.e., which will afford maximal integration." [2]

In addition to describing the foregoing postulates as the essentials of a dynamic theory of personality, Mowrer and Kluckhohn draw further on the fields of anthropology, psychoanalysis, and psychology for development of their theory.

THE INDIVIDUAL IN SOCIETY. Anthropological studies provide the authors with an insight into the role of the individual in society. They conceive of personality as the result of the process of socialization of the individual; "every individual has motives, but must pattern his adjustment so as to make these motives conform to the expectations and limitations of other individuals." [3]

The biological and instinctual emphasis which Freud accorded to personality development is not accepted by this school. Nevertheless, much of Freud's delineation of psychosexual development is used, though in modified form.

MOTIVATION AND BEHAVIOR. From learning theory developed out of

[2] O. H. Mowrer, and Clyde Kluckhohn *ibid.*, pp. 73–74.
[3] *Ibid.*, p. 86.

experimental research, it is held that all behavior is motivated and that all learning involves reward. The basic formula that is applied in this attempt to understand all learned behavior, including learned aspects of the personality, is: *Motivation leads to variable behavior, which ultimately results in reduction of tension. A motive is seen as a problem situation; the response that leads to a solution of the problem is reinforced by the reward of decreased tension.*[4] Modifications and elaborations of this reinforcement concept of learning are used by this group of investigators to explain the etiology of abnormal as well as normal behavior and to provide a basis for treatment.

Constitutional Theories. From the time of the pre-Christian Greeks attempts have been made to correlate body type with temperament. Based on a comparatively crude knowledge of human physiology, these early theories have more literary and historical than scientific significance. In the mid-nineteenth century, Lombroso's work in describing criminal types reawakened interest in this approach to the understanding of personality. More refined systems of measurement and statistical analysis have provided a basis for a series of investigations out of which constitutional theories have evolved. The foremost of such studies are those of Kretschmer and of Sheldon.

ERNEST KRETSCHMER (1888–   ). Kretschmer has described four types of physiques and their related personality characteristics: The *pyknic type,* with stocky build and short limbs, possesses an extroverted personality and is subject to mood fluctuations; this type of person when mentally ill is inclined to manic-depressive psychosis. The *asthenic type,* with slender build and long limbs, possesses an introverted personality; this type of person when mentally ill inclines to schizophrenia. The *athletic type,* with a strong, solid, and muscular body build, shows comparable introvertive tendencies. The *dysplastic type,* characterized by body disharmony and therefore not classifiable under the foregoing types, is also temperamentally introverted.

WILLIAM SHELDON (1899–   ). Sheldon, in analyzing several thousand standardized photographs of American male college students, found that three basic factors accounted for all variations observed, and that, furthermore, differences in the relative predominance of any of the factors can account for all existing body types.

The anatomical basis for Sheldon's theory lies in the fact that in

[4] *Ibid.,* p. 79.

the human embryo there are three layers of tissue—endoderm, mesoderm and ectoderm. Although there are some minor exceptions, in general the body structures developing from the endoderm are the digestive system and viscera; those from the mesoderm are the bony structure and muscle, those developing from the ectoderm are the nervous system and skin. Correspondingly, Sheldon names his three body-type components endomorphy, mesomorphy and ectomorphy.

Somatotypes. All three components are present in everyone, but the degree of predominance of one component or another varies greatly. The components are listed as follows.

1. endomorphy—relative predominance of soft roundness in various parts of the body with large digestive viscera.

2. mesomorphy—relative predominance of bone, muscle and connective tissue with a strong muscular physique.

3. ectomorphy—relative predominance of linearity and fragility, a large surface area in relation to body mass, long delicate bones, a relatively large brain and central nervous system.

Each component is represented in Sheldon's system on a seven point scale with 1 the minimal and 7 the maximal degree of dominance. The individual's constitutional classification, or "somatotype" is given in terms of his degree of endomorphy, mesomorphy and ectomorphy, with a number from the seven point scale representing the respective degree of dominance of each component.

Varieties of Temperament. Sheldon also presents three basic temperamental components.

1. Visceratonia—characterized by a love of comfort and luxury, relaxation, a fondness for fine foods, sociability and a need for other people when troubled.

2. Somatotonia—characterized by a need for energetic exercise, aggressiveness, immunity to fatigue, directness and a need for physical action when troubled.

3. Cerebrotonia—characterized by overly fast reactions, social inhibitions, functional complaints, hypersensitivity, intentness, insomnia and a need for solitude when troubled.

Very high coefficients of correlation have been obtained between endomorphy and visceratonia (.79), between mesomorphy and somatotonia (.82), and between ectomorphy and cerebrotonia (.83).

The Existential Approach. The existential approach has grown out of an increasing awareness among a group of European psychiatrists and psychologists of the significant weaknesses in their modes of understanding human beings. Many psychotherapists have felt the futility of fitting a specific person—their patient—into an objective catalogue of syndromes or attempting to structure their understanding of this person within a previously conceived theoretical framework. They have realized that the knowledge of theory alone does not alleviate anxiety, nor does it cure a patient. The reader can perhaps understand more clearly the concern of the therapist in terms of this illustration: a hallucination is defined as perception without an adequate objective stimulus and, thus, when a patient shows certain symptoms he is "understood" as experiencing hallucinations. This labeling of a symptom is a far cry from actually understanding or really knowing what this patient is experiencing and as such is little more than a descriptive approach. Through such descriptive approaches we have no adequate way of entering into the world of the patient or experiencing existence as he does. Existentialism as a psychotherapeutic approach to mental disorder attempts to become aware of the patient's daylong subjective experiences in relation to the patient himself, his world, and the people about him.

Existential therapy traces its etiological roots to such existential philosophers as Kierkegaard and Heidegger, whose principal philosophical concerns dealt with the science of being. Early existential psychiatrists were Binswanger, Von Gebsattel, and Minkowski. Contemporary interpretations of existential therapy are presented in a series of essays and case studies brought together under the title "Existence." *

BASIC POSTULATES. Existential therapy attempts to get behind the dynamisms and specific behavior patterns of the patient and to know them from the patient's point of view.

Several of the more important postulates held by the existentialists are:

1. That the individual person not only continuously experiences his existence but also is constantly aware of and perhaps threatened by the possibility of nonexistence or nonbeing.

2. That anxiety is the experience of the threat of nonbeing.

3. That guilt is a state of being in which the individual finds himself as a result of failing to fulfill his potentialities.

---

* Rollo May, Ernest Angel, and Henri Ellenberger, *Existence* (New York: Basic Books, 1958).

4. That to understand the patient is to understand him in the context of the world in which he lives.

5. That the world of the patient has three simultaneous aspects: (1) his relationship to the physical world, (2) his relationship to the people around him, and (3) his relationship to himself.

6. That time is a distinctive dimension of human personality and that existence is an ever-moving process and is never static. Existence can never be defined in static terms.

7. That existence is a continuously emerging process in which man is neither limited to his immediate present nor determined by his past, but can transcend both and thus can move freely to the future.

THERAPEUTIC PRACTICE. From these considerations the existentialists draw certain implications for therapeutic practice. *First*, they are variable and flexible in their approach to the patient, eschewing rigid adherence to specific technical practices. *Second*, the interpretation of mental dynamisms found in the patient must always be made in relationship to the existence of the patient in *his* world. *Third*, the therapeutic relationship is perceived as a real relationship between two persons in which the therapist attempts to understand and to participate in the patient's world. (Rollo May speaks of this as the *presence* of the therapist.) *Fourth*, an important part of the therapeutic process is to analyze the forces disrupting the experience of presence. *Fifth*, the goal in existential therapy is to bring the patient to a point where he can experience his existence as real. *Sixth*, existentialists use the term "commitment" to describe the patient's readiness to accept insight, pointing out that this "commitment" must precede insight and the acquiring of knowledge about one's self and one's world.

Points of Agreement. Personality theory is still evolving and among the current approaches of schools of thought, differences of opinion will be found. However, there is a growing core of agreement that is based on continuous clinical work. Points of agreement include the following.

1. Personality is a resultant of the interaction of a person's unique biological make-up or constitution, his individual psychological development and the influence of the cultural setting in which he grows. The emphasis given to any of these factors varies among different approaches.

2. Personality is dynamically developing and not a static entity.

3. Early childhood experiences and especially parent-child relationships, are determinants of extreme importance in the formation of personality.

4. Personality dynamics operate on an unconscious as well as a conscious level.

5. Repressed material can find expression in the form of symptoms.

6. Disordered personalities can be treated by specialized techniques.

PSYCHODYNAMICS
OF HUMAN BEHAVIOR

Every human being evolves through the interaction of hereditary and environmental forces which vary in their relative importance from person to person. In the individual there are certain inherited potentials and the degree to which they are realized is a function of the environment in which he develops. The uniqueness of the human organism can be appreciated when one takes into account the myriad possible gene combinations and the infinite variety of environmental experiences that are brought to bear upon the particular combination of genes. From the very moment of his conception, every aspect of the environment which surrounds the individual interacts with the genetic potential provided by heredity.

At birth the infant responds to the first stimuli wholly on the basis of his constitutional make-up, or temperament, which remains throughout his life as a substratum operating as a partial influence on his responses to all subsequent reality. Each response is the product of basic temperament as it has been modified by experience (learning). As the developing infant continues to experience reality, the psychologically unformed mass is differentiated and the ego, or self, evolves. In this process of ego development the personality, from the psychodynamic viewpoint, is organized around a core of biological and psychological needs; the ways in which the individual attempts to satisfy these needs are an important factor in ego development. Inevitably, frustrations and conflicts develop, and in his effort to maintain, protect, and enhance the integrity of his ego, the individual resorts to the defense mechanisms described later in this chapter. Some responses of the individual operate consciously, others unconsciously.

THE EGO OR SELF

The infant develops a self, or ego, from his varied experiences. This process is not merely a passive molding of the organism by

47

the environment; it involves an active reaching out by the individual. As the ego develops, it becomes the integrating core of the personality which organizes, evaluates, and acts upon all subsequent life experiences. The developing ego adopts as its own the norms imposed upon it by persons in positions of authority; and the degree of ease and emotional comfort with which this is accomplished determines in large measure the direction of future personality growth. The earlier life experiences generally have greater impact on the development of the ego than later ones, but at all times the relationship between the ego and the environment is a dynamic one and the ego cannot be regarded as inflexibly fixed at any point in life.

It is important not to confuse the ego which has just been described with the "concept of self." Whereas the ego is the core of the personality, the "concept of self" is the individual's evaluation of his own worth as a person. Whereas the ego is the individual's potential for performance, the "concept of self" delimits his actual performance. The "concept of self" develops, in part, from the individual's own reality-testing experiences, but it is also significantly influenced by evaluations he receives from the emotionally important people in his life and by his interpretations of their responses to him. For example, a child of high-level intelligence who is constantly berated and belittled by rejecting parents (regardless of his performance) may develop a concept of himself as an inadequate person unable to fulfill his potential.

Thus the ego, within the framework of the individual's concept of himself, becomes a focus for examining and knowing reality, for developing ideas of right and wrong, and for evaluating his own potential in relation to the world about him. It serves as the means by which he remembers the past, knows the present, and anticipates the future, and in this way enables him to experience life as a continuing pattern. In addition, the ego provides the guiding principle for meeting life's problems. For these reasons the individual is continuously devoted to maintaining, defending, and enhancing the ego.

MOTIVATION

The human organism is so constituted that at birth it immediately experiences needs which only the environment can satisfy. These earliest needs are purely biological, such as the needs for air and food. Their satisfaction is essential for the maintenance of *homeostatic balance* (the optimal physical and chemical condition for sustaining life). The early learning experiences of the individual give rise to additional personal and social needs the satisfaction of which is required for maintaining *emotional balance*. Examples of such later needs are: security, social approval, and achievement. These more complex needs function in interaction with each other, and they may operate consciously or unconsciously.

Unsatisfied needs create *tension,* which motivates the organism to initiate action (drive) toward their satisfaction with consequent reduction of the tension. At any given time and in any given situation the action or actions selected to accomplish this purpose will depend on the individual's previous learning as well as his constitutional potentialities and limitations.

Biological Needs. Unlearned needs which grow out of the biological nature of the human organism are present at birth and account for much of the early behavior of the newborn. The principal unlearned biological needs are classified as: *visceral* (need for food, oxygen, and water, need to eliminate, and need to rest); *sensory* (need to experience the environment through touch, smell, hearing, taste, and vision); *activity* (need to relieve tension through muscular action); and *emotional* (needs producing generalized reactions of receptivity or avoidance in response to pleasant or unpleasant stimuli).

Although in the very early months of life the biological needs are most important and their frustration at this time can be critical, the cultural pattern routinely provides to some extent for their satisfaction or modification. Thus, they become so interwoven with the psychological needs about to be described that of themselves they usually contribute little to an understanding of the individual's later behavior.

Psychological Needs. Just as the organism strives to maintain biological balance through homeostasis, so does it strive to maintain psychological balance. The individual can preserve the integrity of his ego only if he can satisfy the personal and social needs which have been superimposed upon his biological needs as the result of early learning experiences. The following three classes of personal and social needs are found in the writings of contemporary psychologists:

Social recognition. These have also been labeled *affiliative* needs because they involve the establishment of relationships with others. Such relationships include: belongingness, love, approval, acceptance, companionship, dependency, and prestige.

Self-realization. In order to maintain integrity of the ego, the individual is motivated to bring to fulfillment all his potentialities. Efforts to satisfy this need are directed toward: mastery, achievement, and independence.

Security. The essence of this type of need is the continual concern with maintaining conditions which will assure need gratification, whether the needs are of a biological or psychological nature. Emotional security, the most significant of the security needs, results from the individual's feeling that he will be able to maintain stable and satisfying relationships with the people who are emotionally important in his life.

Sexual Needs. Because sexual activity satisfies both biological and psychological needs, it is here considered in a separate category. Although sex is a visceral need, its satisfaction (unlike that of other visceral needs) is not essential to the life of the organism. From the biological point of view, sexual activity relieves physiological tensions; from the psychological point of view, it is important in the satisfaction of many of man's personal and social needs. The degree and manner in which sexual needs are satisfied are highly varied and individualized, with life circumstances and individual learning experiences playing an important role in their determination.

The complexity of the sex drive in our culture may be appreciated when one considers the extent to which apparently unrelated human activities are affected by aspects of it. (Note, for example, the widespread use of sexual symbols as attention-getters in advertising and the emphasis on sex in many forms of entertainment.) The pervasiveness of the sex drive and the consequences of its frustration are fundamental factors in the psychodynamics of human behavior.

Individual Differences and Relationships Among Needs. While the needs themselves are almost universal in human society, the manner in which any of them may be satisfied varies widely from one individual to another (for example, food preferences, choice of marital partner, or choice of career). The relative importance of needs also varies from person to person and within any individual from one time to another.

Variation in the intensity of a need is dependent on previous learning experiences and the degree of deprivation. It must be borne in mind that the needs function in an integrated organism and that they operate always in interrelation with all other needs.

Emotions as Drives. The satisfaction or lack of satisfaction of a need is always accompanied by emotional reaction. If the need is satisfied, the accompanying feeling tone is pleasant; if not, it is unpleasant. In time the emotion itself may come to serve as a drive and thus psychodynamically influence behavior. The pleasant emotion is sought for its own sake; attempts to avoid extremely unpleasant emotion become drives in themselves and may bring about changes in the total behavior pattern of the person. Thus, the need which gave rise to the pleasant or unpleasant emotion is subordinated to the emotion itself. Of particular significance is the effect of anxiety as a motivating force in human behavior, with anxiety-reduction becoming a need in and of itself.

LEVELS OF AWARENESS

Mental experiences (such as the awareness of a need, wishes, aspirations, and emotions) may be said to operate on three levels: the conscious, the preconscious, and the unconscious. To Freud we owe our appreciation of the importance of the unconscious in influencing personality development and human behavior, since the concept of the unconscious is one of the cornerstones of the Freudian approach to personality structure.

Conscious processes are mental experiences of which the individual is here and now aware; they are generally susceptible to control. The sharpness with which one is aware of conscious experiences is a function of attention.

Preconscious processes concern mental experiences of which one is not here and now aware but which one can bring to awareness with relative ease (the preconscious is also referred to as the *foreconscious*).

Unconscious processes are mental experiences which cannot be readily recalled and are not susceptible to control but which continue to influence the individual in his behavior and attitudes in a manner not constrained by limitations of time, space, or logic. The existence of these processes can be demonstrated experimentally through hypnoanalysis and narcoanalysis. Exploration of the mental and emotional life of patients undergoing psychotherapy also provides abundant evidence of the existence of unconscious mental processes and of their continual impact on behavior. Examples frequently offered as manifestations of the unconscious mental life are slips of speech and the phenomena of dreams. Attitudes, feelings, desires, and ideas are incorporated into the unconscious as a result of repression and forgetting.

FRUSTRATION AND CONFLICT

It is of course inevitable that some needs experienced by the individual cannot be satisfied. The very nature of society demands that men accept the frustration of some of them and exercise a degree of self-denial. Frustration resulting from the clash of two motives that exert their force in different directions produces the psychological state of *conflict*. Everyone is aware of the frustrations and conflicts that are the everyday occurrences of life; less well recognized, but of extreme importance to abnormal psychology, are those which operate beneath the surface—i.e., on the level of the unconscious.

Types of Frustration. There are two types of frustration: personal and environmental. Personal frustrations result from personal insufficiency, such as inadequate intelligence, lack of physical strength, disabling diseases, or other handicaps. Environmental frustrations result from obstacles existing in the environment, such as parentally imposed restrictions, lack of money, or physical restraint.

Patterns of Conflict. There are three patterns of conflict:

The *double-approach* conflict, in which the individual must choose between two attractive goals (for example, marriage versus career).

The *double-avoidant* conflict, in which the choice must be made between two evils (for example, doing distasteful work or having no money).

The *approach-avoidant* conflict, in which the individual must decide whether or not to move toward a pleasurable goal the attainment of which involves painful consequences (for example, seeking the glory of heroism at the expense of personal danger).

The majority of conflicts that are significant in personality development involve opposition between drives which are in conflict with moral and social codes. Typical of such conflicts is the adolescent's adjustment to his sexual drives in the face of cultural and social restrictions.

Reactions to Frustrations and Conflicts. Because they are unpleasant, tension-loaded states, frustrations and conflicts motivate the individual toward activity which will reduce or eliminate the discomfort thus engendered. Such activity, called the *adjustment process,* may be undertaken either consciously or unconsciously. When the frustration or conflict is severe or prolonged, the individual may experience a threat to the ego, with consequent feelings of anxiety, and this combination of stress and anxiety propels the individual toward the basic reactions of "fight" or "flight." The specific form these reactions will take is determined by the individual's previous learning and life experiences, particularly as they have influenced his attitude toward socially approved patterns and, to a greater or lesser degree, motivated his desire for social acceptance. As the individual experiences and accepts the patterns and demands of society, he tends to control, conceal, or modify his reactions. The more extreme expressions of "fight" or "flight" are found in children and immature adults.

THE "FIGHT" REACTION. John Dollard, the American psychologist, in his extensive analysis of frustration and aggression, has described the manifestations of the "fight" reaction as follows: The primitive "fight" response is a destructive physical act directed against the frustrating person or object. However, as the person learns to understand the social disapproval attached to such behavior in our society and the danger of punishment and counteraggression that must follow, he seeks more devious methods of fighting back. He may then resort to various forms of verbal aggression (angry name-calling, barbed wit, argument, or criticism, either open or veiled). In some circumstances the individual may find it impossible to express any aggression toward the frustrating person and he may seek to vent his feelings by displacing them onto other persons, usually those who cannot retaliate effectively or those who are not members of his own group. Examples of displacement of aggression from adult to child, from employer to employee (and the reverse), and from persons in authority to persons subject to authority are frequently seen. The hostility directed toward minority groups, expressed as discrimination based on prejudice, is an example of displaced aggression.

In extreme cases the aggressive impulses arouse such feelings of guilt as to become completely inhibited. Frequently, such blocked aggression and the accompanying need to reduce the feelings of guilt arouse patterns of self-directed aggression. Occasionally, suicides and "accidents" have been so interpreted.

THE "FLIGHT" REACTION. Regression as a form of flight reaction to frustration has been experimentally demonstrated and has been observed in the case histories of many patients under therapy. Other forms of "flight" reaction include daydreaming, disinterest, and apathy.

The reactions of "fight" or "flight" just described constitute *acting-out* responses to frustration and conflict, and must be differentiated from defense mechanisms, which are *indirect and unconscious* adjustive efforts.

OTHER REACTIONS. Still another reaction to frustration—the development of rigid and repetitive patterns of behavior—has been suggested by Norman Maier, an experimental psychologist, who, in a series of experimental animal studies, induced neuroses in his subjects. From these studies, he concluded that, in frustration situations, variability in response and goal-oriented behavior give way to fixed and stereotyped behavior.

THE ADJUSTMENT PROCESS

The majority of the frustrations and conflicts experienced in day-to-day living can be resolved on the conscious level. More deeply rooted frustrations and conflicts which cannot be resolved on that level lead to the development of unconscious adjustive efforts, the *defense mechanisms*. Along with the frustrations and conflicts that gave rise to them, these mechanisms constitute significant elements in the personality structure of the individual.

Conscious Attempts at Adjustment. The most commonly employed conscious attempts at adjustment in the face of frustration or conflict are: increasing the effort to overcome the obstacle; lowering or changing the goal; realistically reappraising the frustrative or conflictive situation. In some instances, conscious adjustments may resemble the pattern of a defense mechanism. The difference between them lies in the person's degree of awareness, or insight; a true defense mechanism always functions unconsciously.

Unconscious Attempts at Adjustment (Defense Mechanisms). Defense mechanisms are the unconscious attempts of the individual to protect himself against threats to the integrity of the ego and also to relieve the tension and anxiety resulting from unresolved frustrations and conflicts. All people employ these self-deceptive measures to some extent, attempting in this way to maintain their self-esteem and soften the impact of failure, deprivation, or sense of guilt. It must not be assumed that defense mechanisms invariably signify abnormal personality structure. In fact, such mechanisms frequently result in gains for the individual in his adjustment efforts; his reactions may be a constructive form of compensation, sublimation, or identification. On the other hand, excessive dependence on defense mechanisms as a means of resolving frustration or conflict may indicate abnormal modes of adjustment. The principal defense mechanisms follow.

Compensation—the mechanisms whereby the individual devotes himself to a given pursuit with increased vigor in an attempt to make up for some feeling of real or imagined inadequacy. The compensation may be direct or indirect. *Direct compensation* refers to the generation of an intense desire to succeed in an area in which one has experienced failure or inferiority. The classic example is the effort of Demosthenes to become an outstanding orator because of his childhood speech disabilities; the very existence of this frustrating handicap provided the motivation to work more intensely to overcome it. *Indirect compensation* consists of the effort to find success in one field when there has been failure in another. This is seen in the vigorous efforts frequently made toward social achievement by students who fail to make their mark in academic circles or on the athletic fields. *Overcompensation* is compensatory effort which is made at the expense of a well-rounded and complete adjustment to a variety of life's demands. The individual who devotes all or an unreasonable amount of his time to a very narrow area in response to failure or a feeling of inadequacy, even though he may enjoy great success from his efforts, is said to have "overcompensated" if he finds adjustment in other areas of life difficult.

Conversion—the mechanism in which emotional conflicts gain external expression through motor, sensory, or somatic manifestations. The resulting disability frequently represents both escape from painful or ego-threatening situations and gain through illness. The physical manifestations may be dramatic, often occurring in association with some minor accident or illness. The "shell shock" reactions of soldiers in wartime have provided excellent illustrations of the conversion defense. As a result of having been near an exploding shell, these men developed purely psychogenic paralysis, blindness, or other disabilities, thus escaping further anxiety-producing combat and, moreover, being rewarded with sympathy and medical care.

Denial—the process whereby an individual avoids painful or anxiety-producing reality by unconsciously denying that it exists. The denied reality may be a thought, a wish, or a need, or some external object or condition. Denial may take on verbal form in an occasional statement that something is not so or in a compulsively repeated formula which is resorted to as a means of keeping the thought, wish, etc. out of consciousness. Completely ignoring unpleasant aspects of reality is one way of denying that they exist. In an extreme form, such a denial may result in complete loss of contact with surrounding reality. Examples of this defense mechanism range from less serious manifestations such as denying that one has unpleasant traits (e.g., cruelty, stubbornness, and dishonesty) to the extreme cases, such as denying, despite conclusive evidence, the fact that some loved person has died.

Displacement—the process in which pent-up emotions are redirected toward ideas, objects, or persons other than the primary source of the emotion. Displacement may occur with both positive and negative emotions. For example, feelings of love which cannot be expressed openly toward a married member of the opposite sex may be displaced toward a child of that person. Another way in which displacement may be manifested is by changing the channel of expression for the emotion; for instance, physical aggression may be inhibited but expressed verbally.

Dissociation—the mechanism in which a group of mental processes are separated or isolated from consciousness and operate independently or automatically. The end result may be a splitting of certain mental content from the main personality or a loss of normal thought-affect relationships. Examples are: amnesia, development of multiple personalities, and somnambulism. A dramatic illustration of dissociation is seen in the case presented by Thigpen and Cleckley in "The Three Faces Of Eve."

Fantasy—the process in which daydreaming or some form of imaginative activity provides escape from reality, with satisfaction obtained through imagined achievements, or martyrdom. A certain amount of daydreaming, especially in the earlier years of life, must be regarded as normal. As a preparation for creativity, fantasy is not only desirable but even essential. But fantasy becomes a dangerous and sometimes a disabling mechanism if it is consistently preferred to reality and is indulged in as a method of problem-solving. In extreme forms of fantasy, characteristic of psychotic adjustment, the individual is unable to differentiate fact from fancy.

Identification—the mechanism in which the individual enhances his self-esteem by patterning himself after another person. This may be done in fantasy or in actual behavior. Employed in moderation, identification may be both helpful and stimulating, and it frequently leads to superior achievement. Used to excess, it may deny the individual gratification of his own personality needs. The popularity of motion pictures and spectator sports as diversions is largely due to the satisfaction obtained through identification.

Introjection—the process of taking into one's own ego structure all or a part of another person or an object, which is then reacted to as if it were an element of oneself. An example would be a suicidal act in which aggression is directed against a hated parental figure which has been introjected.

Negativism—the process of active or passive resistance to demands on the individual: active, when the person does the opposite of what he is asked to do; passive, when he avoids doing what is expected. An extreme form of negativism is seen in the mutism of the catatonic patient. A more common example is the child who fails in school as an expression of resistance to undue parental pressure.

Overcompensation—See *Compensation*.

Projection—the mechanism by which the individual protects himself from awareness of his own undesirable traits or feelings by attributing them to others. In its function of self-deception this mechanism is particularly injurious to personality adjustment, since it tends to undermine or completely destroy insight. There is no constructive use of projection and its overuse is often dangerous, for it is the mechanism underlying suspiciousness and, therefore, can be especially harmful to effective interpersonal relationships.

Rationalization—the mechanism through which an individual justifies inconsistent or undesirable behavior, beliefs, statements, and motivations by providing acceptable explanations for them. Examples are: the "sour-grapes" mechanism, which implies that what was sincerely wanted is not worth trying for; and the "sweet-lemon" form, which finds desirable qualities in that which was not truly wanted. As a defense mechanism, rationalization operates unconsciously and must be differentiated from the conscious "alibi."

Reaction Formation—the process in which urges that are not acceptable to consciousness are repressed and in their stead opposite attitudes or modes of behavior are expressed with considerable force. Overprotestations of sincerity or of willingness to help may often mean the very opposite. Scrupulosity is often a reaction formation in response to unacceptable desires or wishes.

Regression—the mechanism whereby the individual returns to an earlier and less mature level of adaptation. An extreme form of regression is seen in the infantile behavior of some psychotic persons. Milder regression is seen in the return of an older child to babyish mannerisms upon the birth of a sibling. Regression as a mode of adjustment may, however, occur at any period of life.

Repression—the process of complete exclusion from consciousness of impulses, experiences, and feelings which are psychologically disturbing because they arouse a sense of guilt or anxiety. Repression is essential for the existence and operation of all other defense mechanisms. It must be distinguished from *suppression,* the conscious control of unacceptable impulses, feelings, and experiences. Repression is especially operative during early childhood.

Sublimation—the process by which unconscious and unacceptable desires are channeled into activities that have strong social approval. The unacceptable desires are usually sexual in nature and their expression may be sublimated as creative effort in music, art, and literature. Other areas of life that provide avenues for sublimation are social welfare work, teaching, and the religious life.

Undoing—the mechanisms in which the individual symbolically acts out in reverse (usually repetitiously) something he has already done or thought which is unacceptable to his ego or to society. Through this behavior he strives to erase the offending act or thought and with it the accompanying sense of guilt or anxiety. An example of undoing is the behavior of a mother who, having punished her child, feels guilty and attempts to undo the punishment by smothering the child with affection.

Failure of Defense Mechanisms—Decompensation. As previously stated, the function of a defense mechanism is to maintain the integrity of the ego and thus to keep the individual in a state of psychological equilibrium. When the stress is too great for the personality to resist, the defenses are weakened and the personality begins to disintegrate. This process is called *decompensation*. In the process of decompensation, the individual may at first attempt to use other defensive measures: for example, he may pass from superficial rationalization to severe projection. The decompensation may produce a panic state of anxiety as the individual is confronted with the break-through of unconscious material. From a psychological point of view, the final stage of decompensation for some individuals may be a florid psychotic reaction.

5

CAUSATIVE FACTORS (ETIOLOGY)

The causes of abnormal behavior are many and complex. Even in a single individual the etiology of personality disorder is, without exception, multiple; simple one-to-one cause-and-effect relationships are practically unknown. In general the causative factors are classified as biological, psychological, and cultural. Most mental disorders result from some combination of all these factors; few are caused by one class of factors alone.

To understand the etiology of mental illness, one must also distinguish between predisposing and precipitating causes, both of which are found in any of the aforementioned classes of factors. *Predisposing causes* are those factors which have produced in the individual a susceptibility to some form of mental illness. They may lie in the genetic origin, the physical history, or the family and social background. For example, a history of rejection and emotional deprivation in childhood may leave a person ill prepared to cope with the stresses of later life and so predispose him to a neurotic breakdown. *Precipitating causes* are those immediate stresses or traumatic incidents which trigger a mental disturbance. Some common precipitating causes are: bereavement, financial reverses, accident or injury, severe or debilitating illness, and marital difficulties. Such events are not of themselves sufficient to cause a personality disorder, for they are borne by many persons who find ways to adjust satisfactorily, either in the course of the traumatic experience or soon afterward. In the susceptible individual, precipitating causes have a special significance which is derived from the context of his entire life pattern. Frequently, the mentally disturbed person is unaware of the stress to which he is responding.

BIOLOGICAL FACTORS

Among the factors influencing the development of abnormal behavior, the biological factors seem to play a vital part. The extent and manner of this influence have not been specifically identified in all forms of personality disorder. The principal biological factors are heredity, constitution, and physical disease and injury. They may exert their effects alone or in combination.

Heredity. By heredity is meant the biological endowment transmitted (through the genes) from the parents to the offspring at the instant of conception. The particular arrangement of genes for any individual may be considered unique, except that identical twins will have identical gene patterns. Every human trait is the result of the interaction between hereditary potential and environmental forces. A trait is regarded as hereditary when its presence can be traced to particular gene combination. Such characteristics as eye color, color blindness, and certain types of baldness are commonly believed to be determined by heredity. A distinction must be made between hereditary traits and *congenital traits;* while the latter are present at birth, they are due not to gene patterns but to the influences of prenatal (intrauterine) environment. A congenital trait is therefore properly regarded as *environmental* in nature.

Throughout literature and folklore the significance of heredity in the production of mental illness has been magnified, but extensive research has shown that only a few specific disorders, of statistically minor importance, can be inherited directly. Two of them are *amaurotic family idiocy* (also known as Tay-Sachs disease) and *Huntington's chorea;* but even in these the evidence has not been conclusive. On the other hand, the possible existence of a genetic factor in predisposing an individual to mental illness (schizophrenia, manic-depressive psychosis, and epilepsy) has been demonstrated by studies of identical twins. The close relationship between schizophrenia and identity of genetic structure has been indicated by the genetic studies of Kallmann. Other studies showing similar results have been reported for manic-depressive psychosis by Rosanoff and for epilepsy by Lennox. The role of heredity as a principal cause of mental deficiency was once generally accepted, but the extent of its influence is believed to be much more limited than was previously held.

The assumption that mental disturbances seem to "run in families" is widely accepted. If true, however, it would not necessarily prove that the causes are genetic factors, for the similarities of environment, life experiences, interpersonal reactions, and accompanying stresses in families might suffice to account for the disturbances.

Constitution. This term refers to the biological make-up of the individual. It is a comprehensive term, for it includes the individual's innate characteristics and his very early environmental experiences. (In this sense, early environmental experience refers to: the germinal state; prenatal development; the birth process; and, in varying degrees among individuals, the critical formative influences of the early postnatal period. The specific role of each of these has not been identified.)

Principal constitutional factors are: the physique, temperament, endocrine functions, and other aspects of body physiology. Various constitutional factors have been shown to have a high degree of correlation with certain types of mental illness, but no cause-and-effect mechanism has been established.

PHYSIQUE. Numerous studies of physique in relation to behavior have been made, beginning as far back as Hippocrates; the most significant contributions have been those of the modern period, particularly the recent studies by Kretschmer and Sheldon. In his *Physique and Character* (published in 1925), Kretschmer described four basic types of physique and sought to correlate them with various "personality types." He was able to demonstrate that asthenic people who develop a mental illness will most frequently develop schizophrenia, while pyknic people will most often develop one of the affective disorders (for example, manic-depressive psychosis). Sheldon evolved a system of body measurements, called *somatotyping,* by which he attempted to correlate physique with temperament and mental illness. Although the conclusions of these two investigators have been the center of much controversy and no exact statement of causal relationships has emerged from their findings, the factor of physique merits attention in any study of etiology of abnormal behavior. For a discussion of the theories of Kretschmer and Sheldon, see pages 42–43.

TEMPERAMENT. This attribute may be considered the constitutional core of the personality. Temperament can be recognized early in life, is relatively persistent, and sets the general tone of the individual's response to his environment. Manifestations of temperament are: prevailing mood, tempo and intensity of response, energy level, and sensitivity to stimulation. Some types of temperament have been hypothesized as predisposing the individual toward the development of mental or emotional disorders. For example, hypersensitivity tends to limit the individual's capacity to tolerate stress and enhances the likelihood of a neurotic breakdown.

Endocrine Functions. Endocrine (ductless) glands are those glands which secrete directly into the blood stream. Their functioning is closely interrelated with that of the autonomic nervous system. The accompanying table lists the principal endocrine glands, their

THE ENDOCRINE GLANDS AND THEIR FUNCTIONS *

Gland	Location	Function	Disorders
1. Pineal	Under surface of cerebrum	Unknown	Sexual development disturbed in pineal gland tumors
2. Pituitary	Under surface of cerebrum	Controls growth and development (ant. lobe) Influences on blood pressure and water regulation (post. lobe)	Hypofunction: retarded development; diabetes insipidus Hyperfunction: giantism or acromegaly
3. Thyroid	Front of trachea	Regulation of metabolism	Hypofunction in infancy: cretinism; adult: myxedema Hyperfunction: Goiter, increased metabolism
4. Parathyroid	On surface of thyroid glands	Regulation of calcium metabolism	Hypofunction: tetany, death
5. Thymus	Anterior mediastinum	Inhibitory effect on sexual development. Atrophies in adult	Hypofunction: Precocious sexual development
6. Adrenal cortex	Over kidneys	Influences sodium and water metabolism. Sexual glands	Hypofunction: Addison's disease Hyperfunction: Accelerated sexual development
7. Adrenal medulla	Over kidneys	Autonomic nervous stimulation (adrenalin production)	Hypofunction: No disease entities. Hyperfunction: none
8. Islets of Langerhans	In pancreas	Carbohydrate metabolism	Hypofunction: diabetes mellitus Hyperfunction: none
9. Gonads	Pelvis in female Testicles in male	Growth and reproduction	Hyperfunction: Sexual precocity Hypofunction: Under-development of secondary sex characteristics

* After Lawrence I. O'Kelly and Frederick A. Muckler, *Introduction to Psychopathology*, 2nd ed. (Englewood Cliffs, N.J.: Prentice-Hall, 1955), p. 449.

functions, and the disorders associated with their dysfunction. It can be seen from the table that these glands play a significant role in regulating growth and development and are important determinants of variations in temperament.

OTHER ASPECTS OF BODY PHYSIOLOGY. These include: individual differences in receptor and effector functioning, in the make-up of the autonomic and central nervous systems, and in circulatory functioning. While specific roles in the causation of abnormal behavior cannot be accurately described for these physiological variations among individuals, their possible significance as contributing factors to abnormal behavior cannot be dismissed.

Physical Disease and Injury. Alterations of body structure or function owing to disease or trauma may bring about mental abnormalities. *Head injuries* constitute the single most important class of traumata altering behavior. General *reduction in the adjustive capacity* of the body may prevent adequate response to a stress situation; examples of this are the effects of fatigue, malnutrition, and infection. *Chronic or severe ailments* such as heart disease, cancer, tuberculosis, or diabetes may give rise to maladaptive personality changes. The *prolonged high fever* that is often associated with childhood diseases is a factor of special significance since it may result in encephalitis, convulsive seizures, or arrested mental development. Prolonged or severe biological stress involving *extreme physical exertion or states of semistarvation* has been known to produce radical personality changes or even mental breakdown. Experimental evidence suggests that minor personality changes are related to *nutritional factors* such as vitamin deficiency.

PSYCHOLOGICAL FACTORS

Of particular concern to the psychologist is the individual's life history of interpersonal relationships, in which may be found the causes for many forms of personality disturbances. Not only do these psychological causative factors reflect basic personality structure, they also influence the individual's response to physical or cultural factors. For example, the personality changes following a head injury may be specifically influenced by the pretraumatic personality, for it has been noted that the same extent and localization of tissue damage in several people do not necessarily result in the same psychological symptoms. Psychological causative factors are usually multiple, and they operate in a complex and overlapping fashion. Rarely, if ever, can abnormal behavior be traced to a single psychological factor.

The chief facet of the life history is the pattern of the individual's interpersonal relationships, and the most convenient approach to the interpersonal history is the chronological one, dividing the life span into seven periods: infancy, early childhood, late childhood, adolescence, early adulthood, middle age, and old age. These arbitrary divisions are not intended to suggest breaks in the continuity of the interpersonal history, for the changes which take place in any given period are inescapably interwoven with the entire interpersonal history up to that point. Chronological age may, indeed, be a poor index of psychological maturation of the individual.

Infancy. The period of infancy is one of complete helplessness and dependency during which the infant's functioning is chiefly oriented toward the satisfaction of physical needs. It is normally assumed to extend from birth to the latter half of the second year—in which time the infant should have learned to walk and to communicate. This period is marked by rapid development of the organism; perceptions of the milieu are gradually differentiated, though simply; the elementary aspects of social response begin to appear; major muscle groups are brought under rudimentary control. Psychologists in general (and psychoanalysts in particular) emphasize the critical nature of this period for subsequent personality development.

The major problems of infancy revolve about the "mothering" and feeding of the infant. Although problems of toilet training are frequently listed as problems of infancy, actually they do not emerge until the individual becomes more aware of authority and discipline, and they are therefore properly categorized under problems of early childhood, particularly in the preschool period.

"MOTHERING." Because the infant's first and most meaningful contact with the world outside himself is his physical relationship with his mother, the extent and quality of this relationship lays the foundation for his basic outlook and his attitude toward the world and himself. The extent to which the mother provides warm, affectionate, and abundant contacts determines whether the individual's responses to the world about him will be of an accepting-and-satisfying nature or a rejecting-and-depriving nature. Holding, caressing, and talking to the infant help to generate feelings of basic security. The "mothering" may be further enriched by participation on the part of the father and other members of the family constellation. Absence or inadequacy of mothering contacts has been proven to result in severe physical retardation and has been found in the life histories of many psychotic and neurotic persons. Anxieties and emotional upsets of the mother during pregnancy can be harmful and be a source of feelings of insecurity manifested later in the life of the individual.

FEEDING. The principal need the infant feels is engendered by hunger; consequently, the feeding situation is of critical importance in early personality development. The satisfaction of this need in a calm and relaxed fashion and in accordance with the infant's demands rather than under a rigidly fixed schedule constitutes another requisite for emotional security. In the feeding situation the infant not only satisfies his need for food but also derives pleasure from the activities of sucking, mouthing, and swallowing.

The principal problems arise from improper feeding techniques or from parental attitudes unsatisfying to the child and from too early or abrupt weaning. These feeding problems develop when a mother is improperly informed about feeding procedures or when her own fears and anxieties interfere with her carrying them out properly. Problems which grow out of the feeding situation may be carried forward to later stages of development and may serve as a focus for more extensive problem behavior, especially when they are magnified and perpetuated by the anxieties of the mother.

Not all irregularities in the infant's feeding pattern should be considered as problems, since a mature, flexible, and secure approach can keep them from becoming sources of difficulty. Some of these irregularities may occur as a result of such physical factors as allergic reactions or malformations of the digestive system. Failure to recognize and adequately treat such conditions may, however, lead to further unnecessary psychological complications.

Early Childhood. This is the period in which the first earnest attempts at socialization are made. It is initiated during the latter part of the second year for, at such time, the infant becomes aware of his individuality and is confronted with problems of authority and discipline. In early childhood the individual makes considerable advance from his prior dependency and helplessness, exhibiting independence in locomotion, self-care for simple needs, and development of social behavior. The period of early childhood is generally regarded as ending at some time in the sixth or seventh year.

During this period the *family* is the setting in which the child develops his social skills and learns to control his behavior in accordance with the norms set up for him. Parental approval or disapproval is the principal guide, and the way these are used by the parents is one of the strongest psychological determinants of personality development. Consequently, psychological problems which arise in early childhood involve one or another aspect of the socialization process. Some of the causative factors of later abnormal behavior which may be attributed to the early childhood period are: parent-child relationships, authority and discipline, toilet training, sexual development, aggression and hostility, relationships with siblings, and extreme frustrations and other traumatic experiences.

PARENT-CHILD RELATIONSHIPS. Extreme behavior in any direction between parent and child can be the source of emotional disturbance and later abnormal behavior. The deviations from sound parent-child relationships most frequently seen are: rejection, overprotection, and marital discord or broken home.

Rejection. Since the child is dependent on his parents for evaluation of himself and of the outside world, any rejection on their part will produce in him some form of negative reaction. Prolonged, extreme, or cruel rejection constitutes a definite source of insecure feelings and later maladjustment. Parental rejection is characterized in many ways: it may be overt and explicit, or subtle and unconscious; it may be shown as a persistent pattern of the parents' behavior, or inconsistently displayed by one parent or both; it may be expressed by denial or deprivation, nagging, criticism, insistence on standards impossible of attainment, favoritism among siblings, or sheer neglect.

The individual child's reaction to rejection will depend not only on the mere fact of being rejected but also on the manner and degree of its expression and, of course, on the temperament of the child. He may conform or rebel, withdraw or attack. Abnormal behavior stemming from parental rejection ranges from minor psychological symptoms to major personality disturbances.

Overprotection. When the parent consciously or unconsciously prevents the child from developing normal independence in his interactions with the environment, the situation of overprotection is said to prevail. This may be expressed in the form of overindulgent "smother" love or in cold and dominating control. Overprotecting parents either submit abjectly to every demand of the child or tyrannically impose their own values, ambitions, and desires. Often overprotection serves the parents as a mechanism to compensate for guilt feelings arising from their unconscious rejection of the child. It may also stem from the anxieties aroused in the parent by feelings of personal inadequacy, difficulties in conceiving the child, loss of previous children, or serious illness. Overprotection interferes with the child's efforts to test his powers for meeting the stresses of his environment, leaving him poorly prepared to face the realities of life outside the home. Overprotected children tend to grow into submissive or overdemanding, anxious, insecure persons.

A prolonged pattern of overprotection leads to adult patterns of emotional instability and immaturity. Overprotected children frequently exploit human relationships in a selfish manner and thus are poorly prepared for marriage and parenthood.

Marital Discord and Broken Home. Basic to the proper development of the child's personality is the parents' role in providing him with an environment of parental affection, an opportunity to experience authority and discipline in an acceptable manner, a value system, and a healthy masculine and feminine identification. Evidence consistently shows that the wholesome personality development of the child takes place most smoothly when both the father and mother are present in the home. Under this condition the child will be best able to (1) achieve a mature and healthy adjustment in which he can accept the norms of society without being dominated by them, (2) relate warmly to others without becoming too dependent upon them, (3) find satisfactions in work and play, and (4) learn to satisfy his drives in an acceptable fashion. Through a satisfactory relationship with both parents in the home he is able to achieve a sense of his own personal warmth and dignity.

Marital discord and its possible consequences of separation and divorce is probably the most disruptive and malignant condition that challenges healthy personality growth. The hostility and confused emotionality that confront a child in the midst of such a marriage make it difficult, and in some cases impossible, for him to use this relationship for normal growth in interpersonal relations. His own role identifications are not clear. He is made to feel anxious and insecure, and the foundation for a personality or behavior disorder may thereby be laid.

Marital discord, however, is not the only factor which can upset the home structure. Circumstances beyond individual control may block wholesome development. Among these are: death of one of the parents; extended absence from the home of either or both parents owing to illness, military duty, or work assignment. The extent of damage wrought upon the individual child will depend on the child's previous adjustment and on other relationships which may be available to him in or outside the home.

AUTHORITY AND DISCIPLINE. The ability to adjust adequately to reality situations in our culture demands that the child learn to accept authority. The manner in which this acceptance of authority develops depends on the child's relationship with his father and mother. He begins life as a completely egocentric individual, sensitive to nothing but his own needs and desires. His earliest deprivations result from simple limitations imposed on him by various reality factors (for example, the delay that is often necessary before he can be fed or comforted). As growth continues, he learns that the sources of some deprivations are the wishes of his parents rather than physical necessity. This represents the first authority relationship and is *the beginning of the child's socialization,* by which process he gradually absorbs the standards of society.

Where the parents set standards appropriate to the maturity of the child and hold the child to these standards in a firm but benevolent fashion, the child usually finds it possible to accept the reality demands imposed on him. Where, on the other hand, the parents introduce standards which are beyond the child's reach or which are enforced in arbitrary and dogmatic fashion, the child will respond with either rebellion or oversubmissiveness. Where no standards are provided or where those provided are enforced inconsistently, the child is confused, does not develop adequate frustration tolerance, and ultimately finds it impossible to adjust to the demands of maturity.

TOILET TRAINING. A specific and highly critical phase of the child's process of socialization is the development of bladder and bowel control. Attempts to impose standards of control and cleanliness upon the child before he is physically or emotionally ready for such training is often the cause of early feelings of inadequacy and fear. Persistent stress on this aspect of the child's behavior can be the cause of later personality problems. Psychoanalysts particularly emphasize this feature of parent-child relationships and attribute to unsatisfactory toilet training such traits as mischievousness, stubbornness, and compulsive cleanliness and neatness. Training of the child in satisfactory toilet habits often constitutes the first critical authoritative relationship between parent and child. Exaggeration of its importance is frequently a reflection of the mother's own anxiety about cleanliness or her own feelings of inadequacy in the role of mother.

SEXUAL DEVELOPMENT. The child's acquaintance with sex begins with his awareness and exploration of his own body. Further development takes place when he becomes aware of anatomical differences between the sexes. Parental reactions to these learning experiences of the child condition his basic attitude toward sex. Healthy parental approaches include willingness to answer questions immediately, frankly, objectively, and on an appropriate level, thus providing an opportunity for the child to integrate his sexual knowledge as a natural part of his entire learning experience. Parental reactions which arouse in the child feelings of shame, guilt, or mystery can be the beginnings of difficulties in the wholesome acceptance of the sexual function in life. Excessive fondling by the parents may lead to overstimulation of the erotic zones of the body and, thus, condition the child to this form of satisfaction. On the other hand, prolonged affectional neglect may cause the child to turn to self-stimulation as a form of satisfaction.

During this early childhood period the emotional attachment between the child and the parent of the opposite sex may be intense. This is what Freud has described as the Oedipal relationship (or Oedipus situation), which involves not only the attachment to the parent of the opposite sex, but also feelings of jealousy and rivalry against the parent of the same sex. When this intense relationship exists, the manner of its resolution is critical for later emotional development. Sexual intimacies between the parents observed by the child may have a traumatic effect upon him, for he may interpret the situation as being a demonstration of aggression rather than of affection. In some cases even the viewing of the parent's unclothed body will cause emotional distress.

The attitude toward sex inculcated in the period of early childhood lays the groundwork for important areas of the adult personality, such as relationships with the opposite sex, capacity to exchange love and affection, and ability to assume adequate masculine or feminine roles in life. Warped attitudes provide the basis for a variety of later personality difficulties.

AGGRESSION AND HOSTILITY. As the child develops and learns to control his skeletal musculature, he discovers his capacity to respond to the environment with aggressive action. Feelings of hostility growing out of frustrations, humiliations, or threats may cause the child to express this aggressive capacity directly and openly. The consequences of his expressions of aggression, his own reaction to the experiences, and the reactions of other persons constitute important influences in this testing and learning process and eventually in the development of the total personality. Repeated experiences with hostile feelings and their expression through aggression help to determine the patterns of control which will be carried into adult life. Children must be led to understand that their hostile feelings are natural and acceptable but that the manifestation of these feelings in aggression must be controlled. The degree of control of aggressive impulses must, of course, be related to the age level of the child as well as to the provoking situation. For example, more aggression can be tolerated in the behavior of a three-year-old child than in that of a seven-year-old.

Where the parents' reaction to aggression tends to be extreme in either direction, difficulties in personality adjustment may be expected. Thus, a child who is made to feel anxious and guilty about all hostile feelings and any expression of aggression may develop unhealthy patterns of control; his feelings of guilt and fear of counter-aggression or punishment may cause extreme inhibition and timidity. But too rigid control by the parents may also lead to overrebellious behavior on the part of the child. In contrast, another pattern may result when the parents fail to exert any control over the child's expression of his aggressions. In this way they may foster continual aggressive behavior as a mode of adjustment. Difficulties in developing control of aggression constitute a principal cause of disabling symptoms; many authorities believe aggressions are the most significant sources of feelings of guilt. In addition, aggression can be the basis for a vicious cycle in which the sequence is: frustration—aggression—guilt—anxiety—intensified frustration.

SIBLING RELATIONSHIPS. Although a child's most significant relationships are with his parents, interaction with brothers and sisters plays an important part in personality development. The principal problem of adjustment which they present to the child is that *parental love must be shared.* Such enforced sharing inevitably arouses feelings of jealousy and hostility which the child discovers can further threaten his feelings of security. The child's adjustment to the sibling problem is colored by the number of children in the family, the child's own rank in order of birth, the age and sex distribution of the children, and any marked physical, intellectual, or emotional differences which may generate in the child either a feeling of inferiority or a sense of dominance to be exploited. The role which the child assumes in the family constellation also determines the patterns of adjustment in later social life.

Over and above the foregoing factors, the way the parents handle the sibling relationships determines the extent of their impact on the individual's personality. Favoritism can intensify the child's feelings of jealousy or hostility toward the favored one, and conscious or unconscious "playing of one child against the other" can step up the rivalry, sometimes with unfortunate results.

Within reasonable limits, sibling rivalries must be accepted as a normal characteristic of the struggle for growth and development. However, persistent and exaggerated rivalry relationships can function as basic etiological factors of abnormal behavior in childhood and may extend into adult life. Thus, deep-seated and repressed hostilities toward brothers or sisters can constitute the focal point for pathological prejudice, extreme compensatory behavior, and depression, which may be expressed in a variety of syndromes.

EXTREME FRUSTRATIONS AND TRAUMATIC EXPERIENCES. A stereotyped notion about abnormal behavior is that it can be traced to a single traumatic experience. This point of view is an oversimplification which has been perpetuated by stage, motion picture, and TV presentations, in which causation must be uncomplicated and compressed into small capsules of time. Studies of countless case histories, however, show that the impact of any traumatic experience on a child's development is always influenced by the child's development up to that time. A psychological trauma can, of course, influence personality development; the more drastic the experience, the stronger will be its effect in the causation of maladjustment. But even this result depends on the child's interpretation of the traumatic experience in terms of his inner feelings. The death of a parent, for example, is more critical if it occurs at a time when the child is experiencing a strong hostility toward the parent; unconsciously he may assume responsibility for the death.

The way people significant to the child handle the experience also determines the impact of the trauma; where the child is intelligently supported in such an experience, there will be less force in the trauma, but if the child is discouraged from expressing appropriate feelings and must repress them, the effect of the trauma may be long-lasting and perhaps injurious.

Common traumatic experiences which have been found to be important in the development of emotional maladjustment are: death of parents or siblings, surgery, accident or severe illness, sudden or prolonged separation from parents, intense or protracted frustrations, and deprivation of basic physical needs. Psychoanalytic theory also calls particular attention to the influence of traumatic sexual experiences in the background of abnormal behavior.

Late Childhood. The late childhood period normally begins during the sixth or seventh year of life, usually coinciding with the beginning of school for the child. It is a period characterized by vigorous physical growth and the emergence of significant intellectual abilities. During late childhood the child extends his sphere of social activity beyond the family circle. Critical areas of adjustment fall into three categories: physical development, school adjustment, and socialization.

PHYSICAL DEVELOPMENT. Physical handicaps, deformities, or gross discrepancies in growth may cause severe adjustment problems for the child in this period of his life. Such limitations place him at a disadvantage in normal movement toward group participation, especially since at this stage of life the understanding and support of the family are less and less available to him as he moves out into the community. Children are notoriously cruel in their proneness to exploit the physical limitations of other children. The child's capacity to adjust to problems of this kind will depend, therefore, upon the feeling of security that he has achieved in the family setting.

Physical handicaps, deformities, and growth problems do not, however, in themselves cause emotional maladjustment. Maladaptiveness arises out of the child's attitudes and his evaluation of his body image, both of which are strongly influenced by the reactions of the people in his environment. One of the most common adjustments to physical handicap is compensation, which may be expressed by the overdevelopment of a specific (perhaps nonphysical) ability, the development of an attitude of bravado, or even flight into delinquency and other deviant behavior.

School Adjustment. Going to school involves separation from parents, submission to sets of standards established by nonfamily groups, and participation in group activities, all of which are potential sources of stress for the child. The management of these demands by parents and teachers can make the school experience either a healthy and positive one or a stumbling block in the path of the child's personality development. Common experiences that are hazardous for the child's healthy development in the school milieu are: extreme pressures to overcome his resistance to separation from home; imposition of standards of achievement beyond his capacity; a practice of threatening and bullying the child to conform in a model way; criticism and nagging over his performance or social behavior; and parental overprotection that restricts the child's growing independence.

Few problems of school adjustment are due to the school situation alone, but are instead problems of maladjustment, the groundwork of which was laid in the preschool years and which were precipitated by school-centered stresses. Of particular concern (because of their long-range impact on the development of the child's potential for making his way in the world as adult) are reading and arithmetic disabilities. These are sometimes the outgrowth and symptomatic expressions of underlying personality disturbance; in other cases the scholastic failures may cause the personality disturbance by the increased pressure they place on the child during the school years.

Socialization. As the child moves into the late childhood years, he normally begins to join groups and find a place for himself among his peers. Through this process of socialization he begins to differentiate the male and female roles, to test his own abilities in relation to those of his associates, and to learn certain rudimentary social skills. Anything that interferes with the process can be a source of stress and possible personality disturbance. For example, extreme demands on the child's time in the form of burdensome home chores, of lengthy homework assignments, and of other tasks which circumscribe his group behavior can interfere seriously with his social development and create in him long-lasting resentment. Other potentially damaging conditions are: imposed isolation, extreme restrictions on the child's behavior, and the habitual insistence of parents that the child participate in activities which please the parents more than they do the child.

Children who come into this period of life feeling shy, inhibited, or inadequate experience difficult problems of adjustment, as do those who have been pampered and have become egocentric. Satisfying and successful group experiences can bring out the shy or inhibited child; they can also suppress the overdemanding and egocentric one. However, all the child's group experiences cannot be planned and supervised, and, frequently, the problems that he carries with him into the group are intensified by ridicule, exclusion, and bullying.

Adolescence. The period of adolescence is heralded by the onset of a series of critical physiological changes, which bring the individual closer to physical and biological maturity. These changes occur earlier in girls (sometimes as early as nine or ten years); in boys corresponding changes are not likely to take place before the twelfth year. Adolescent changes generally include: (for girls) the development of mammary glands and subcutaneous fatty tissue, and the menarche; (for boys) development of improved muscular tonus, deepening of the voice, and growth of beard. It is in this period that biological sexual maturity is approached and gradually attained in both sexes. The individual's reaction to these changes and to the sex impulse thereby generated constitutes one potential source of psychological disturbance for the adolescent. Along with the fundamental biological changes there appear several psychological changes, such as growing independence of family ties, heightened heterosocial interests, self-consciousness, feelings of frustration at the threshold of maturity, and the maturation of vocational interests and ambitions.

BIOLOGICAL CHANGES. The fundamental biological changes that take place during adolescence are integral in the maturation of every individual, and their potential for causing personality disturbance lies more in their timing, their sequence, and the child's reaction to them than in the changes themselves. The "early maturer" sometimes is embarrassed or made to feel guilty by the appearance of the changes, especially when he or she has not been prepared to understand their meaning. On the other hand, the "late maturer" feels inadequate when he falls behind his peers in this area of development. Parental lack of understanding or unwillingness to discuss these changes intelligently and objectively with the child will accentuate his difficulties. Because our culture places severe limitations on early gratification of sex needs, the presence of biological sexual maturity in the adolescent requires sensitive understanding.

Adequacy of physique and physical appearance preoccupies the adolescent and is an important factor in his development and maintenance of self-esteem and good social relations. Mishandling of the problems of physical change in this period of life may lead to adult patterns of overcompensation or inadequate social and sexual adjustment.

PSYCHOLOGICAL CHANGES. In our society the period of adolescence serves to test the individual's capacity to function in the role of man or woman and to develop skills in the appropriate role. A part of this capacity resides in the physical changes described in the previous paragraphs, but the greater part lies in the psychological adjustment that is achieved. The individual's problems become complicated at this point in his life, for, as he approaches maturity with its manifold responsibilities, he is expected to develop independence and assertiveness but he must develop these traits in the face of continued adult controls. Conflict over authority relationships, sometimes rising to the level of rebellion in the eyes of parents, is a typical adolescent problem. When independence is allowed too early and too fully, or when it is withheld or severely restricted, adjustment problems present themselves which may have an impact on the adult personality that will follow.

The adolescent's concern with the testing of his capacities leads to preoccupation with self, and this preoccupation often expresses itself in behavior that is selfish, isolated, or introverted. Given an understanding family atmosphere and the opportunity for social experiences with his peers, the adolescent ultimately resolves his egocentricity. When such a favorable milieu is lacking, the egocentric adjustment may prove to be lasting and may be the core of the adult personality.

The ultimate resolution of the self-testing process, then, lies in the achievement of satisfactory heterosocial, sexual, and vocational adjustments. Beset by frustrations in each of these areas, the adolescent gradually reaches out for experiences appropriate to his level of maturity and, in the long run, with full maturity and increased self-confidence, he assumes responsibility for satisfactory adjustment in each.

Factors which interfere with adequate heterosocial and sexual adjustment are: delayed physical development, overrestrictive control by parents, and overwhelming feelings of inadequacy. Progress in vocational adjustment may be hampered by inadequate guidance, limited educational or work experience, parental interference, lack of interest on the part of the adolescent or of encouragement from parents, or the individual's own unwillingness to assume the responsibilities of adulthood.

Early Adulthood. With the end of adolescence the individual's developmental process is deemed complete, and society then regards him as a mature person. However, at many levels of American society the adolescent dependence is prolonged beyond the teen years because of the maintenance of emotional family ties and because of the long years of education required for many business and professional careers. In general, the individual is considered adult when he assumes responsibility for setting up his own family unit and is able to maintain it independently. Another major criterion of adulthood is satisfactory vocational adjustment.

Although the young adult faces a number of crises which influence his personality development, few if any of these experiences constitute basic causes *per se* of abnormal behavior. Such crises are more often secondary or precipitating causes of personality disturbances which might ensue. The individual who comes to adulthood with feelings of security and confidence in his own abilities may experience anxiety and disturbance in the midst of a crisis but ultimately will face them realistically and work out an adequate adjustment. On the other hand, the young adult with a history of childhood or adolescent insecurity or other personality maladjustment, confronted with the same crisis, may be precipitated into one of a number of personality disturbances such as depression, prolonged anxiety, or psychosomatic disorder.

COURTSHIP, MARRIAGE, AND PARENTHOOD. Adjustment to the problems of courtship and marriage is largely dependent on the individual's previous interpersonal relationships. Of primary importance is the relationship with parental figures. The individual's manner and success in assuming his sex role and in relating to the opposite sex are a direct outgrowth of his or her identification with the parent of the same sex and the relationship with the parent of the opposite sex. Research tends to show that the single factor most predictive of a successful courtship and marriage is the happy marriage of the parents of the new couple.

Marriage is in fact a test of emotional stability and maturity. In a happy marriage two people share love and affection in a secure and creative sense and face the ordinary problems of intimate adjustment in a realistic, flexible, and mutually understanding manner. Unhappy marriages must be regarded as *symptoms* of personality weaknesses in the partners. Marriage is, therefore, not a cause of abnormal behavior any more than it is a solution to one's life problems. An unhappy marriage can, however, intensify and expose latent personality disturbances.

Statistics indicate that in the United States one out of every four marriages results in divorce and a third of the remaining marriages are unhappy. These figures reveal the extent of emotional maladjustment and portend an increasingly high incidence of maladjustment in the children these marriages will produce. The principal factors underlying maladjustments are: emotional deprivation in childhood, broken homes, and inadequate preparation for the physical and emotional demands of marriage as well as its socioeconomic responsibilities. To these must be added the further complications of war, housing shortages, the increased number of working mothers, various economic pressures, and the uncertainties and apprehensions of life in the atomic age.

Unhappiness in marriage expresses itself in such further maladjustments as: development of psychosomatic illnesses, depressions, anxieties, infidelity, alcoholism, and cruel and exploitative treatment of children. Other factors that may complicate marriage and contribute to emotional distress are: inability to have children, fears and guilt feelings concerning the marital relationship, pregnancy, and the responsibility of parenthood; differences in role expectation; in-law interference; and financial insecurity. A happy marriage enhances feelings of self-fulfillment and security, enables the individuals concerned to deal more effectively with everyday problems, and promotes a family unity which assures the happy development of its children.

VOCATIONAL ADJUSTMENT. The highly complex, changing, and technological nature of our society makes the problem of selecting a vocation for the modern young adult a difficult one. In general, occupational choice in our society is made in one of two ways: Either the individual, having completed secondary school education (or interrupting it), looks for a "job" primarily as a means of economic support; or he makes plans to prepare himself for a particular career and undertakes advanced training to qualify for it.

Where the job-hunter is willing to experiment and to shift jobs in the early stages of his adjustment until he finds one with opportunities meeting his interests and capacities, the adjustment can be quite satisfactory. On the other hand, where the job is selected on a chance basis and opportunities for shifting are limited by increasing financial responsibilities (early marriage, dependency of parents, etc.), the outcome may be one of dissatisfaction, failure to use one's full capacities, and feelings of inferiority and guilt. Prolonged job dissatisfaction of this sort provides the focus for the development of an array of personality disturbances. Absenteeism, accidents, physical symptoms, and family tension are frequently associated with an unsatisfactory job adjustment.

When the individual makes a choice of career intelligently, assuming there are opportunities for him in the field, his vocational adjustment will enable him to experience a sense of personal satisfaction and fulfillment. Such choices of vocation are often aided by recourse to psychological testing and counseling. If, however, the choice is forced on the individual by parental demand, or if it is based on neurotic compensatory mechanisms, subsequent vocational adjustment is likely to be poor and personality disturbances are a possible outcome. Satisfactory vocational adjustment can be a source of security and strength, offsetting many other factors which otherwise might have a damaging effect on the personality. Poor vocational adjustment can be a continual source of frustration and the precipitating cause of even major personality breakdown.

Middle Age. While this period is difficult to delimit in terms of years and could well be called "later adulthood," it may be assumed to extend from the time when the individual's marital, vocational, and social status have become reasonably fixed through the period of the climacteric or menopause. It is at this stage of life that one sees the highest incidence of overt expression of emotional and mental illness. Age distribution in hospital patient populations and consultation statistics support this point. The disturbances which come to the fore in middle age cannot, however, be said to have their causation solely in either the biological or the psychological phenomena of this period of life. It is rather that the changes occurring at this time make it possible for underlying disturbances to break through in the form of overt illness.

The principal areas of adjustment which the individual must face in middle age are: decline of physical vigor, change of family constellation, restriction of the possibility of future change, and the menopause or climacteric.

DECLINE OF PHYSICAL VIGOR. During middle age physical illness is of more frequent occurrence; endurance of and tolerance for physical stress are less abundant, and sexual potency diminishes. The individual is forced to an awareness of gradual physical decline. How he will react to these changes depends on previous psychological adjustments, and the reaction may be more disturbing than the changes themselves.

CHANGE OF FAMILY CONSTELLATION. By the time middle age is reached, one's parents and older relatives may have become dependent or died; children usually have married and left the home; brothers and sisters have grown apart and settled in distant regions. Such changes disturb the familial roots from which the individual's original security was derived. The individual who has not achieved personal security through various adult adjustments may respond to these changes with emotional illness.

RESTRICTION OF POSSIBILITY OF FUTURE CHANGE. During this period the pattern of life has usually become so fixed that little opportunity for change exists. The middle-aged person becomes aware that he is committed to a particular way of life. If he is dissatisfied with his lot, he usually feels that he can no longer do anything about it. Whatever expectations he has for the future are not likely to compensate adequately for present unhappiness, and the individual may feel trapped. Such attitudes are important precipitants of emotional illness.

THE MENOPAUSE AND CLIMACTERIC. This is commonly referred to as "change of life." During the latter part of the middle years, as a result of specific changes in sex glands, the individual loses the ability to procreate. The sexual drive and the ability to engage in satisfactory sexual relations continues, but in diminished intensity. These changes, which are accompanied by widespread adjustments in the endocrine system, are more dramatic in the female since they cause gradual cessation of menstrual activity. In some women the reaction to these changes is extreme and may include severe depression with agitation and anxiety, overwhelming feelings of guilt and unworthiness, as well as suicidal attempts. This type of reaction is called involutional melancholia. Milder changes include loss of self-esteem, feeling of futility and pessimism, loss of energy, and psychosomatic complaints. In many individuals, however, specific reactions to such involutional changes are transitory and undramatic. Lack of insight on the part of the family into the reasons for the behavioral changes of the afflicted person may accentuate the problem and lead to a disruption of previously adequate family relationships.

Old Age. The period of old age cannot be clearly delineated because of wide individual variability. Previous attitudes, life situation, and physical vigor influence the adjustment during the later years of life. The principal problems and causes of personality disturbance in old age are: severe physical restriction, dependency, feelings of decreasing usefulness, and feelings of isolation.

SEVERE PHYSICAL RESTRICTION. Aging may bring with it loss of sensory acuity, particularly in the visual and auditory areas, and impaired mobility. Limitations in psychological functioning such as impaired memory and restricted learning ability may result from changes in brain tissue. Such changes attack the security feelings of the individual and intensify his feelings of inadequacy. Impaired sensory acuity, restricting the individual's awareness of his surroundings, may induce feelings of suspiciousness and exclusion. Severe cerebral changes may bring on psychotic behavior.

DEPENDENCY. At this stage of life there is often a forced state of physical, social, and economic dependency, which may be further complicated by feelings of rejection and may result in the use of childish patterns of sulking, attention-seeking, and contrariness.

FEELINGS OF DECREASING USEFULNESS. For both the male and the female this period reduces the areas of life in which the individual feels able to make a useful contribution to others. Family and vocational responsibilities are usually behind them, and, unless avocational activities in the form of hobbies or minor responsibilities (such as baby-sitting) are provided, a feeling of emptiness and futility may develop. The person may "die" psychologically, even physically, because there is nothing left for him to do.

FEELINGS OF ISOLATION. Loss of lifelong friends, restricted mobility, and limited income all serve to isolate the aged individual from social relationships. If his life has been relatively empty of cultural pursuits, or if he cannot or will not take refuge in reading or in some hobby, effective emotional adjustment will be extremely difficult for him to achieve.

CULTURAL FACTORS

Aside from the most extreme conditions of environmental stress, cultural factors rarely are primary causes of psychopathology. Such factors are more likely to provide the setting for the precipitation of emotional upset or to determine the nature of the symptoms than to cause the illness. The cultural milieu in which the individual moves influences his personality development through the child-rearing practices it encourages, the value systems it engenders, and the stresses that are peculiar to its environmental pattern.

Abnormal Behavior in Cultural Groups. There is no conclusive evidence that any given ethnic or cultural group has a particular propensity to mental illness. However, there is evidence that when mental illness does develop in a given group, there is greater tendency for the development of one type of illness than for another. Thus, for example, schizophrenia tends to be more characteristic of highly civilized societies than of primitive societies. Also, when compared with norms for other ethnic groups, the incidence of alcoholism is somewhat higher among an Irish population, whereas the incidence of manic-depressive psychoses is greater in New Zealanders. The specific dynamic (or constitutional) factors producing these differences are not clearly understood.

Child-Rearing Practices. Perhaps the most notable way in which cultures differ is with regard to the practices in child-rearing. Feeding, toilet training, emotional displays, sexual practices and the imparting of information on sex, preparation for marriage, and authority relationships are of particular significance for personality development. A culture in which the home and the school system emphasize a rigid authoritarian relationship between children and their elders tends to contribute to suppression and repression of normal developmental responses, which may then be expressed deviously and in a harmful fashion. In such a cultural milieu one would expect to find strongly aggressive, markedly withdrawn, or over-submissive adult personalities. Adjustment to sexuality is certainly influenced by childhood sexual practices, which are generally fixed within the cultural mores; rigid and irrational sexual taboos found integral in whole cultures have been shown to ill prepare the young for marriage. Sexual promiscuity in some societies, on the other hand, makes subsequent stable heterosexual adjustment difficult. Differences in child-rearing practices are, however, being reduced by the far-reaching effects of mass communication and other widespread exchanges of knowledge.

Value Systems. Development of personality and character tends to be organized around the principal standards and values set up by the cultural milieu. Conflicting values within the individual's own culture or between different cultures to which he may be exposed may generate serious problems of adjustment for him. A high rate of delinquency is often seen in first-generation Americans who encounter conflict between old-world and new-world standards and values. The value-system conflicts which confront many children in our society and which may have serious impact on personality development arises from: differences between moral values taught at home, school, and church and those practiced by adults in the society; a marked discrepancy between wished-for and actual reality; and the suppressed and delayed gratification of normal desires.

DIFFERENCES BETWEEN MORAL VALUES TAUGHT AND PRACTICED. This conflict of value systems threatens the basic security of the child, causes a loss of esteem and respect for the authority figures in the society, and may lead to guilt-producing behavior.

DISCREPANCY BETWEEN WISHED-FOR AND ACTUAL REALITY. The developing individual in our society is exposed to glittering, fanciful, and appealing descriptions of life in advertising, magazine and newspaper accounts, and in television and cinema programs. The disparity between these descriptions and the life the individual is actually leading is so great that he may develop chronic feelings of dissatisfaction and a sense of overwhelming competitive stress, and he may, thus, adopt unrealistic and unattainable aspirations. If there is in the personality the groundwork for maladjustment, the individual may express his feeling of frustration by retreating in the face of impossible odds or rebelling in abnormal, perhaps socially disturbing or destructive, behavior.

SUPPRESSED AND DELAYED GRATIFICATION. In a cultural milieu so complex as American society it is necessary to institute controls over the expression of many desires which in a simpler society may require less control. This affects particularly the adolescent group in our culture, who find their desires for economic independence, heterosexual activity, and freedom from adult control long delayed. No matter how necessary these controls may be, they do provide problems of adjustment for the individual adolescent. The complete lack of such controls, however, would create even greater problems for the group as a whole, resulting in delinquency and irresponsibility.

Technological and Economic Factors Creating Stress. In a highly industrialized and urbanized society there are many conditions that may contribute to personality disturbance. The more significant of these are: working and housing conditions, mobility of family units, and availability of basic necessities.

WORKING AND HOUSING CONDITIONS. Extremely unpleasant working conditions or exploitative working situations such as "sweat-shops" can interfere with normal personality development by lowering self-esteem, producing intolerable frustration and providing limited time for recreation and family life. Slum housing which may develop around such industrial conditions can further contribute to personality maladjustment. The high incidence of working mothers tends to reduce the importance of the home as a haven of love, security, and personality development. Some of the worst of these evils are gradually eliminated by modern housing projects, legislation to improve working conditions, and the combined activities of enlightened business and community groups. It must be borne in mind, however, that mere physical change such as slum clearance does not in itself prevent personality disturbance.

MOBILITY OF FAMILY UNITS. The rapid pace of living made possible by improved transportation and communication facilities tends to increase the mobility of family units, thereby destroying the sense of family stability and "rootedness." Frequent moving about, long periods of traveling to and from work, and many job changes can create psychological tensions that handicap personality development.

AVAILABILITY OF BASIC NECESSITIES. On the margin of any society exist groups of people who find it difficult to provide themselves with the basic necessities of life. Examples of such people are migrant farm workers and dependent individuals such as those on relief, the chronically ill, and the severely handicapped. Under such extreme conditions where all attention is focused on a struggle for survival, there is little time or energy available to provide psychological support for the family unit. Again it must be said, however, that these circumstances are not of themselves causes of personality disturbance, though they may provide a pattern for the precipitation of personality maladjustment. It is generally recognized that many people survive these exigencies and achieve wholesome personality adjustments.

Problems of Minority Peoples. The individual normally should have the opportunity to develop feelings of self-esteem through inter-action with others in his social milieu. Where this is hindered, as in the case of minority groups in some cultures, hazards to person-ality development are created. Pervasive prejudice and discrimina-tory behavior may lead to feelings of inferiority and insecurity, which may be compensated for by aggression, withdrawal, or delin-quent behavior. Where racial segregation in housing, in education, and in the use of public facilities is enforced, the resultant inequitable opportunities offered minority groups breed resentment and discon-tent.

Cataclysmic Events. The psychologically traumatic effect of any disaster is dependent on the individual's emotional stability and his life history. This is supported strongly by evidence of human behavior under widely varying conditions of environmental stress. There can be no question that war, economic deprivation, civilian disaster, and starvation all tax the individual's psychological resources and may bring an already unstable personality to the breaking point. However, the impact of such events on personality development and behavior is more likely to come from their long-range after-effects than from the immediate stress of the event itself. For example, family dislocations in Europe following World War II contributed more to psychopathology than did the bombing raids. The persistent crumbling of one's feelings of self-esteem resulting from long-lasting unemployment is more damaging than the first shock of loss of job.

6

TRANSIENT SITUATIONAL PERSONALITY DISORDERS

Not all the symptoms of mental upset are the result of underlying personality disturbance. It is possible for a relatively stable individual to be confronted with a situation so stressful or unpleasant that he displays symptoms identical in many respects with those seen in serious mental disorders. Such reactions, which are more or less transient in nature and appear to be acute responses to situational factors, are considered a separate diagnostic entity from neurotic reactions or the other more disturbed and lasting forms of emotional disorder. The current classification system of the American Psychiatric Association labels them "transient situational personality disorders." They may be conveniently discussed under two broad categories: *stress reactions* and *adjustment reactions*.

The relative incidence of transient situational personality reactions is not known. Studies of civilian catastrophes suggest that as many as half the people directly involved develop stress reactions. Military studies of the incidence of disordered reactions to combat have not clearly discriminated between transient disorders and true neurotic or psychotic reactions. Nevertheless, it may be safely surmised that situational reactions frequently occur in combat.

Many transient situational personality reactions are resolved without benefit of treatment. Where treatment is needed, short-term, relatively superficial psychotherapy, accompanied by rest and appropriate physical care, usually is effective.

GROSS STRESS REACTIONS

Normal personalities may react with overwhelming fear to situations of stress. As a consequence, they will resort to established patterns of reaction to deal with their fears. Under extreme stress, the reactions are exaggerated and often of no avail to the individual in meeting the crisis. The individual's capacity to carry on breaks down, and the resulting disturbance resembles the symptoms of the more serious personality disorders. These transient disturbances may be distinguished from the graver mental conditions on three grounds:

1. There is usually no previous history of the kind of behavior that is displayed under the stressful situation.

2. The reactions are reversible; eventually the individual resumes his customary mode of behavior.

3. The reaction is short-lived.

The main criteria for establishing the diagnosis are the transient nature of the disturbed reaction and the certainty that it occurred in response to a stressful situation. If, however, it can be determined that the reactions are merely an exacerbation of previously existing symptoms, or reactions which progress into lasting patterns, they must then be considered as different diagnostic entities. As far as reactions to combat and to civilian catastrophes are concerned, while there are no significant differences in symptoms or in the required treatment, such reactions are regarded as a separate category.

Transient Reactions to Combat Stress. At the time of World War I the dynamics underlying situational reactions were not clearly appreciated, with the result that a rather broad variety of psychiatric reactions were classified as "shell shock." In World War II, however, a series of differential diagnoses was gradually worked out, in which a larger measure of recognition was accorded the transient situational reaction.

In general, the reaction of the patient to combat is one of overwhelming anxiety. Prominent symptoms are: hypersensitivity, accelerated startle reaction, disturbed sleep, tremors, loss of weight, and an assortment of psychosomatic symptoms. More serious symptoms of mutism and disorientation may also be present. While differences observed in the symptom pattern may be produced by variations in the nature of the combat situation, more important in determining this symptom pattern are the life history of the individual and the question of whether the stress is cumulative over a long period of time or is acute and intense. The similarities of the symptomatology at the onset are more striking than the differences.

The influence of dynamic factors underlying stress reactions to combat are relatively clear. Constant, inescapable stress produces intense fear and mobilizes the body's resources to deal with the situation. Because the situation does not provide opportunity for reactions to reduce the stress, the emotional stress persists. Continual and intense autonomic response without adequate release produces a disorganization of the body's functioning. An added factor is the burden of the actual physical debilitation and fatigue generated by combat conditions. Under the circumstances it is understandable that the individual will resort to unconscious means of escaping the situation. This accounts for the severe dissociation states, amnesia, mutism, disorientation, and stupor. Although these combat reactions are considered largely situational, the fact that 90 per cent of military personnel who experienced combat conditions did not develop incapacitating symptoms strongly suggests that predisposing conditions must have influenced the behavior of those who did break down.

Almost invariably, the most effective treatment was that administered in the combat area. Rest, physical rehabilitation, and psychotherapy which allowed expression of repressed, disturbing feelings proved helpful in most cases. The technique of narcosynthesis (discussed in detail in Chapter 18, The Diagnostic Process) was widely used during World War II, both to help the patient to obtain much needed rest and enable him to bring to the conscious level the disturbing emotional experiences which he had repressed.

Transient Reactions to Civilian Stress. Any terrifying experience, prolonged stress, or traumatic bereavement undergone in civilian life may produce a transient psychological breakdown. The symptoms, except as they may be related to the particular situation, do not differ significantly from those seen in combat reactions. They range from milder symptoms such as "nervousness," hypersensitivity, and fatigue, to the more extreme patterns of amnesia, disorientation, and stupor. Recurrent nightmares reenacting the stressful event may follow for some time. Dynamic factors are more likely to play a role in transient reactions to civilian stresses than in combat because the former more often involve spouses, parents, children, relatives, and long-standing friends, all of whom have had some impact on the individual's personality formation, and about whom a large amount of unconscious material has been accumulated. Where there is question of responsibility for the event, feelings of guilt may complicate a relatively simple fear reaction; for example, in accidents where relatives or friends have been killed or maimed, hostility or bitterness may be present.

Effective treatment includes reassurance and rest, induced by sedation if necessary. A working-through of some of the guilt or the hostile feelings may be required. Prospects for the recovery from the immediate symptoms are good. There is even a relatively good chance that the individual may enjoy permanent freedom from anxiety and stress over the situation.

When the individual himself has suffered incapacitating injuries, two special conditions must be taken into consideration. *First,* in certain cases of this type psychiatric symptoms are not observed for some time after trauma. The posttraumatic reaction appears when the patient realizes the extent of his injuries or the loss of his family or possessions. The reaction may also occur as a response to the inevitable return to an unpleasant life pattern (for example, a disturbed family situation or a frustrating vocational picture). *Second,* the patient may be influenced by the possibility of financial compensation. As a result the stress reaction may be prolonged or the individual may develop guilt with relation to the acceptance of the payments.

ADJUSTMENT REACTIONS

Unsatisfactory life circumstances of some duration or new and trying environmental conditions may produce psychological breakdown of a transient nature. As in the case of the gross stress reaction (where the reaction is clearly a relatively superficial response to the situation and symptoms of underlying personality disorder are lacking) the adjustment reaction must be considered a separate diagnostic entity, with a good prognosis. Transient adjustment reactions differ from gross stress situations in that the former result from long-lasting circumstances and, when manifested, there is a lesser degree of intensity. The symptom picture and the type of situation eliciting the response vary with the age of the patient. For this reason, adjustment reactions are identified with respect to the stage of life of the individual.

Adjustment Reaction of Infancy. Transient psychogenic reactions of apathy, excitability, or feeding or sleeping problems may be aroused in the infant who experiences disturbances in his significant interpersonal relationships. Separation from the mother or her absence for long periods may produce such changes. Careful attention in diagnosis must be given to the possibility of organic pathology.

Adjustment Reaction of Childhood. This category includes symptomatic reactions to immediately disturbing situations or emotional conflicts. The symptoms vary, and they may be mixed. Among those most prevalent are: habit disturbances (such as nail-biting); enuresis; masturbation; conduct disturbances at home, at school, or in the community (stealing, destructiveness, truancy); and neurotic manifestations (tics, phobias, sleep-walking). When any of these symptoms persists or is accompanied by radical alterations of behavior and personality, the possibility of deeper pathology must be suspected. (See Chapter 10, Special Symptom Reactions, for further discussion.)

Adjustment Reaction of Adolescence. The turmoils of the adolescence adjustment may become extreme enough to produce symptoms of transient personality breakdown. The wide variety of transient neurotic manifestations characteristic of this diagnostic entity usually can be traced to difficulties the individual experiences in achieving independence or his failure to adjust satisfactorily to the new heterosexual demands of this period of life.

Adjustment Reaction of Adulthood. This category includes reactions which were formerly classified as "simple adult maladjustment." Such reactions may be stimulated by marital discord, occupational maladjustment, or confining or harsh circumstances which present the individual with a difficult problem of adjustment. The symptoms include: excessive fatigue, depression, impaired efficiency, heavy drinking, unconventional behavior, and anxiety. Treatment should be directed toward changing the environment where this is possible. Otherwise, as long as the reaction pattern is not chronic and no insidious pathological process is at work, relatively superficial psychotherapeutic efforts are usually helpful.

Adjustment Reaction of Later Life. Unhealthy new reactions, or the accentuation of previous undesirable personality traits may accompany the psychological, biological, and social adjustments required in later life. Involutional changes, retirement, the breaking up of the home or family, may prove too taxing. Symptomatic disturbance in the personality may ensue. The problem requires investigation of the complex patterns of the patient's family relationships.

7

PSYCHOSOMATIC DISORDERS (PSYCHOPHYSIOLOGIC REACTIONS)

One of the major contributions to abnormal psychology made during the latter part of the nineteenth century, mainly through the work of Janet and Freud, was the discovery that some physical disorders could have their origin in strictly psychological causes. It is this class of disorders to which the term "psychosomatic" is applied. The term is derived from two Greek words: *psyche,* meaning spirit, soul, or mind, and *soma,* meaning body. Combining them into one word suggests that man functions as an integrated whole with continuing interrelationships and interdependence of psychological and physiological functions. Today, this orientation is universally accepted in the fields of psychology and psychiatry.

PSYCHOSOMATIC DISORDERS IN GENERAL

A psychosomatic disorder is the result of chronic or severe disruption of the delicate homeostatic balance of the body arising from psychological stress. Such a condition may involve any of the organ systems and usually requires both medical and psychotherapeutic attention.

Incidence. The prevalence of psychosomatic disorders can only be estimated, and estimates vary widely. Reports from mental health authorities generally indicate that from 40 to 60 per cent of patients consulting physicians for all kinds of illness suffer from a psychosomatic disorder. Research in industrial medicine suggests that a very large proportion of absenteeism is due principally to psychosomatic complaints. Military experience indicates that the most important cause for attendance at sick call is some psychosomatic disorder. For other evidence of the high incidence of illnesses within this category one has only to witness the huge industries that are built on the sale, without prescription, of laxatives, stomach powders, and headache remedies.

Etiology (Causation). Although in many cases it is difficult to pinpoint the exact causation of psychosomatic symptoms, it is agreed that such disorders are the result of prolonged or intense emotional stress. This stress is a function of the manner in which the individual responds to some life situation, regardless of whether his perceptions of it are objectively justified. When the emotions generated by the situation cannot be discharged through acceptable verbal or physical activity, the tensions are internalized and they disrupt the normal functioning of some organ system. Fear, anxiety, and anger which the individual does not feel free to express openly are the most common causes of such disruption. Psychosomatic relationships are best understood through an analysis of human emotion and its physiological correlates.

EMOTIONS AND BODILY CHANGES

An emotion is a response of the *total* organism (or person) in which the normal pattern of physiological balance is altered to prepare the organism for extensive and more or less specific emergency action. It involves: subjective experiences, observable changes in behavior, and changes in the activities of the viscera. The *subjective experiences* include such feelings as pleasantness or unpleasantness, excitement or lassitude, and tension or relaxation. Among the *observable changes in behavior* one sees facial expressions, postural adjustments (including gestures), and changes in voice quality and volume.

The *visceral changes* may be extremely complex. In general, they are concerned with the maintenance of *homeostatic balance*—a sensitive physicochemical balance in the internal environment of the body which includes such factors as temperature regulation, fluid balances, heart rate, blood pressure, and rate of respiration. These adjustments are necessary in the midst of severe emotional experience because the individual is making unusual demands on the fine balance and physical limits of his organ systems.

Action of the Autonomic Nervous System. The physiological correlates of behavior in an emotional crisis are seen in the functioning of the autonomic nervous system, the normally involuntary mechanism through which homeostatic balance is maintained. There are two divisions of the autonomic nervous system: the parasympathetic and the sympathetic. They function antagonistically (in the same sense that some muscles relax so that others may contract): the *parasympathetic division* tends to maintain normal biological functioning: the *sympathetic* prepares the organism for emergency response. Under emotional stress the normal physiological activities maintained by the parasympathetic division are blocked so that the body may function under the emergency direction of the sympathetic division.

Normal and Abnormal Emotion. All people experience emotion in normal living. Such emotion is transitory, rising to a peak of intensity appropriate to the situation and subsiding as the individual faces and copes with the situation or as the disturbing phenomena disappear. The ability to experience a full range of normal emotion is a mark of good adjustment and serves to enrich the life of the individual. It is when emotion becomes chronic or too intense that homeostatic balance is seriously disrupted, and the continued imbalance results in some psychosomatic disorder.

PSYCHOSOMATIC REACTIONS THROUGH THE VARIOUS ORGAN SYSTEMS

A psychosomatic disorder may occur as the only illness or it may be seen in conjunction with some physical or mental illness. It may take on the form of a specific disability or generalized malfunction. The specific organ system that will be affected by a psychosomatic reaction is dependent on (1) the possible constitutional weakness of the particular system, (2) previous illness and accidents in the person's life history, (3) the presence of some illness affecting the organ system in relatives of the patient, (4) the nature of the emotional stress, (5) the symbolic meaning to the patient of a given organ system, and (6) the secondary gain the patient may achieve through the selected symptom. The relative significance of these factors can be determined only through a complete study of the individual's life history. In general, the life histories of patients with psychosomatic disorders reveal a lack of maturity. These disorders express the inability of relatively immature individuals to move on to more mature levels of responsibility. They may reflect a pattern of repression and strong childhood conditioning.

In the accounts which follow, the conditions are identified as reactions in terms of the organ system principally or exclusively involved. The principal psychosomatic disorders are exhibited in gastrointestinal, cardiovascular, respiratory, skin, musculoskeletal, and genitourinary reactions. Other such disorders include those involving the blood stream, the endocrine system, and the special sense organs.

Gastrointestinal Reactions. Psychosomatic disorders in which the gastrointestinal system is principally involved include: peptic ulcer, disorders of elimination, chronic gastritis ("nervous stomach"), and anorexia ("nervous loss of appetite").

PEPTIC ULCER. Although the immediate cause of peptic ulcer is the excessive secretion of stomach acids which irritate, inflame, and ultimately break down the stomach wall, the oversecretion is most often generated by the chronic stress state resulting from unrelieved emotional tension. Peptic ulcer is commonly found in persons with ambitious, driving personalities, whose outward behavior is in conflict with their dependency needs. Peptic ulcers are more prevalent among men than among women.

DISORDERS OF ELIMINATION. Chronic diarrhea (mucous colitis), constipation, and enuresis have important psychological significance. Psychoanalytic theories propose a meaningful connection between these disorders and early toilet training experience. The functions of elimination are said to be involved with problems of giving or retaining, conformity or rebellion. Although such theories are challenged by some experimental work, it is generally accepted that patients with disorders of elimination show emotional stress arising from anxiety, guilt feelings, and resentment.

CHRONIC GASTRITIS. This term covers a variety of gastric symptoms such as belching, stomach rumbling, heartburn, and "indigestion." When these symptoms are associated with emotional stress they are usually regarded as psychosomatic.

ANOREXIA NERVOSA. In this disorder appetite and food intake are suppressed as a result of emotional strain. The association between eating and the emotions is largely a matter of individual background. Some psychological factors found in various cases are: resistance to growing up, aggressive resistance to parental demands, and self-punishment for feelings of guilt. Clinical findings also suggest that loss of appetite may result from childhood misunderstanding of the process of conception, with consequent fear of pregnancy due to oral intake.

Cardiovascular Reactions. Illness involving the heart and the blood vessels in which psychological factors may play a role are:

cardiac neurosis, essential hypertension, fainting (syncope), and headache.

CARDIAC NEUROSIS. This term is used to describe a group of symptoms referable to the heart but psychogenic in origin. The symptoms are palpitation of the heart (tachycardia), shortness of breath (dyspnea), spasm, pain, and murmur. Because these symptoms also occur in organic heart disease, careful medical examination must be made before the disturbance may be diagnosed as a psychosomatic disorder. Nor can the diagnosis of cardiac neurosis be offered unless there are positive findings of emotional conflict and tension. Experiences that are frequently seen to precipitate a cardiac neurosis are: a physician's statement of concern over the patient's heart, the patient's failure to pass a physical examination, the occurrence of heart disease (and possible sudden death) in some friend or a member of the patient's family, and the sudden and unexpected appearance in the patient of some isolated heart symptom (perhaps transitory) which is actually caused by a secondary agent such as excessive use of coffee or tobacco.

The aforementioned precipitating causes will tend to develop cardiac neurosis only in those persons who have major basic anxiety and are preoccupied with bodily functioning. There is no universally accepted pattern of personality adjustment in the disorder, but a persistent fear of dying and the secondary gain to be obtained from manipulating the environment through invalidism are significant factors.

ESSENTIAL HYPERTENSION. Chronically elevated blood pressure for which no organic basis can be found is called essential hypertension. In its earliest stages it is characterized by occasional, transient periods of elevation of the pressure; then, if the emotional problem of the patient is unrelieved, in time the pressure stabilizes at some high level. The persistence of this heightened pressure puts undue strain on the blood vessels and can give rise to such vascular accidents as cerebral hemorrhage or excessive strain on the heart, either of which may be fatal. Since persistent essential hypertension produces destructive organic changes, it must always be considered a medical as well as a psychological problem.

Psychodynamic factors associated with essential hypertension suggest a picture of external friendliness and self-control beneath which there are strong aggressions and anxiety. The anxiety is intensified by the patient's fears of the consequences of expressing his aggression, and a constant conflict ensues. The life history of such patients frequently reveals dependency on overprotective and domineering mothers, with underlying resentment of this relationship.

FAINTING. Loss of consciousness often results from a sudden drop in blood pressure associated with circumstances arousing intense fear. Fainting as a cardiovascular disturbance must, however, be distinguished from fainting as a dissociative reaction found in hysteria.

HEADACHE. A wide range of emotional factors may cause headache. Those headaches caused by such emotional tension may result from cardiovascular changes producing an increase in intracranial pressure; they are frequently encountered as secondary symptoms of essential hypertension.

From the psychodynamic point of view headaches are most often associated with unexpressed hostility. Migraine headaches ("sick headaches"), which have both a constitutional and a psychodynamic basis, are severe and are accompanied by nausea, vomiting, and visual disturbances. Some investigators have regarded this type of headache as allied to epilepsy. (See Chapter 15 for further discussion of this disorder.)

Respiratory Reactions. Psychophysiological reactions through the medium of the respiratory system include: bronchial asthma, hay fever, recurring bronchitis, and sinusitis. While nearly all the systematic studies in this field have been concentrated on bronchial asthma, in general it may be said that respiratory symptoms are expressions of the commonly accepted association between breathing and the maintenance of life. Thus, such respiratory disorders always express feelings of anxiety. Because of the complexity of the allergy problem, extreme care must be exercised in evaluating these conditions, and psychogenic origin can be assured only on the basis of strong and direct evidence.

BRONCHIAL ASTHMA. The spasm of bronchial asthma may be the direct result of a physicochemical reaction to an allergen, or it may be a response to some emotional stress. The extent to which it is accepted as a strictly psychogenic illness is decreasing as a result of discoveries in allergy research. In cases where a psychogenic origin is established, the predominant pattern is an excessive, unresolved dependence on and fear of separation from the mother. There is also some evidence of unacceptable erotic attachment to the parent. This conflict is noted in a variety of personality patterns; as a result, asthma may be found in individuals showing such contrasting traits as hypersensitivity, aggression, ambition, and compulsion.

OTHER RESPIRATORY CONDITIONS. Little specific research has been directed toward an understanding of the psychodynamic factors in hay fever, chronic bronchitis, and sinusitis. Psychiatric literature does, however, turn up an occasional case in which emotional stress is seen side by side with these conditions.

Skin Reactions. While relatively little is known of the psychogenic factors involved in the production of such skin reactions as eczema, hives, acne, and itching, as well as the neurodermatoses, clinicians have uncovered case histories where patterns of psychodynamic significance are seen. The underlying factors reported are strong aggressive tendencies, unconscious voyeuristic and exhibitionist needs, and associated feelings of guilt and shame. The guilt feelings may lead to "self-mutilations" in the form of skin eruptions. Whereas the skin may be thought of as simply an outer coating of the body, in reality it is a sensory organ responding constantly to stimuli of contact, pressure, and temperature, and as such it constitutes a wall between the inner self and the outside world. In this role, it is vulnerable to the development of symptoms which express feelings of insecurity, inadequacy, and hostility.

Musculoskeletal Reactions. The muscular and skeletal systems may react to emotional stress with rheumatoid arthritis, backache, and muscle cramp. The role of emotional factors in the production of these and other musculoskeletal reactions is readily understandable in view of the close relationship between the experiencing of tensions and their release through the medium of muscular activity. When such tensions are prolonged or intense, and remain unrelieved, the resultant muscular strain produces aches and pains.

RHEUMATOID ARTHRITIS. The physical symptoms of this condition are pain, swelling of the joints, and limitation of movement. Systematic investigations have been few and have been essentially limited to studies of female patients, among whom the incidence is reported to be three to five times as large as among men. The most authoritative study describes the arthritic personality as self-sacrificing, overconscientious, self-sufficient, demanding, domineering, and having little capacity for emotional involvement. In female patients there is strong evidence of masculine protest with a history of tomboyish behavior in early life. The central psychodynamic reaction in arthritic patients so far as psychosomatic disorder may be involved is a chronic, inhibited, hostile, and rebellious state with resistance to any outside control. The chronic inhibition produces prolonged muscular tension which ultimately brings on the arthritic symptoms.

BACKACHE. Low back pain is reported frequently in a variety of neurotic disorders. It may arise from prolonged unrelieved tensions or it may be the symbolic expression of the patient's resentment toward overburdening responsibilities. This symptom was one of the most commonly stated complaints at sick call in the military service during wartime. In only a very small percentage of cases was any organic background discovered, and while it was most often attributable to malingering, this latter characteristic itself was usually an indication of some psychological causation.

MUSCLE CRAMP. Dynamic interpretation of muscle cramp or muscle spasm must be sought in relation to the particular muscle groups involved. An example of a symptom which expresses a conflict through muscle cramp might be the development of pain and spasm in the arm as a result of unconscious pugnacity.

Genitourinary Reactions. In no other body system are there more striking illustrations of the interaction between bodily functions and psychological influences than are seen in the genitourinary system, in particular with regard to sexual function. The relationship with parents, especially the one of the opposite sex; strong taboos and mystery which surround early introduction to the phenomenon of sex; and the many and complex cultural and emotional concomitants of this function tend to make of it a fertile ground for the creation of an infinite variety of factors influencing the functioning of the organic components of the system.

DISORDERS OF SEXUAL FUNCTION. *In the male* the principal sexual dysfunction is impaired potency, which ranges from delay in ejaculation to inability to maintain or even achieve tumescence. Still another manifestation of psychosomatic disturbance in male sexual adjustment is premature ejaculation. From a dynamic viewpoint male sexual dysfunction may result from basic immaturity leading to an inordinate fear of impregnating the partner and thus inhibiting the sexual function, uncertainty and feelings of inadequacy about one's ability to achieve the masculine role satisfactorily, and generalized anxiety. Psychoanalytic studies suggest that the neurotic choice of this particular symptom may be the result of an unresolved Oedipus conflict in early childhood. *In the female* the principal sexual dysfunction is frigidity, which expresses itself in disinterest towards the sexual act, orgasm inadequacy, or vaginismus (a constriction or spasm of the vaginal muscles which renders penetration difficult or impossible). The psychodynamic factors are in general similar to those mentioned for impaired potency (substituting the Electra complex for the Oedipus).

DISORDERS OF REPRODUCTIVE FUNCTION. These include various disturbances in the menstrual cycle (irregularity, unusual pain or tension associated with the menses, disturbances in parturition and lactation, and extreme reaction to the climacteric). The essential psychodynamic focus is the patient's insecurity and her immature approach to fulfilling the role of wife and mother.

DISORDERS OF URINARY FUNCTION. The most common urinary symptoms which may suggest psychosomatic disorder are excessive urinary frequency and blocked urination. Urinary frequency is most often the result of anxiety and tension. Blocked urination may also arise out of anxiety, but it often suggests problems of false modesty and sexual conflict. Perhaps the most common psychologically based example of blocked urination is the inability of many persons to urinate in the presence of others.

Other Organ Systems. Emotional conflict and consequent tension may be expressed in the malfunctioning of organ systems other than those previously described in this chapter. *Blood chemistry* changes can be generated by intense emotional activity. The *endocrine glands,* which have a close association with the functioning of the autonomic nervous system, are undoubtedly affected under stress. The *special senses,* which are so often the portal through which the stimuli for strong emotional reaction enters, can easily become the precipitating agents for psychophysiological (psychosomatic) disorder. Systematic research in these areas is, however, extremely limited, and a statement of the psychodynamic factors involved would be only speculative.

8

PSYCHONEUROTIC DISORDERS

While psychoneurotic disorders may be less dramatic in their manifestations and less incapacitating than other forms of mental illness, they constitute a major health problem; they are said to be as common among the mentally ill as upper respiratory ailments are among the physically ill. The psychoneuroses are not only generally characterized by inner struggles and discordant interpersonal relationships, but they also give rise to a broad range of other symptoms, the principal ones being: psychogenically developed physical ills, anxiety, feelings of depression, feelings of irritability or hypersensitivity, unreasonable doubts, obsessions and compulsions, phobias, and disturbances of sleep and of appetite.

The evolution of the approach to the psychoneuroses should provide the student with a clue to an understanding of this class of mental disorders. Freud set forth a dichotomy of "true neuroses" (which he believed to result from variations in the supply of hypothetical sexual toxins) and the "psychoneuroses" (which he considered to be of mental origin). Later, a classification was generally accepted, and universally employed until the time of World War II, which separated the psychoneuroses into four types: anxiety, conversion hysteria, psychasthenia, and neurasthenia. Now it is generally agreed that the principal etiological factors are psychological, although neuropathic or constitutionally predisposing factors are not ignored. The current classification of the neurotic reactions is discussed in detail under "Types of Neurotic Reactions" later in this chapter.

"Psychoneurosis," "neurosis," and "neurotic reaction" are synonymous terms and throughout this chapter are used interchangeably.

INCIDENCE

Estimates place the incidence of psychoneurotics in this country at about eight million. However, precise figures are difficult, if not impossible to obtain, since only a fraction of neurotics are admitted

100

to mental hospitals and these constitute only 4.5 per cent of the first admissions for all mental illnesses. The fact is, a very large number of these individuals continue to suffer without ever being treated for their neuroses. It is characteristic of them to go through life continually seeking treatment for physical illness, and even when the true nature of their difficulty is recognized they tend to reject any diagnosis that is psychologically oriented. Many psychoneurotics go on for years, frequently changing doctors in the hope of finding one who will uncover some organic basis for their suffering and provide either medical or surgical relief.

Some reports state that 40 to 60 per cent of patients consulting general practitioners suffer from neuroses. One study indicates that 60 per cent of time lost in industry through illness is really due to psychoneurotic disorders.

The incidence of diagnosed psychoneurosis is higher among women than among men. This may be explained by the greater opportunity offered to men in our society to act out their difficulties, thus relieving them of neurotic tension, and the greater likelihood of women to seek treatment.

RELATION TO PSYCHOSES

Although there is some opinion suggesting that a neurosis is an early stage of a psychosis, there is good statistical evidence that psychoses and neuroses are separate entities. Follow-up studies of psychoneurotics have revealed that only 4 to 7 per cent later developed psychosis, and there is the strong possibility that some of this group were incorrectly diagnosed in the first place. Further, since 5 to 10 per cent of the general population exhibit psychotic behavior at one time or another, the suggestion is made that neurotics have no greater tendencies to psychosis than do the non-neurotics. Studies of the parents of neurotics indicate a much lower incidence of psychosis than would be expected if the two disorders were related. The accompanying table prepared by James D. Page offers a detailed comparison of psychoses and psychoneuroses (p. 102).

ETIOLOGY (CAUSATION)

In understanding the causes of neurotic reactions four kinds of factors must be evaluated: predisposing, possibly constitutional factors; childhood developmental patterns; factors in the immediate life situation that precipitated the reaction; and cultural factors,

COMPARISON OF SEVEN CHARACTERISTICS IN PSYCHONEUROTICS AND PSYCHOTICS*

Characteristic	Psychoneurotics	Psychotics
ETIOLOGY	Psychogenic factors are of primary importance; hereditary factors are undetermined.	Constitutional and/or hereditary factors are critical in most cases; neurological and toxic factors are often determining agents; psychogenic factors are contributory.
GENERAL BEHAVIOR	Speech and thought are logical and coherent; loss of contact with reality is limited; delusions and hallucinations are not observed.	Speech and thought processes are incoherent; behavior is bizarre and irrational; delusions and hallucinations are common.
SOCIAL ADJUSTMENT	Behavior is in general conformity with accepted standards of society.	Social habits are lost; behavior is at odds with accepted standards of society.
SELF-MANAGEMENT	Can manage self although are not always self-supporting; suicide is a possibility.	Institutionalization is usually necessary to prevent harm to self or others.
INSIGHT	Frequently is good.	Is partial at best, frequently totally lacking.
TREATMENT	Psychotherapy is the treatment of choice.	Emphasis is on controlling behavior, with chemical and physical agents prominent; when contact is established, psychotherapy should be used.
PROGNOSIS	No deterioration; improvement can be expected.	Deterioration may be present in chronic cases; previous high incidence of lifetime hospitalization is being lowered.

* After James D. Page, *Abnormal Psychology* (New York: McGraw-Hill, 1947), p. 101.

which seem to play a part in determining the form of the reaction. Of these, early childhood experiences leading to conflictive tendencies appear to be a basic factor not only in determining whether there will be a neurotic reaction but also in prescribing in large measure the form it will take.

Predisposing Factors. The extent to which biological or possibly constitutional factors predispose the individual to a neurotic reaction is unknown. While the amount of emphasis given to this factor varies from one school of thought to another, by no school is it considered to be of primary importance. Heredity as a determining cause *per se* has been practically eliminated from consideration. Still, there is abundant evidence that the incidence of neurosis and other psychopathology is higher in the family histories of neurotics than in those of non-neurotics. Although such findings can be interpreted as evidence of hereditary influence, it is more probable that they suggest the importance of early environment and psychological contagion. The most that can be said with assurance about the existence of predisposing factors is that the type of neurotic reaction which develops is related to the nature of the premorbid personality structure and that the existence of certain personality traits (such as heightened sensitivity) renders the individual more susceptible to neurotic breakdown. Whether or not the background for this is constitutional is not certain.

Childhood Developmental Patterns. It is generally agreed that unsatisfactory early parent-child relationships are the primary determinants of later neurotic reactions. Such relationships which arouse in the child conflict feelings and faulty evaluations of the environment have been described as the "nuclear neurotic process." While it is possible for this process to be initiated by some traumatic childhood experience of frightening dimensions, it is more likely to be an outgrowth of a chronic condition which exerts its influence gradually over a long period of time.

A childhood atmosphere in which desertion or violent punishment is continuously threatened or implied can lead to attitudes of insecurity and fearfulness. Parents who are rejecting can arouse hostile impulses in the child, who in turn cannot express them for fear of loss of love or retaliation; this situation can lead to a cycle of anxiety and hostility, each replacing the other in endless fashion. Sexual impulses stimulated by unconsciously seductive parent-child relationships can generate feelings of guilt, fear of punishment, or conflict. Childhood experiences of this kind constitute the nuclear process which later life experiences can precipitate into a neurotic reaction.

Precipitating Factors. Usually a careful study of the current life circumstances of the neurotic makes possible the identification of factors that have precipitated the neurotic reaction. These may be classified as follows:

1. Circumstances which constitute a reenactment or intensification of early childhood experiences that created conflicts or anxiety.

2. Circumstances which arouse fears of a weakening of the defensive processes—for example: (a) arousal of dangerous desires which the individual fears may break through ego defense; or (b) unusually stressful or traumatic life experiences.

3. Circumstances which necessitate an intensification of defensive processes which proves to be too burdensome. Failure to achieve goals, that may in the first place have been neurotic and unrealistic, may set in motion extensive defense mechanisms to protect the ego against feelings of inadequacy. An impossible life situation may also generate a need for defensive behavior which rises to intolerably burdensome levels, precipitating a neurotic reaction.

Cultural Factors. Statistical analysis of the incidence of various types of neurotic reaction by social class level, national origin, or racial identification have revealed differences in the type of reaction which indicate possible cultural determinants of the form of the neurosis. In general, however, it must be stated that all forms of neuroses are found in all cultural groups. Cultural factors influence the development of neurotic patterns through the type of child-rearing practices which are encouraged, and by the development of conflicting value systems within the culture or between two cultures to which the individual may belong or be exposed. In general, cultural practices have more influence on the type of symptom formation than on the presence or absence of a neurotic reaction itself.

GENERAL CHARACTERISTICS

Although neuroses manifest themselves in the greatest degree of variation—each neurotic being almost unique in the particular symptom pattern shown—certain common characteristics are found in all neurotic reactions. These are: presence of anxiety, inability to function at capacity level, patterns of rigid or repetitive behavior, egocentricity, hypersensitivity, immaturity, somatic complaints, unhappiness, and a great deal of unconsciously motivated behavior. The prominence of any one or all of these characteristics varies from one form of reaction to another.

Anxiety. It has been stated that the hallmark of the neurosis is the presence of anxiety. A feeling of dread, fearful anticipation, and apprehensiveness in even the most routine circumstances are essential features. Neurotic anxiety must be distinguished from fear. Fear is an emotional response appropriate to the dangers presented by reality; neurotic anxiety is a reaction that is disproportionate to the amount of danger present. It is frequently, although not always, vague and generalized. In this form anxiety is said to be *unbound* or *free-floating*. In some types of neurotic reaction the anxiety is channelized or bound into a specific physical symptom or a specific area of activity.

Neurotic anxiety is aroused by feelings of insecurity developed in the individual by apparently innocuous or only mildly stressful environmental situations. The neurotic person experiences the situation as more hazardous than it really is because it threatens a neurotic defense that has been set up. The individual's anxieties may be aroused, for example, because of the threatening implication of impulses which are experienced, most often if they are of a sexual or aggressive nature. Loss of job, as a threat to the basic self-esteem of the individual, may also arouse feelings of insecurity and thus become a source of anxiety.

Inability to Function at Capacity. For any one of many reasons and despite the fact of possible high intelligence or superior talent, the neurotic usually fails to realize his potential and frequently fails miserably in his achievement efforts. Effective functioning is interfered with by disabling somatic symptoms, fearfulness and timidity, time spent in self-preoccupation, and inability to effect sound human relationships. Occasionally, the neurotic reaction will motivate intense drive for accomplishment in a narrow area of life in a compensatory fashion to counterbalance feelings of inadequacy or failure. The outstanding accomplishment that may result is obtained, however, by neglecting all other areas of life. The end result is failure to achieve well-rounded accomplishments, despite the superior functioning in the particular area selected.

Rigid or Repetitive Behavior. This feature of neurotic behavior has sometimes been called *neurotic stupidity*. The individual seems incapable of learning new means of adjusting to life's problems. He adheres to rigid patterns which he uses maladaptively in a wide variety of situations, making the same inappropriate response time after time. Compulsive behavior patterns provide only one example of rigidity. Other examples are: setting up dependency relationships indiscriminately, attempting to please all people at all times, seeking power relationships in all personal contacts, responding with anxiety regardless of the presence of a real threat. The explanation for this repetitive, fixed pattern is that the individual is responding, not to the ever-changing reality factors, but to complex unconscious needs within himself which he carries with him into all life situations.

Egocentricity. The neurotic is constantly self-preoccupied. He is more keenly aware of himself than is the normal person and as a consequence is habitually comparing himself and his situation with other persons and their situations. He is frequently demanding and exorbitantly selfish, though he is often driven to express these feelings indirectly. Symptoms are developed for secondary gain which is obtained through imposing unreasonable demands on others that would not otherwise be met. Phobias necessitating the continuous presence of a spouse, or somatic attacks developed just in time to prevent undesired action by another, are examples of symptoms providing the neurotic with secondary gain.

Hypersensitivity. Because of the high degree of tension he experiences, the neurotic characteristically overreacts to life situations. This trait is manifested in a low threshold for irritation, inability to tolerate criticism, overreaction to praise or flattery, frequency of complaints about even minor physical discomforts, and reactions of agitation to normal stress situations.

Immaturity. Neurotics, generally, are people who have failed to develop mature emotional and motivational patterns. Their emotional relationships are often typified by dependency and exaggerated needs for affection and social approval. Childish needs are retained and frustration is reacted to with sullenness, pouting, or temper displays. In some instances a false bravado is employed in ways not to be expected from adults.

Somatic Complaints and Symptoms. Uncomfortable or disabling physical symptoms are the things which most frequently lead the neurotic to consider himself a sick person. The physical ailment, which is psychogenically oriented, may take on any form: pain in any area of the body, dysfunction of any organ system, hypersensitivity, even muscular paralysis. Occasionally, the symptoms and complaints are quite specific, but they are often vague and multiple. Although the symptoms develop on an emotional basis, they are not unreal. The organic dysfunction can, as a matter of fact, produce structural changes which must be treated along medical lines (for example, peptic ulcer). For many psychoneurotics, medical care turns out to be the only treatment, and the underlying emotional disturbance goes unrecognized. The particular symptoms which will be selected by the neurotic, albeit unconsciously, may be influenced by: previous illness or injury; symptoms which have been demonstrated by other members of the family; constitutionally vulnerable parts of the body; and symptoms which hold a symbolic value for the patient.

Unhappiness. Beset with many handicaps, it is easy to see why the neurotic will be an unhappy person. Feelings of loneliness, of being hurt, or of missing the "good things in life" are characteristic of these patients. The prevailing mood for the neurotic is one of depression, despair, and pessimism over the future. His misery is two-edged, for while the neurotic feels imposed upon he also feels himself entangled in a web of his own making. Rarely does he experience joy.

Unconscious Motivation. While unconscious motivation forms the basis for much of the behavior of the "normal" individual, it dominates the major reactions of the neurotic to life situations. He has much greater need for the unconsciously developed defense mechanisms. His awareness of reality is to a much greater extent colored by unconscious fears and hostilities, which constitute the basis for the neurotic behavior pattern.

TYPES OF NEUROTIC REACTION

For many years a fourfold classification of psychoneurosis was recognized, by which patients were diagnosed under the categories of anxiety, conversion hysteria, psychasthenia, or neurasthenia. As a result of experience with large numbers of individuals who came under clinical observation in the military medical services in World War II, it was felt that a broader categorization was needed since some psychoneurotic patients could not be accurately assigned to any of these subtypes. Since then further consideration of the problem has given rise to the current classification by the American Psychiatric Association, which lists six types: anxiety reaction, conversion reaction, dissociative reaction, phobic reaction, obsessive-compulsive reaction, and depressive reaction. Note how this classification speaks of "neurotic reaction" rather than "neurosis" or "psychoneurosis." The virtue of this approach is that it emphasizes the disorder as a reaction to a life pattern rather than as the development of a disease process.

Even this official classification presents problems to the clinician, since the reactions listed rarely occur in completely differentiated form and there are still some patients whose illness cannot with assurance be fitted into any one of the six subtypes. Accordingly three other types will be discussed in this chapter: asthenic reaction, hypochondriacal reaction, and somatization reaction.

The Anxiety Reaction. The anxiety reaction manifests itself principally in diffuse and consciously experienced feelings of anxiety and apprehension for which there seems to be no specific basis in reality. The condition may be chronic and continuous, with the patient always tense and worried, easily upset, and preoccupied with future calamities or past errors.

CAUSATION. As with all neurotic manifestations, the anxiety reaction is a response to an unconsciously experienced threat, which may be suggested by some environmental condition. Repeated unsatisfactory life situations, conditions which threaten goals or status, or events which arouse fears of the breakdown of defensive processes—any of these may constitute the precipitating cause of the anxiety. More frequently, however, the reaction is built upon a lifetime pattern of insecurity and immaturity. The patient, having become anxious through either overprotection or rejection, relives his early apprehensions in the many subsequent minor stresses that are absorbed by the healthy adult.

SYMPTOMS. The moderate, chronic anxiety characteristic of the anxiety reaction may be precipitated periodically into acute anxiety attacks of high intensity by minor environmental stresses. Such attacks are accompanied by palpitation of the heart, tremor, difficulty in breathing, and profuse perspiration; sedation may be required. Vague fears of death or catastrophe may be expressed.

TREATMENT. While the anxiety reaction is the most prevalent of the neurotic adjustments, it responds well to therapy. Alleviation of the acute symptoms may be accomplished with relatively superficial psychotherapy, but attack on the deeper core of the neurosis itself requires more protracted treatment.

The Conversion Reaction. For many years labeled "conversion hysteria," this neurotic reaction is at the same time one of the most intriguing and diagnostically apparent of adjustments through illness. The patient, facing some difficulty which he cannot accept, develops a physical ailment which in one way or another protects him in his situation. It is understandable that while the symptom, if it were organically based would handicap him dreadfully, the patient shows little real concern about it. The reason is that he feels better with the symptom than he would in facing the reality he is escaping.

Although this reaction, particularly in its more dramatic manifestations, is becoming relatively rare in modern clinical practice, it has both historical and dynamic significance in the field of abnormal psychology. Its recognition early in the development of modern psychiatry helped to establish more firmly the emotional and psychological basis of numerous mental disorders. Many of Freud's patients were hysterics ("conversion hysteria") and the study of them led to some of his significant insights.

CAUSATION. The conversion reaction typically occurs in highly immature, exhibitionistic personalities given to ready dramatization of their life problems. These persons frequently have histories of seeking protection from emotional conflict through a flight into physical or psychogenic illness. The reaction is almost always precipitated by trauma or impending emotional conflict, and the form of expression is frequently dependent upon a minor accident, previous illness, or example set by a parent.

SYMPTOMS. The disability into which the patient "converts" his anxiety ranges over the whole field of illness and physical handicap. The symptom pattern reflects the patient's own knowledge of the medical nature of the illness he is hysterically simulating. In many cases the symptoms are difficult to distinguish from those of organic illness without laboratory tests. Among the less informed patients, the discrepancies may be almost amusingly apparent.

During World War I many hysterics were identified as "shell shocked" when in actuality these patients were making a neurotic adjustment through a conversion reaction. The reaction manifested itself in dramatic loss of motor and sensory functioning, blindness, loss of bodily sensations, paralysis of the arms or legs, and loss of speech function. During World War II, such cases were recognized as psychological in origin, and through early diagnosis and treatment they were successfully rehabilitated.

TREATMENT. Symptoms can be removed readily through suggestion or hypnosis, sometimes with the aid of narcoanalytic agents. To achieve a deeper change in the personality is a much more challenging task demanding prolonged psychotherapeutic effort.

The Dissociative Reaction. Dynamically, this reaction is identical with the conversion reaction, save that the patient's flight is into unawareness rather than into sickness. Until the most recent psychiatric classification was adopted, dissociative reactions were, in fact, classified as "conversion hysteria."

CAUSATION. The personality picture and the psychodynamic influence in all dissociative reactions resemble those found in the conversion reaction. The patients are immature, very suggestible, and usually show a history of highly developed fantasy life in their earlier years. The reaction is almost always precipitated by an emotional crisis to which escape into unawareness seems the only solution.

SYMPTOMS. The principal common aspect of all dissociative reactions is an interruption or breakdown of the conscious contact with reality, thus giving rise to some loss of personal identity: a brief amnesia, a fugue state, development of multiple personalities, or somnambulism.

Amnesia. Amnesia, which literally means "forgetting," may result from a number of organic conditions as well as from a neurotic conflict. In the dissociative reaction, amnesia is an obliteration through repression of awareness of self and of the historical data of all or part of one's previous existence. The hysterical amnesic is readily helped to a remembrance of his forgotten life data through hypnosis or hypnotic drugs.

Fugue. A fugue is a long-lasting amnesic state in which the patient leaves his original environment and may even take up a totally new way of living. Clinical literature describes dramatic cases of patients who have lived for long periods in a fugue, pursuing new occupations and in some cases even remarrying.

Multiple Personality. Multiple personality is a form of dissociative reaction in which patients develop two or more separate and usually markedly different personalities. The personalities achieve varying degrees of completeness, and they may or may not be consciously experienced. Morton Prince described the most widely known instance of this type of reaction in the Beauchamp case, in which five(!) distinct personalities were identified. While they are widely known in lay circles and highly dramatized in fiction, true multiple personalities are extremely rare, with fewer than one hundred cases reported in psychiatric literature.

Somnambulism (*Sleepwalking*). Somnambulism is a relatively common dissociative reaction. In this reaction the patient attempts to act out socially unacceptable unconscious impulses in the sleeping state. Most sleepwalking behavior is simple and undramatic, although there have been reported occasional instances of extremely complex behavior carried out during sleep.

TREATMENT. In treatment, the correction of the dissociated state is frequently accomplished with hypnosis. Prolonged and intensive therapy is required for the deeper personality changes.

The Phobic Reaction. A phobia is an irrational dread of an object, person, act, or situation. A phobia may be developed toward any imaginable aspect of the environment. From this, a host of terms have arisen with the prefixes describing the stimulus for the phobia. The more common phobias appear to be: *claustro*phobia (fear of closed-in places), *agora*phobia (fear of open places), *acro*phobia (fear of heights). The possibilities are, of course, almost limitless.

CAUSATION. In general, it is believed that neurotics whose early history reveals timidity, fearfulness, and feelings of inadequacy tend toward the phobic reaction. Four different conditions under which phobias may develop have been identified:

1. The phobia may develop as an intense conditioning experience in the early life pattern.

2. Most typically, the phobic reaction is the outcome of displacement of more generalized fears onto a symbol, which can then be avoided more adequately. For example, a basic feeling of insecurity and uncertainty may be displaced onto a phobia of high places (fear of falling). For a while such a patient may handle his fears simply by avoiding high places, but if the underlying fears are intense and pervasive they prevent this neat evasion by spreading and creating a whole series of phobias which ultimately paralyze the patient psychologically.

3. A phobia may develop as a means of protecting the patient from unconscious unacceptable wishes. Thus, a woman may develop a fear of being out alone which protects her from the possibility of giving way to extramarital sexual relations which she may unconsciously desire.

4. Finally, phobias, especially those of an obsessive type, may develop as a result of feelings of guilt over certain behavior which the patient considers reprehensible. Fear of syphilis is a common reaction to guilt aroused by the actual engagement in unacceptable sexual behavior.

Under any of the foregoing conditions the phobia may have secondary value for the patient in gaining for him special attention or enabling him to control the people around him.

SYMPTOMS. Phobic reactions are neurotic adjustments in which the outstanding symptom *is* the development of disabling phobias. Usually, however, the reaction is accompanied by anxieties and somatic complaints. The phobic features of the illness severely limit the patient's capacity to move about in his normal pursuits. When he is confronted with the feared object or situation, he is beset by overwhelming anxiety. Phobias are also found as part of the symptom picture in anxiety reactions, and they are seen associated with obsessive-compulsive reactions (see below).

TREATMENT. Treatment must be adapted to the dynamic factor that has led to the development of the phobia. Recently developed phobias are readily relieved with short-term psychotherapy. A more intensive program is necessary to treat phobias that are long-standing or to develop insight into the dynamics underlying the phobic reaction.

The Obsessive-Compulsive Reaction. Originally included under the term *psychasthenia* (by Janet in the nineteenth century), the obsessive-compulsive reaction has received considerable clinical attention in recent years. The symptoms that make up this reaction are organized around a core of obsessions (which occasionally include phobias) and compulsions.

OBSESSIONS. An obsession may be simply defined as a useless or irrational *thought* which persistently forces itself into the consciousness of the individual. Mild, transitory obsessions beset practically all people in such forms as: a persistent strain of music, concern over the locking of a door, or occasional superstitious worries. In their neurotic form, however, they are usually morbid in content and they dominate the waking behavior of the individual for long periods of time.

COMPULSIONS. Compulsions, useless or irrational *acts* which the person feels compelled to carry out, are also manifested occasionally in normally adjusted persons (for example: knocking on wood, straightening things out when orderliness is inconsequential, pulling small particles of lint off coat sleeves, etc.). In their neurotic form compulsions are more persistent and more absurd, and they may grow to such dimensions as to interfere seriously with the patient's ability to carry out his normal routine. (Note that although obsessions and compulsions have been discussed separately, in the neurotic patient they are often intertwined.)

CAUSATION. Psychoanalytic theories of personality development trace the origin of the obsessive-compulsive type of reaction to repressive and rigid measures imposed on the child during the early childhood toilet training period. Reference is frequently made to such individuals as *anal* personalities; their development has become fixed at this stage of psychosexual growth. Although not every case has this type of past history, it is true that the pre-neurosis history suggests a childhood pattern wherein the basic conflict of resistance or conformance to adult demands has been exaggerated. Carried back to the earliest phase of personality development, this conflict can be readily related to one of the earliest demands on the child, namely, to be clean in his toilet habits.

The obsessive-compulsive reactions thus develop in personalities having typical premorbid patterns which seem to lend themselves to the development of obsessions and compulsions. The history of this type of neurotic personality always reveals overemphasis on orderliness and cleanliness; persons in this category are also prone to carry conscientiousness and idealism to extremes. They are individuals who are often making too obvious efforts to be kind and considerate and to suppress angry feelings; close study uncovers stinginess and stubbornness.

SYMPTOMS. Morbid obsessions and compulsions vary widely in the forms they take, but certain classical reactions are seen. Some *obsessions* frequently encountered are: thoughts about viciously aggressive acts toward parents, children, or spouses; concern with disease and infection; blasphemous thoughts occurring to highly religious people; and thoughts colored by obscene language or the details of extreme, perhaps perverse, sexual acts. Some common *compulsions* include: counting, hand-washing, throat-clearing, mumbling; they frequently take the form of complex ritualistic behavior, particularly in regard to dressing or undressing.

GENERAL OBSERVATIONS. In reference to the over-all clinical picture of the obsessive-compulsive reaction these general observations may be made:

1. The predominating unconscious pressure seems to be aggressive in nature, and of such overwhelming proportions as to make it impossible for the individual to accept its existence at the conscious level. Although conflict over sexual impulses may be present, these, too, are aggressive in nature.

2. The patient's defenses are rigidly structured with strong intellectualizing efforts to study his own illness but only within the safety of ideation (reflective thoughts) or verbalization. There is frequently a real blocking of affective response in relation to the symptoms and the underlying conflict. Overt anxiety is typically well avoided. These factors make the treatment difficult and prolonged.

3. Either in spite of the defenses, or possibly because of the strength of the defenses, in the obsessive-compulsive reaction much more of the basic neurotic conflict is represented in consciousness. These basic elements are revealed in the particular obsession or compulsion which persists in the patient, but because he so firmly disavows the underlying conflict, he can allow them expression in his consciousness.

OTHER UNDERLYING FACTORS. Neurotic obsessions and compulsions reduce tensions by relieving the underlying unconscious conflicts and needs. The obsessions and compulsions, when expressed, may serve as a symbol of the conflict, or they may serve as defensive measures to prevent the conflictive material from intruding entirely into the conscious mind.

As a *symbolic measure,* the obsessions and compulsions are employed so that hostile or sexual impulses can emerge in a more acceptable form. Obsessions dealing with strong aggressions represent real but unconscious hostile feelings which the patient harbors. However, the real underlying emotion is not allowed expression, and it is perhaps for this reason that the overt content of the obsessional thoughts will rarely be carried out.

Compulsive behavior, too, allows expression of unconscious impulses; perhaps because the compulsion deals only with a symbol of the impulse, or because the compulsion stops short of the complete impulse, it can gain conscious expression. Both obsessive and compulsive reactions can temporarily discharge tension; but as the core of the conflict is never resolved, the tension reduction is short-lived and the obsessions and compulsions must be recalled.

As a *defensive measure,* both obsessions and compulsions may be called upon to reduce tension; the reactions can be used to drive away awareness of the unacceptable impulse or to prove that the impulse is not there. A simple example of obsessional activity used as a defense is the need to engage in useless, obsessional counting to keep other thoughts from entering into consciousness. Or the obsession may develop as a reaction formation which causes the individual to be obsessively concerned about the very thing he is unconsciously rejecting (for example, the parent who worries obsessively about the welfare of a child whom he unconsciously rejects). Feelings of guilt about unconscious sexual or aggressive wishes can also lead to obsessional scruples or compulsive attempts to protect the safety of others; examples of this are obsessional concern over modesty or compulsive checking of the possible danger of fire. Compulsions may also be used as a distraction from the obsession or as a magic gesture that will dispel it.

TREATMENT. The treatment of long-established obsessive and compulsive reactions always requires a long-range and intensive program. In many cases little more can be accomplished than to shift the patient to less disturbing or encumbering symptoms or to reduce the intensity of the symptoms.

The Depressive Reaction. Also labeled "neurotic depressive reaction" and "reactive depression," this neurotic reaction must be distinguished from psychotic depressions (for example, involutional melancholia and manic-depressive psychosis). The principal points of distinction are: The neurotic depressive reaction is always precipitated by a saddening stress situation (for example, a bereavement or other shock) to which the depressive reaction is immediate, although it may deepen somewhat as time goes on. While it may be severe, the depression is not accompanied by delusional beliefs.

CAUSATION. Though this type of neurotic reaction is apparently precipitated by environmental stress, it is seen only in neurotically predisposed personalities. The characteristic predepressive personality is marked by feelings of inferiority, hypersensitivity, and fears of a hostile world. There is often considerable repressed hostility. When the patient is reacting to a bereavement, he may employ the depressive reaction to protect himself from awareness of his own ambivalent feelings of hate and love toward the deceased. In a basically immature personality, the depressive mode of reaction may be related to an inordinate feeling of dependency toward the deceased.

SYMPTOMS. The psychoneurotic patient in a reactive depression is dejected, and his motor reactions are slow and dull. There is difficulty in sleeping and the patient complains of restlessness, lack of concentration, and tension. Frequently, the patient becomes aware of his illness only when he realizes he is not recovering (after an appropriate lapse of time) from the effects of the bereavement or other shock.

TREATMENT. Since the depression is real, there is definite danger of attempted suicide. Electroshock therapy is used frequently to arouse the patient from the depression. It should be accompanied by psychotherapy.

The Asthenic Reaction. Formerly labeled "neurasthenia," the asthenic reaction is characterized by heightened irritability, chronic fatigue, and vague aches or pains. The reaction ranges from a mild and transient form producing chronic somatic complaints, listlessness, and a loss of interest in the surroundings or life situation, to symptoms of such severity as to disable the patient, keeping him from holding a job or even from doing simple household chores. The milder form is a very common condition.

CAUSATION. At one time there was a tendency to interpret neurasthenia as a result of overwork and strain which "drained the nerves of their energy." Freud's thinking placed the cause of this ailment in sexual conflict. There has even been the suggestion that the disorder was a result of excessive masturbation. Today, the condition is identified principally as a reaction to unhappy and frustrating life experiences and circumstances in individuals already conditioned by unhappy childhood relations. Similar fatigue reactions in the patient's parents or parental overconcern about the patient's health in childhood seems to sensitize some individuals to this type of reaction.

SYMPTOMS. As with most neurotic reactions, asthenic symptoms are often used to control the actions of others and thus obtain secondary gain for the patient. Symptoms, which are not sharply focused, shift from time to time. Along with headaches, backaches, dizzy spells, bilious attacks, and indigestion, the patient habitually complains of being tired and lacking in energy. Even when the patient is motivated to an occasional spurt of energy, he regards this as a meaningless exception when he "happened to feel better," and he soon falls back into his tired, irritable pattern.

TREATMENT. Treatment of the asthenic neurotic reaction is frequently hampered by the patient's need to explain his illness along physical lines. Medical research has shown that prolonged fatigue reactions can produce organic pathology. Another obstacle to therapy is the fact that the unsatisfactory life situations which have precipitated the reaction cannot readily be changed. Nevertheless, the attention and understanding given the patient during therapy often help to make him a more tolerable person to live with.

The Hypochondriacal Reaction. The outstanding manifestation of this type of neurotic reaction is an all-dominating preoccupation with the bodily processes.

CAUSATION. Isolated and immaturely self-centered personalities are especially prone to develop hypochondriacal reactions. The life history will usually reveal habitual overconcern with health and body. One should look also for similar patterns in the parents. The hypochondriacal reaction is characteristically an illness of middle age precipitated by feelings of inadequacy and lack of fulfillment in persons predisposed to this type of reaction. As with the asthenic reaction, much secondary gain accrues to the patient through his attention-getting efforts.

SYMPTOMS. Characteristically, the patient expresses the suspicion that he suffers from all manner of diseases, offers odd explanations of his bodily processes, and complains of specific and nonspecific aches and pains. Despite all this, the patient has little anxiety. Care must be exercised to distinguish this reaction from both the asthenic and depressive reactions, which it resembles. When the hypochondriacal complaints are of a bizarre nature, it is necessary to consider the possibility that a schizophrenic reaction is present.

TREATMENT. Treatment is difficult because the patient usually breaks off any therapeutic relationship in which the focus is not on his physical complaints. The hypochondriacal reaction is seen more frequently in women than in men.

The Somatization Reaction. There are neurotic reactions in which the outstanding symptom is disordered functioning of some part of the body as the result of emotional disturbance. This type of reaction is discussed in detail in Chapter 7, Psychosomatic Disorders.

THE PSYCHONEUROTIC REACTION:
TREATMENT AND PROGNOSIS

It is generally agreed by clinicians that some form of psycho-therapy which leads to the development of insight and to a more effective solution of personal problems is the treatment of choice for neurotics. In addition, social casework which strives to make changes in unsatisfactory environmental conditions can be helpful. Under some circumstances the symptoms may be so extreme or disabling as to require symptomatic relief before the major program of psychotherapy can be begun.

Symptomatic Treatment. Where symptomatic treatment is deemed necessary, symptoms can be relieved by hypnosis, sugges-tion, or various types of medication. In offering this kind of treat-ment there is a risk that the patient will not persist with the psychotherapeutic process or that with the symptoms relieved his belief in the physical basis of his illness will be confirmed. Another pitfall in symptomatic treatment is the tendency neurotic patients have, after temporary relief, to shift to another symptom as an expression of the underlying difficulty.

Psychoanalytic Treatment. Although much success has been reported in the psychoanalytic treatment of psychoneurotics, its expense and the long period of treatment required make it impracti-cal for the greater number of such patients. Fortunately, less inten-sive psychotherapy can also produce entirely satisfactory outcomes. In this less ambitious program, patient and doctor in face-to-face interviews examine the patient's life history with particular reference to the origin and meaning of his problem. Together they work through new modes of adjusting. Recent developments suggest that such a procedure can also be practiced in small groups of patients with good success. A more detailed description of treatment tech-niques is provided in Chapter 19, The Therapeutic Process.

The chief problem encountered in the treatment of neurotic patients is their hidden resistance to treatment, and the working through of this resistance frequently prolongs the course of therapy. They are apt to terminate treatment at the first sign of improve-ment, or blame the treatment for any exacerbation of their symptoms and use this pretext for discontinuing therapy.

Prognosis. In general, it may be said that of all the forms of mental and emotional maladjustment, the neurotic reaction offers the best chances of successful treatment. Unfortunately, however, the largest number of neurotics never actually enter into any psychotherapeutic program. The best prognosis seems to be in cases of anxiety reaction and those of depressive reaction. The obsessive-compulsive and hypochondriacal reactions are the most resistant to treatment. In the conversion and dissociative reactions, symptomatic relief is rather easily accomplished, but beneficial modifications in personality structure are attainable only by means of intensive therapy. In all instances, however, the individual's motivation for treatment is essential and the degree of success in treatment is proportionate to his desire for change, which is in turn proportionate to the pain inherent in his symptoms.

9

PERSONALITY DISORDERS
(CHARACTER DISORDERS)

Personality, or character, disorders are essentially differentiated from other mental disturbances in that there exists a developmental defect in the *structure* of the personality rather than in its functioning. In most instances the structural defect is responsible for a lifelong pattern of maladjusted behavior that is characterized by an "acting-out" of the disturbance in place of the subjective experience of anxiety, or the development of mental or emotional symptoms manifested in other disorders. The occasional "acting-out" behavior seen as an accompaniment of such organic conditions as epidemic encephalitis, head injury, or convulsive disorders must be distinguished from that observed in true personality disorders.

There are three main groups of personality disorders: personality pattern disturbances, personality trait disturbances, and sociopathic personality disturbances. A fourth group, in which the psychopathology seems to be expressed largely in the form of a single symptom (such as enuresis or stuttering) is called special symptom reactions (discussed in Chapter 10). While these groupings of the personality disorders are in general descriptive of the behavior that is typical of each group, the fourfold classification is also based on the differing dynamics of personality development. Thus, while a diagnosis of personality pattern disturbance is descriptive of a kind of behavior (compulsive, antisocial, etc.), it is also indicative of a particular type of developmental defect in the personality structure.

About 12 per cent of first admissions to public mental hospitals are categorized as personality disorders. This figure, however, represents a minimal indication of the incidence of these disorders, for the following reasons: (1) Most individuals suffering from personality disorders are not ill enough to be hospitalized; accordingly, when they are treated at all, it is on an outpatient basis. (2) Many of these persons do not consider themselves to be ill and so do not even seek treatment. (3) An appreciable number of these individuals are convicted as criminals; as a result, their numbers are merged with the statistics of penal institutions.

PERSONALITY PATTERN DISTURBANCES

This group includes cardinal personality types in which the maladjustment is expressed in a lifelong pattern of abnormal behavior. The disturbances, though not psychotic, occur in personalities that are frequently described as "prepsychotic." While such persons resemble the psychotic more than they do the neurotic, they may show some features of both and are actually in borderline states of adjustment. Personality pattern disturbances are deep-seated disorders which provide the individual with little capacity for handling stressful situations except through escape into psychosis. In some cases constitutional factors are present, and they may be critical. Prolonged therapy may help the individual to achieve a more satisfactory adjustment while he is under the treatment program, but there is little evidence that a change in personality structure can be effected.

The principal types of personality pattern disturbance are: inadequate personality, schizoid personality, cyclothymic personality, and paranoid personality.

Inadequate Personality. Persons who exhibit a lifelong pattern of failure and chronic inability to satisfy the demands of everyday living are classified under this heading. Their lives are series of emergencies none of which can they satisfactorily resolve. They are not mentally defective, nor do they appear to be physically deficient, yet they cannot live up to the capacities which they seem to have. Their behavior is generally characterized by poor judgment, ineptness, and inadaptability. Their life patterns show lack of foresight, planning, and perseverance. Energy and drive are low. Unless these persons are supported by unusually favorable environmental conditions, such as wealth or protective parents, they become completely dependent on the community. Thus, they are often found on family welfare service or relief rolls, in jail, and among the lower social and economic levels of society. From a psychodynamic point of view, these are people who have never developed a strong personality structure and, thus, are poorly equipped to meet the usual tensions and pressures of life.

Schizoid Personality. The outstanding characteristics of the schizoid personality are his aloofness and his inability to enter into warm interpersonal relationships. Such persons seem to be avoiding direct contact with life, showing a strong dependence on daydreaming or autistic thinking in which they can express hostility or even normal aggression which other persons would express directly and openly. They seek compensation and satisfaction in fantasies of glory or omnipotence.

The pattern of the schizoid's unsociability is seen early in the life history, and it is usually accompanied by fearfulness, avoidance of competition, and emotional detachment. As children these individuals are usually overobedient, extremely shy and retiring, and hypersensitive. The onset of puberty is especially acute for them, with accentuation of their withdrawal and introversion.

Schizoid personalities frequently engage in overidealistic and unrealistic schemes and as a result their behavior is often considered eccentric by others. If they are intelligent individuals, they engage in writing books that are never published, in planning inventions that are never patented, or in conducting experiments that are never completed. They are frequently thought of as the typical prepsychotic schizoid personality, though it must be noted that not all schizophrenics show this premorbid personality picture. When the schizoid personality does become psychotic, the prognosis is poor. There is a strong suggestion of the influence of constitutional components in the formation of the schizoid personality. The weak personality make-up does not permit the schizoid individual to risk the uncertainties or possible pain of emotional attachment and as a consequence he has little or no emotional drive.

Cyclothymic Personality. Exaggerated extroversion and friendliness and an indiscriminate need to reach out in a generous, expansive, and energetic fashion toward all aspects of the environment are characteristics of the cyclothymic personality. Such individuals frequently indulge in outbursts of irritability and rage when their drives are blocked. Mood swings from depression to feelings of elation, apparently stimulated by internal factors and relatively independent of surrounding circumstances, are frequently observed. Usually these mood swings are contained within nonpsychotic proportions, but in extreme cases intermittent and alternating psychotic manic and depressive reactions may develop.

Milder forms of the cyclothymic personality are common among those who are successful in our society. These people are capable of sustained and energetic activity; they can devote themselves to organizational and promotional efforts with much enthusiasm and are almost inexhaustible in their efforts. The cyclothymic personality can create trouble for himself by overexpansive commitments in business ventures, through protracted social drinking, and in marital and extramarital exploits.

Paranoid Personality. Exquisite sensitivity in interpersonal relationships accompanied by a tendency to project into these relationships suspiciousness, extreme jealousy, and envy is the outstanding characteristic of the paranoid personality. In his over-all adjustment to people, he frequently resembles the schizoid personality, though he is somewhat less withdrawn, more rigid, and better organized. Paranoids are frequently cantankerous persons, difficult to deal with, and react to frustration with a move to "get-even." They are often found in the ranks of zealous cultists, ardent supporters of any *cause célèbre,* and reformers. They account for a fair percentage of lawsuits that are filed. Severe stress may push them into a paranoid psychosis.

PERSONALITY TRAIT DISTURBANCES

The most important feature of the personality trait disturbance is inability to adjust in the face of environmental stress because of immature or faulty development of the personality. It is expressed in the individual's inability to maintain his equilibrium or independence of function. Persons with these trait disturbances may resemble neurotics, although they show relatively milder expressions of anxiety, phobias, conversion, and so forth. Individuals with trait disturbances differ from persons suffering from pattern disturbances (see preceding section) in that the manifestations of their illness seem to be more dependent on stress, either environmental or endopsychic. Trait-disturbed individuals are also less likely to progress to psychotic reactions. From a dynamic point of view, personality trait disturbances may be considered to result from fixation at an earlier level of adjustment, with an exaggeration of certain behavior patterns, or from a pattern of regression to these earlier levels in the face of stress.

The principal types of personality trait disturbances are the emotionally unstable personality, the passive-aggressive personality, and the compulsive personality.

Emotionally Unstable Personality. In this category are found persons who display a variety of extreme emotional outbursts in minor stressful situations. The popularly used term "hysterical attack" well describes their behavior. They are blustering, argumentative, and subject to temper tantrums. Emotionally unstable persons are the ones who "lose their heads" in accidents and fires, and thus are often the cause of panic. They become uncontrollable when faced with family tragedy or personal difficulty. Characteristically fluctuating and fickle relationships are set up with others. In their emotional excitement, judgment is frequently impaired and their behavior is ineffective. Their reactions seem to develop out of their need for a too-quick mobilization of their defenses to protect them against strong and poorly controlled hostility, guilt, and anxiety. These individuals were formerly described as "emotionally unstable psychopaths."

Passive-Aggressive Personality. Because of the similarity of the underlying psychopathology, three types of personality trait disturbances are grouped here: the passive-dependent type, the passive-aggressive type, and the aggressive type. All three types may be occasionally seen in the same person. Although there may often be a veneer of neurotic anxiety, these patients are not properly considered psychoneurotic, for their disturbance is the result of faulty development of personality structure and not a result of malfunctioning of the personality.

PASSIVE-DEPENDENT TYPE. As children, these individuals have been passive and dependent in an infantile fashion; as adults, they act in the manner of dependent children toward a supportive parent. Their principal characteristics are helplessness, indecisiveness, and a tendency to cling to others. When they are required to assume responsibility or exercise initiative, they become anxious and panic-stricken. They need strong emotional support in most situations. Passive-dependent persons tend to engage in one-sided human relations which are unsatisfactory to themselves and others. When they are offered any kind of service at a clinic or by a family welfare agency, they are apt to make persistent efforts to perpetuate the relationship.

PASSIVE-AGGRESSIVE TYPE. While they are similar in their passivity to the passive-dependent type, these individuals add subtle and indirect patterns of aggression to their relationships with people. Their hostility is manifested in pouting, sulking, stubbornness, inefficiency, and dawdling. They frequently are able to block the activity of others with relation to themselves by passive resistance and subtly obstructionist maneuvers. Psychiatrists report that this personality disturbance is seen frequently in our culture.

AGGRESSIVE TYPE. Related in their behavior to the emotionally unstable and antisocial personalities, these individuals show outbursts of irritability, temper tantrums, and destructiveness in response to even minor frustrations. The reaction may take the form of a morbid or pathological resentment. Their behavior is usually the expression of underlying, unconscious dependency. Overt forms of their aggression are: spreading of rumors and gossip, throwing objects, and bearing vindictive grudges. Individuals exhibiting this reaction have not learned to handle their aggressions, as mature persons do, with a flexible system of controls and outlets.

Compulsive Personality. These are the meticulous, rigid, over-systematic people who are overinhibited and overconscientious in their adherence to social and moral standards. They are hard workers; many of them make constructive contributions to their environment. Their perfectionism and exactness frequently distress those about them and often create problems in interpersonal relationships since they tend to impose their standards on their associates. Because they themselves cannot relax, they frequently find annoying the relaxed attitude of those about them.

In their compulsive behavior these individuals resemble the compulsive neurotic and they may occasionally develop such a neurosis, but dynamically and symptomatically they stop short of the full-blown neurosis. Compulsive personalities do not resort to the displacement of affect onto obsessive thoughts or compulsive activities, a type of behavior which is characteristic of neurotics. Case studies of compulsive personalities suggest that the trait may develop through the persistence of an adolescent pattern (fixation) or as a regression from more mature behavior in response to stress.

SOCIOPATHIC PERSONALITY DISTURBANCES

The primary characteristics of this group of personality disorders is behavior which expresses a rebellion against or at least an unwillingness to conform to the demands of society. Although subjectively experienced discomfort or disturbed interpersonal relations may be present, the significant diagnostic feature is the individual's nonconformist behavior. Such behavior may take the form of criminality and delinquency, sexual deviation, and alcoholism or drug addiction. It must be pointed out that not all such behavior is diagnostic of the sociopathic personality; frequently, it may be an expression of other severe underlying mental illness such as a psychosis or a neurosis, or it may result from organic brain damage or disease. Sociopathic personalities are classified into four groups: antisocial reaction, dyssocial reaction, sexual deviation, and addiction.

Antisocial Reaction. Symptomatic of the antisocial reaction are: emotional immaturity, poor judgment, poor sense of responsibility, and an inability to appreciate the consequences of one's behavior. The antisocial individual is chronically at odds with society and seems always to be in trouble. He seems incapable of maintaining genuine loyalties to any person, group, or code. This diagnosis covers behavior that has been traditionally classified as "constitutional psychopathic state" or "psychopathic personality." Exact figures on the frequency of this disorder are not available since only a small fraction of such people are hospitalized, are brought to court, or seek treatment. About 2 per cent of first admissions to mental hospitals are diagnosed "antisocial reaction," while from 15 to 20 per cent of incarcerated criminals fall into this category.

CAUSATION. Attempts to explain the causation of the behavior of individuals diagnosed as antisocial personalities take the form of constitutional and psychological theories.

Constitutional Theories. Those who present arguments in favor of constitutional causation hold that some defect in the neurological functioning of the brain renders the person unable to develop normal control over his behavior. They point out that the normal inhibitory function of the higher brain centers is apparently not fully operative and this denies the individual the capacity to restrain impulsive activity. This may be a congenital defect or it may be acquired as a result of disease (for example, encephalitis) or from head injury which caused brain changes. In support of constitutional causation is the fact that antisocial behavior is a frequent consequence of encephalitis and some head injuries. Further support may be found in the electroencephalographic studies of criminal psychopaths in which as many as 80 per cent of those tested were found by some investigators to have borderline or abnormal brain wave tracings.

Psychological Theories. Here, as in the case of constitutional theories, explanations which are plausible lack factual proof. The dynamic factors must be understood in the framework of the total personality, and any attempt to single out a particular relationship as being a specific causative factor distorts the picture. However, the following patterns of parent-child relationships have been associated with the development of the antisocial personality: rejection, over-indulgence, and lack of identification.

Rejection. Predominantly, these persons come from homes which are emotionally "cold" and in which the child feels rejected. Subsequent behavior can be understood in terms of the individual's desire to disgrace or punish his rejecting parents or to seek self-punishment as expiation for guilt that stems from hostile feelings toward the parents. Another possible factor is the need for immediate satisfaction in a personality which has been chronically deprived of emotional gratification.

Overindulgence. Another source of antisocial behavior is the over-indulgent home where the child never learns to restrain impulses or to postpone gratifications. The overindulgence tends to hold him at an infantile level of egocentricity in which the life pattern is regulated by "what I want *now.*" When such a person is confronted with external sources of discipline, he has developed no capacity to adjust to them and reacts with rebellion.

Lack of Identification. The socialization process which enables the individual to live according to socially approved patterns requires that during the developmental years he be given a model on which to base his conception of his role in life. Through identifying with such a model he achieves desirable patterns of behavior. In the histories of antisocial personalities it is frequently observed that the identification process is blocked because of a rejecting parent, a broken home, or prolonged parental absence owing to the demands of military service or to other occupational situations. Also in this category is the lack of identification caused by the parent who is a weak model, or caused by the parent who demands of his child difficult or impossible achievements and standards.

Nevertheless, there is little that is certain concerning the causation of sociopathic personality. The dilemma persists: Does a biological defect render it impossible for the individual to learn control, or do incapacitating psychological events of early childhood render it impossible for the biologically intact organism to accomplish effective learning?

SYMPTOMS. The symptom pictures of sociopaths are many and varied. In this type of personality trait disturbances the total personality requires special consideration, since there is no symptom which is alone specifically conclusive. Coleman,* in a review of several studies of these cases, provides a list of the *major* symptoms, some or all of which appear in the behavior of the sociopath. A modification of this list follows:

Inability to understand and accept ethical values. Frequently such persons give mere lip service to moral and ethical values whenever this suits their immediate purposes or needs.

Marked discrepancy between level of intelligence and development of conscience. Although the individual's intellectual level may be average or above, his moral development is at a much more immature level.

Egocentric impulsiveness, irresponsibility, lack of restraint, and poor judgment. Selfishness and unwillingness to consider the consequences of their behavior frequently lead to thrill-seeking, malicious destruction, and unconventional behavior.

Inability to profit from mistakes and ordinary experiences. These individuals learn only more effective ways of escaping punishment or of exploiting others. Learning as a socializing process is never fully accomplished. They are generally considered to be incorrigible.

Inability to forego immediate pleasures for future gains and long-range goals. The sociopath is dominated by pleasure-seeking desires, often of a sensuous nature, and cannot postpone satisfaction. Such behavior is exemplified in impulsive automobile theft in which the sole desire is to have the use of the car for a short time.

Ability to put up a good "front" to impress and exploit others. When it is helpful to his purposes the sociopath can be charming and ingratiating. In this way he is not only able to conceal his true personality but can also frequently impose on others to gain entree into select circles and to advance himself financially. However, because of their explosive nature, such contacts are short-lived.

Impaired interpersonal relationships. The sociopath's friendship relationships, if any, are one-sided. He lacks capacity to be a genuine friend but will "use" friends. Interpersonal relationships are usually handicapped by his cynicism, lack of sympathy, and ruthlessness.

Low tolerance for stress. Much of the sociopath's "acting-out" behavior is triggered by situations of minor stress for which he has little tolerance. Thus, altercations of no great significance on the job or unpleasant work assignments will lead to his quitting or to

* After James C. Coleman, *Abnormal Psychology and Modern Life* (2nd ed.; Chicago: Scott, Foresman, 1956), p. 338.

aggressive behavior. In the home, normal problems of family living give rise to exaggerated upheavals and outbursts of emotion.

Rejection of constituted authority and discipline. Often considered the principal adjustment problem of the sociopath, his inability to accept and use authority constructively manifests itself at many points in his life history. The authority of parent, teacher, employer, policeman, and clergyman is resented and frequently this resentment serves as the focus of his rebellion. This rebellion is expressed by vandalism or by senseless or brutal behavior, the sole motive of which is release of aggression rather than premeditated gain.

Facile lying, ready rationalization, and projection of guilt. The sociopath is rarely at a loss for words. He can unabashedly face implicating evidence and attempt to lie away his responsibility by providing excuses or blaming others. Intelligent sociopaths are extremely clever in such attempts at avoiding responsibility for their behavior and people who try to understand them and help them are often antagonized by this tendency.

Talent for being irritating, disappointing, and distressing to others. For those who make any effort to be close to the antisocial personality or to assume any responsibility for his behavior, there is little to expect but anguish. Time after time, reform is promised but never actually achieved.

TREATMENT AND PROGNOSIS. So little has been accomplished in the treatment of antisocial personalities, that many consider the disorder incurable. If constitutional factors are involved, there is as yet no way of identifying or modifying them. The psychological patterns usually involved are of such long duration that a major therapeutic endeavor would be needed to bring about the desired change. For this reason many therapists are reluctant to undertake treatment of the antisocial personality and, when they do, their own negative attitudes interfere with and often foredoom any successful results. On their part, the patients lack insight and do not seek treatment. A note of optimism is found in the reports of those who have followed the plan of consistent therapeutic discipline in a controlled environment, supplemented by psychotherapeutic interviews. Such treatment, to be most effective, requires the placement of the individual in an institutional setting with supervised opportunity for community activity. The therapeutic goals are designed to help the individual to accept authority and to undergo a learning experience through which there is developed a system of ethical values. As the capacity for inner control begins to develop, external discipline is gradually reduced. Ideally, supportive contact with the patient is maintained after his full return to the community. Treatment of this type has been successful in an encouraging percentage of cases.

Dyssocial (Amoral) Reaction. Persons listed under this category manifest disregard for social codes and often come into conflict with accepted mores as the "normal" result of having lived all their lives in an abnormal moral environment. They often become gangsters, racketeers, vagabonds, or prostitutes. They are asocial with reference to organized society but may have strong loyalty to their own group. Within that group they may develop healthy interpersonal relationships.

These people may be distinguished from the antisocial personality in that there is no evidence that weaknesses in their development pattern have weakened the structure of their personality. Their dyssocial behavior is a result of lessons too-well learned rather than inadequacies in personality structure. Their crime is calculated and motivated by gain rather than arising from deep-seated and unconscious hostility against authority figures. As a group they are no more nor less susceptible to neurosis and psychosis than is the general population.

Sexual Deviation. Sexually deviate behavior may be manifested in any of several forms in which sexual gratification obtained by other methods and practices than heterosexual intercourse is the preferred or only form of sex activity. Individuals are classified as sexual deviates when the deviation is not symptomatic of more extensive syndromes such as schizophrenia and obsessional reactions. Patterns of sexual deviation are almost always the result of a long history of difficulty in psychosexual development due to environmental factors and are rarely the result of constitutional deficiencies alone. The principal deviations are: homosexuality, transvestism, pedophilia, fetishism, bestiality, voyeurism, exhibitionism, and sadism or masochism.

HOMOSEXUALITY. Homosexual behavior is sexual activity with a partner of the same sex. In discussing the problem of homosexuality it must be noted that there is no simple dichotomy of the homosexual and the heterosexual. Clinical findings indicate that many individuals who have never participated in any overt homosexual behavior may have unconscious or latent homosexual tendencies, which may be expressed in some outlet other than sexual behavior.

Thirty-seven per cent of Kinsey's male subjects (25 per cent of the female subjects) reported the occurrence after the onset of adolescence of some form of homosexual release to the point of orgasm. However, only 4 per cent of the males reported exclusively homosexual contacts.

Causation. There is no specific cause of homosexual behavior. Many factors are involved, and their relative importance varies greatly.

As for *constitutional factors,* it should be borne in mind that all humans have both male and female hormones present in their bodies. Relative balance, rather than presence or absence of the hormones is the contributing factor to the degree of masculinity or femininity of the individual. Studies of homosexuals have revealed that in some cases hormonal imbalance does exist, but its significance as a causative factor in homosexuality has not been established.

As for *psychological factors,* normal psychosexual development leading to heterosexual adjustment is dependent on a lifelong pattern of effective emotional relationships, primarily obtained in the family circle but also extending beyond it. The homosexual adjustment results when these relationships are inadequate, distorted, or lacking. The following kinds of emotional experiences have been associated with homosexuality:

A homosexual experience at an early age which was pleasurable, either as a result of seduction by an experienced person or as voluntary exploratory participation. The likelihood of the latter type of experience is enhanced when children are left for long periods without supervision, as in dormitory living in boarding schools or institutions. Under such circumstances a child who is in an emotional crisis, and who is experiencing emotional deprivation, is particularly susceptible.

Cross-identification or identification with the parent of the opposite sex. Parent-child relationships which continue intimate affective relationships between mother and son or father and daughter beyond the early years of life intensify the emotional bond and frequently block the acceptance of the life role appropriate to the sex of the child; the boy identifies with the mother, or the girl with the father. Such development may take place when a parent of the same sex is weak or rejecting, when the home is broken by separation or death, or when there exists an unconsciously seductive parent-child relationship wherein the neurotic parent lavishes on the child emotions which cannot be normally fulfilled.

Castration fears provide the focus for a psychoanalytic theory which explains homosexuality as an ego defense against the fear of castration. Fenichel reports that castration anxiety leading to homosexuality may arise in two ways: (1) The discovery by a young male child of the existence of people without penises may suggest the possibility of becoming such a person and thus fortify earlier threats of castration; to avoid the anxiety created by the female genitals, he avoids sexual contact with girls (later, women). (2) The female genitals, as a result of past fantasies and threats of castration, may be viewed as a castrating instrument which endangers the penis. Without evoking such deeply psychoanalytic theory it is possible to see the homosexual adjustment as a reaction to cold, harsh, and rejecting treatment by the parent of the opposite sex. Thus, the individual finds it impossible to set up a love relationship with a member of the opposite sex.

Rearousal of Oedipal fantasies has also been offered by psychoanalytically oriented investigators as a cause of homosexuality in some individuals. Unresolved Oedipal fantasies are revived and the overwhelming guilt feelings over such incestuous desires blocks sexual approach to any female.

Other psychological factors inducing homosexual behavior, which are probably more the side results of the aforementioned factors than basic causes in themselves include: fear of marriage arising from parental strife; fear of the responsibilities of marriage and family life; and fear of relationships with the opposite sex due to previous frustrating and humiliating experiences. Some individuals who are heterosexual in their pleasure-seeking behavior participate in homosexual activity for monetary reward. Still others turn to homosexuality after enforced and prolonged separation from the opposite sex such as occurs in confinement in prison, or correctional institutions, or in some types of isolated military service. The last-named is a situational reaction and usually does not persist when the situation changes.

Symptoms. Overt expression of homosexuality may take the form of mutual masturbation, sodomy (anal intercourse), fellatio (oral contact with the male genitals), cunnilingus (oral contact with the female genitals), or interfemoral coitus (intercourse between the thighs).

Treatment. Psychotherapy can be effective in the treatment of homosexuals only if the individual is strongly motivated to overcome the problem. Those who are satisfied to live as homosexuals show little response to therapeutic endeavor. Treatment may be effective where the individual has some basic value structure or moral code upon which the motivation for change can be based. Many homosexuals have not, however, developed the personality or character structure which would make possible such a set of values; consequently, they are less responsive to treatment.

A note of optimism is suggested in the gradual shift of public opinion which is beginning to recognize the homosexual as a psychiatric rather than a criminal problem. Under the impetus of this change it can be expected that more intensive study of treatment possibilities will take place. Some groups are now experimenting with a "total push" form of therapy, removing the individual from his old environment and providing for him a long stay in a new setting in which other value systems and patterns of behavior can be developed.

TRANSVESTISM. One variant of sexual adjustment may take the form of transvestism (dressing in the clothes of the opposite sex). In extreme cases the transvestite may attempt to live completely in the opposite sex role. Male transvestites may use lipstick, make-up, and elaborate feminine costumes. This may be done to increase the sense of identification with the female role and to become more attractive to other men. Transvestites may or may not participate in active homosexual release. Of particular significance in producing a transvestite adjustment is the parent who, disappointed in the actual sex of the child, rears and dresses the child as a member of the opposite sex. Treatment problems of the transvestite are essentially the same as those of the homosexual.

PEDOPHILIA. Pedophilia is the sexual deviation in which a grown person, male or female, seeks sexual gratification with a preadolescent child. It may be a heterosexual or a homosexual relationship. Genital manipulation is the most common form of activity, although intercourse or sodomy may be attempted. In such attempts, physical injury may be done to the child; psychic trauma for the victim is almost inevitable in cases where force is used. Clinical studies of pedophiliacs suggest that feelings of sexual inadequacy, fear of rejection by adult sex partners, and emotional immaturity are important dynamic factors. Conditions which lower voluntary control, such as alcoholism, paresis, and brain changes accompanying cerebral arteriosclerosis, are often present. In other cases, the act is part of a psychotic pattern of behavior.

This form of sexual deviation is looked upon in our society as a particularly heinous crime and is usually punished by a prison sentence without any attempts at treatment. Unfortunately, as a result, protection to society is afforded only for the term of the sentence since the individual upon release is prone to return to his former habits. The great majority of pedophiliacs apprehended are male.

FETISHISM. Fetishism is a sexual deviation in which sexual gratification is fully achieved only in the presence of or by contact with a particular love object, which may be a part of the body, a piece of clothing, or some other inanimate object. The most usual fetishistic objects are: intimate wearing apparel, hair, shoes, handkerchiefs, perfume, and such parts of the body as the foot, legs, and breasts or ears. To gain inanimate fetishes, such persons may resort to criminal activity such as assault and stealing. The articles so obtained may be hoarded or discarded after sexual release.

Early conditioning, which associates sexual satisfaction with a particular object, may develop into fetishism where there is an overall personality maladjustment, with special weakness in the psychosexual area. Deep-set feelings of sexual inadequacy and fears of humiliation are dynamically significant. Psychoanalytic literature offers abundant complex interpretations of the deep symbolism and dynamics of fetishism.

Closely allied with fetishism are those cases of kleptomania (compulsive stealing) and pyromania (compulsive fire-setting) in which the principal motives for these activities is sexual gratification.

EXHIBITIONISM. A sexual deviation in which gratification is obtained through exposure of the genitals or other parts of the body, usually to members of the opposite sex or to children, is known as exhibitionism. The exposure is often made in public or semipublic places such as trains, parks, libraries, schoolyards, or doorways. The regressive nature of this deviation is suggested by the fact that genital exposure is an almost universal occurrence among small children of both sexes. Among adults, pathological exposure of the genitals is almost exclusively found in males. Exposure of other parts of the body is, to a limited degree, a widely accepted form of exhibitionism among women.

The principal psychodynamic explanation of the exhibition of the genitals resides in feelings of sexual inadequacy leading to the need for reassurance that the penis is adequate. Thus, exposure is designed to elicit the reaction of startle or fear from a viewer, thus providing the needed reassurance. Conditions which reduce normal social restraint, such as alcoholism or organic brain changes, increase the likelihood of occurrence in those who are dynamically predisposed. Life histories of exhibitionists frequently reveal exaggerated dependency on and attachment to the mother with a consequent pattern of emotionally immature development. Because society regards such behavior as criminal, exhibitionists are usually referred for court action rather than for psychiatric treatment.

BESTIALITY. Bestiality is the sexual deviation in which the individual uses an animal for a sexual partner. This behavior may involve various types of sexual stimulation as well as actual intercourse. Bestiality seems largely to develop in rural areas and among those who have little opportunity for human contact. The element of isolation along with the close living with animals, in some cases involving emotional ties, seems to be significant. Under such circumstances mental retardation is an important contributing factor. Kinsey reported orgasm through animal contact in 17 per cent of farm-reared males. From a psychodynamic point of view, it may be understood as a response to feelings of inadequacy together with fear of humiliation and rejection by a human sex partner.

VOYEURISM. Also referred to as "scopophilia" or "inspectionism," this is a form of sexual deviation in which viewing is substituted for more overt sexual activity. The voyeurist may seek satisfaction by looking at nude women or by watching people undress or engage in sexual intercourse. "Peeping Toms" belong in this category. Masturbatory activity may accompany the viewing. The popularity of the burlesque show and pornographic pictures suggests the widespread nature of voyeuristic needs.

Voyeurism may occasionally be seen as the only sexual approach that a shy and overinhibited individual may allow himself. Fears of punishment for more overt behavior effectively block more direct sexual involvement. From a psychoanalytic point of view, Fenichel (see page 39) suggests that the voyeur is dominated by castration anxiety and finds voyeuristic participation a source of sexual satisfaction without danger.

SADISM AND MASOCHISM. Sadism and masochism are deviations in which sexual gratification is associated respectively with the infliction or the suffering of pain. Sadistic or masochistic behavior involves the sexualization of hostile urges against others or against the self. The pain may be physical, such as beating, slapping, pinching, or biting; or it may be psychological, such as disparaging or sarcastic remarks and behavior designed to humiliate the sexual partner.

Sadism and masochism, in a manner similar to other sexual deviations, represent failure to attain adequate psychosexual development. The history of maladjustment usually extends far back into the early life of the individual. Masochism and sadism are basically expressions of the same dynamic pattern and both may be acted out by the same individual. The direction of the deviation toward sadism or masochism depends on early conditioning and development as well as on the basic passive-aggressive components of the individual's personality. Its occurrence grows out of patterns of rejection and intense frustration. Extreme manifestations of sadomasochistic behavior may be symptoms of broader psychopathology, including even psychosis. Rape, mutilation, and some instances of murder and suicide may be expressions of these deviations. Particularly associated with these patterns of sexual deviation are the following dynamic factors:

Early childhood situations in which sexual excitation has been associated with either the infliction or suffering of pain.

Basic attitudes that sex is unnatural and dirty, impelling the individual to punish himself or his sex partner.

Castration anxiety which results in the need to prove one's strength by inflicting pain, or by depriving others of the satisfaction of inflicting pain by hurting one's self.

Unconscious ambivalence toward the sexual partner so that expressions of love and pain become associated.

ALCOHOLISM AND DRUG ADDICTION

Either alcoholism or drug addiction may occur as a symptom of an underlying mental disorder or, in the absence of recognizable neurosis or psychosis, as a disturbance of a sociopathic personality. It is always indicative of the presence of some personality difficulty when an individual uses alcohol excessively or is addicted to a narcotic drug.

Alcoholism. Estimates of the incidence of alcoholism vary considerably. One authority states that there are 750,000 chronic alcoholics in the United States, while another places the figure at 1,600,000. The number of "excessive drinkers," which includes the chronic alcoholics, has been estimated at 3,500,000. Excessive drinking is the greatest single cause of industrial absenteeism. Each day about 175,000 persons are absent from their jobs owing to "hangovers." The annual loss to industry is more than 60,000,000 mandays. Alcoholism occurs in all parts of the world and on all socioeconomic levels, although the frequency varies widely, with rare occurrence among those of Italian or Jewish descent and comparatively high incidence among those of Irish, English, and French origin.

CAUSATION. It was formerly believed that alcoholism was due to some inherited weakness. Also prevalent was the concept of alcoholism as a moral inadequacy constituting a religious or ethical rather than a medical or psychological problem. It is now, however, generally accepted that alcoholism is a surface manifestation of a basic personality disturbance. In some instances it is a form of escape for the person unable to cope with the stress of reality. For such persons drinking is compulsive, and they will regain control over their drinking only through a resolution of the basic personality problem. There are, also, apparently some individuals who find that even small quantities of alcohol will destroy control over their drinking; once having started, they are unable to stop. Possible explanations for this type of alcoholic include: (1) constitutional or physiological factors which may be of genetic origin; (2) body conditioning or tissue changes resulting from a long-continued use of alcohol which create a state akin to addiction; and (3) psychological factors in which the impact of taking the first drink breaks down volitional resistance to further drinking.

SYMPTOMS. In spite of the subjective sense of stimulation that is felt by drinkers, alcohol is, in fact, a depressant. The feeling of stimulation is due to its depressant action on the higher brain centers which, in effect, "inhibits our inhibitions." As the level of alcohol in the blood increases, its depressing action spreads to brain centers controlling motor co-ordination, with resulting loss of clear speech, slowing of reaction time, and loss of ability to move quickly and accurately. The amount of alcohol that will produce these effects varies widely from person to person and depends on such factors as current physical condition, amount of food recently ingested, and chronicity of the person's drinking. Symptoms indicating that drinking is excessive and has become a personality disturbance in itself are: consistent use of alcohol as a tension reliever; "blackouts," or short periods for which there is amnesia without loss of consciousness; surreptitious drinking; preoccupation with the available supply of alcohol; guilt feelings about drinking behavior; and loss of ability to drink in controlled amounts or to refrain from drinking at all.

Most of the *physical* symptoms appearing in the alcoholic are due to nutritional deficiencies which are the result of the alcoholic's failure to maintain a good diet.

Two major categories of alcoholics are offered in recent research by Murphy,* who classifies them as: essential alcoholics and reactive alcoholics. He states:

"Essential alcoholics are addicts who are likely to begin drinking and to experience intoxication at a relatively early age, who commonly or always drink to intoxication, usually display no clear pattern in their drinking, are unable to drink 'socially' for any length of time, and drink addictively in the absence of discernible factors which might, in the case of other addicts, result in a reactive addiction."

"Reactive alcoholics are addicts who do not usually exhibit a history of early and repeated intoxication, may use alcohol 'socially' for a number of years with possibly only occasional instances of intoxication and no severe 'binge' drinking, may display clearly periodic or continuous patterns in their drinking, and tend to begin addictive drinking relatively later in life than essential addicts, apparently in reaction to life situations which they have found intolerable."

TREATMENT AND PROGNOSIS. The prognosis in alcoholism is very poor if the alcoholic himself does not accept the grave nature of his disorder, recognize the need for outside help, and have strong motivation to recover. Older methods of treatment, such as exhortation, moral suasion, or attempts to motivate the alcoholic by increasing his feelings of guilt and remorse, have been found ineffective. Modern treatment thus aims at the resolution of the basic personality disturbance which generated the pathological need for escape through alcohol. Physical and medical aspects of the patient's condition must be cared for initially and the withdrawal from alcohol

---

* Murphy, Donal Gerald, "Psychological Correlates of Alcohol Addictions" (Unpublished Ph.D. thesis, Columbia University, New York, 1957), pp. 23 and 24.

accomplished. Negative conditioning in the form of nauseating medication administered with the alcohol is sometimes used to assist in this withdrawal. Psychotherapy, usually prolonged, is the most important aspect of the treatment program, but this cannot be undertaken until drinking has stopped. Institutional treatment is more effective than attempts to handle such individuals on an outpatient basis, owing to the greater opportunity for control of the patient's entire day.

Alcoholics Anonymous. A nonprofessional treatment program conducted by Alcoholics Anonymous has been successful in 50 to 75 per cent of the cases approaching that organization for help. "A.A.," as it is called, is made up of ex-alcoholics and is, in a sense, a form of supportive group psychotherapy. Essential to this program are the recognition by the alcoholic that he needs help, his readiness to ask for it, and his belief in some power higher than himself. The complete and unquestioned acceptance by the group of the new member as a worthwhile person is a powerful therapeutic factor.

Other Facilities. Adequate treatment facilities for alcoholics are scarce. Few general hospitals will accept them unless they are critically ill physically, and then will keep them only until the critical phase of that illness is over. Local jails are the institutions to which the majority of alcoholics are sent. However, the picture is changing, and research agencies such as the Yale Center for Alcohol Studies and the Research Council on Problems of Alcohol are sources of plans for legislation, public education, and the establishment of treatment institutions to cope with this major problem of public health.

Drug Addiction. Addiction to a drug is usually a symptom of a basic personality disturbance. Similar to alcoholism, drug addiction when occurring in the absence of recognizable neurosis or psychosis, is considered a sociopathic personality disturbance. True addiction means that the body physiology is so altered by the repeated administration of the drug that withdrawal symptoms occur when the administration is not continued. Drug *addiction* is distinguished from *habituation,* the latter condition being characterized by psychological rather than physiological need. The major narcotic drugs used in the United States are morphine and heroin, both derivatives of opium, though cocaine and marijuana are also widely used. Morphine and heroin are administered principally by hypodermic injection; and in some cases smoking, eating, and inhalation ("snorting" or "sniffing") of the drug occurs. Cocaine is most often sniffed but may be taken hypodermically. Marijuana is commonly rolled into cigarettes ("reefers") and smoked.

It is estimated that there are 40,000 drug addicts in the United States. A sharp rise in the use of drugs, especially by young age groups, was observed in the postwar period. About 5 per cent of those addicted are individuals who developed dependence on the drug as a result of prolonged medical treatment.

CAUSATION. The pattern of causation for addiction or habituation to various narcotic drugs are basically similar. In all cases they reflect disturbance of personality structure, leading to the use of the drug as: (1) a total reaction pattern for evading stress and responsibilities; (2) curiosity and thrill-seeking in a setting of group pressure, such as in a gang; and (3) accidental addiction as a result of medical treatment in which the drug was essential, though this does not apply to marijuana, which has no medical use. The thrill-seeking is often spurred and abetted by organized narcotics rings for purpose of profit.

SYMPTOMS. The major narcotics (opium derivatives, cocaine, marijuana, and similar drugs) differ sharply in the symptoms they produce.

Opium Derivatives. On the physiochemical side, the opium derivatives are depressant in their action. They induce reveries, a feeling of relaxation, decrease in sex drive, drowsiness, alteration of concepts of time and distance, and decrease in voluntary movement. The addict is not exhilarated but rather needs the drug to keep him from feeling the intense discomfort of early withdrawal symptoms. True addiction sets in if the individual continues to use the drug for about thirty days. By this time, the drug has become physically necessary to the user, and he has developed a tolerance, so that larger and larger doses are required. Without the drug, severe withdrawal symptoms appear: profuse sweating, loss of appetite, depression, and feelings of impending doom, disturbances of temperature control, vomiting, diarrhea, cramps, and tremors. Delirium and hallucinatory experience may occur, and there is danger of death from heart failure. These symptoms increase in intensity, reaching their peak at the fourth day of withdrawal. Then they subside and are gone by the eighth day.

Cocaine. The initial reactions to the ingestion of cocaine are dizziness and, sometimes, headache. This is followed by a period of stimulation in which the individual is euphoric and hyperactive for a period of four to six hours. The drug is often used to overcome a sense of inadequacy or to provide the individual with the subjective strength to cope with a stress situation. With prolonged use, more serious symptoms appear, including paranoid feelings, depression, hallucinations, and delusions. One classic form of hallucination in this disorder is known as the "cocaine bug," a sensation that bugs are crawling about just beneath the patient's skin. As with all drugs, the behavior of the cocaine addict is centered about his efforts to procure an adequate supply of the drug. To gain this end, there is often a complete collapse of moral and ethical controls, and the individual's life is spent in petty crime, begging, or prostitution in order to obtain money for his supply of cocaine.

Marijuana. Continued use of marijuana causes habituation rather than true addiction. It is used chiefly to induce euphoria, lasting for two or three hours during which the user experiences a loss of inhibition which allows previously controlled sexual or aggressive drives to be expressed. There is an attentuation of the subjective sense of time, an experience which is the source of its appeal to some jazz musicians. The drug is often used in a group setting to touch off libertine sprees. As with alcohol, there is a wide discrepancy between subjective confidence and objective performance, so that reckless driving and accidents often are the consequences. One of the most curious subjective experiences is that in which space and size relationships are disturbed. The marijuana-intoxicated person feels at times so enormous that he is afraid to move for fear he will crush other persons and things in the room; this feeling may give way to a sensation of being very tiny and vulnerable to injury from other persons; these feelings are referred to as "macrocosmic and microcosmic sensations."

When marijuana is used over a long period of time, the economic factor of maintaining a supply may lead to dietary deficiencies and a depreciation of ethical values. Because of the ubiquitous growth of the marijuana plant (it will thrive in seemingly infertile soil, such as the backyard of a tenement house), the extent of its use is unknown.

Other Drugs. Barbituric acid derivatives (e.g., phenobarbital), the amphetamines (e.g. benzedrine), and the bromides are widely used to alleviate anxiety and tension. Some medical authorities believe that a definite physiological dependence is built up and abrupt withdrawal produces physiologic crises. They protest against too free prescription or indiscriminate use of these drugs.

LSD (lysergic acid diethylamide), initially used in controlled experiments for the treatment of schizophrenia, has become a widely used drug, particularly among college students. The taking of LSD unfortunately was given an air of sophistication by reports of its use in scientific research and its suggested use to increase sensory awareness and promote fuller religious experiences. LSD habituation has led to extreme forms of sociopathic behavior and in some cases to homicide and suicide.

TREATMENT AND PROGNOSIS. Until recently, it was thought that the typical addict could be satisfactorily treated only in a hospital. Centers for such treatment were set up in federal hospitals in Fort Worth, Texas, and Lexington, Kentucky. Steps in the program are: withdrawal of the drug, physical rehabilitation of the patient, and prolonged psychotherapeutic assistance. The pattern of treatment here closely resembles that provided for the alcoholic.

More recently, a program was set up in Synanon House (1958) which attempts to establish a therapeutic environment for those who volunteer for treatment. Patients assume responsibility for maintaining the center and participate in group therapeutic sessions. Adaptations of the Synanon concept are important parts of New York City's drug addiction program. Because of the widespread use of heroin (an opium derivative) and other drugs among ghetto residents, some programs of street confrontation and neighborhood orientation have been developed.

Methadone has been successfully substituted for heroin as a treatment for long-term users. The drug seemingly has no euphoric or negative side effects and helps the addict to overcome his habituation to heroin. In a recent study of more than 800 patients treated by methadone, 80 per cent of the total sample were free of heroin use and were pursuing socially useful patterns of behavior.

10

SPECIAL SYMPTOM REACTIONS

There are a number of troublesome symptoms occurring in childhood and occasionally persisting into adulthood, which may exist as the principal difficulty without evidence of any other psychopathology, or which may be the symptomatic expression of a wider pathological picture. These symptoms have been grouped together in the most recent APA classification and are here discussed individually under the heading "special symptom reactions." Although they are not necessarily indicative of serious mental disturbance, they do constitute important practical problems in the family and school life of the child and may be a source of secondary unfavorable emotional reactions. Such conditions need not be in themselves neurotic, psychotic, organic, or sociopathic disorders, but they may be associated with any of them. These special symptom reactions include learning disturbances; speech disturbances; enuresis; sleep disturbances; habit reactions such as tics, thumb-sucking, and nail-biting; excessive masturbation; and lying, stealing, and truancy.

LEARNING DISTURBANCES

The principal learning disturbances are subject disabilities in reading, writing, arithmetic, and spelling. Because these subjects provide the basic tools for almost all subsequent educational development, the deficiencies not only are problems in themselves, but also may lead to the development of secondary problems. Broadly speaking, their primary causation may be either psychological or organic, although most often it is of a psychological nature. Learning deficiencies occurring in children of below-average intelligence or in those with sensory defects are not considered under the heading of special symptom reactions.

Reading Disabilities. Disabilities in reading as a response to emotional maladjustment are more prevalent than is ordinarily realized. They are found four times more frequently among boys than among girls. As one of the child's first school learning experiences, reading is subject to all the negative emotional reactions that the child brings with him to school or develops in the school environment.

CAUSATION. The principal psychodynamic explanations include the following.

Patterns of Immaturity. These lead the child to resist learning to read because reading represents a step toward maturity and further reduction in his infantile dependence on parents.

Resistance to Parental Authority. The child uses the learning situation to express his developing rebellion against overdemanding, rejecting, or overprotective parents.

Traumatic or Maladjustive Early Classroom Experience. Where the teacher is harsh, coercive, unfair, or even punitive, the anxieties raised in the child may seriously hamper his attention and concentration, thereby crippling his learning efforts. Failure to lay a sound foundation in reading makes it difficult for the child ever to catch up. Certain traumatic experiences in the classroom such as ridicule, teasing, or rejection by classmates have the same effect.

Other Traumatic Experiences. Traumatic or upsetting experiences occurring at home or at a time coincident with his learning to read may also interfere with the child's learning process. Among these may be death of a parent, breaking up of the family, serious illness, parental discord, or changes of school and neighborhood.

Faulty Methods of Teaching. Not all children respond favorably to any one method of instruction. Where only one method is used and all children are forced to conform to it, some will inevitably suffer.

TREATMENT. In most instances when learning disturbances are recognized and treated promptly, they can be corrected by remedial instruction without more extensive psychotherapy. For example, one investigator reported that 80 per cent of cases of reading disabilities responded to remedial teaching alone. On the other hand, where the disability is allowed to go unrecognized or untreated its effect may spread to other aspects of adjustment and may then require both psychotherapeutic effort and remedial instruction. Of paramount importance in all these problems is the creation in the child of a healthy motivation toward learning. The current development in many school systems of special remedial reading programs for acceleration of speed and comprehension in reading attests to the widespread occurrence of such problems.

Writing Disabilities. The principal expressions of writing difficulty are illegibility and "mirror writing," wherein certain letters are written in reverse form. Illegibility is in many cases corrected by improved motivation and training. Mirror writing generally requires special psychological analysis.

Causation. The mirror writing phenomenon may result from a lack of clear-cut cerebral dominance or it may be an expression of strong unconscious resistive tendencies on the child's part. In addition to the dynamic factors applicable to reading, the diffusion of any emotional tensions into motor activity can seriously interfere with learning to write.

Treatment. Treatment of writing difficulties includes remedial instruction and psychotherapeutic assistance where this is deemed necessary.

Arithmetic Disabilities. The aura of difficulty in which this subject is too often clothed may in itself create anxiety or intensify anxieties already present.

Causation. Factors of particular significance in explaining arithmetic disabilities are:

Attention-Concentration Difficulties. Arithmetic functioning requires a relatively long span of attention with a maintenance of a high degree of concentration. Any anxieties that the child may be experiencing will reduce his span of attention and ability to concentrate, thereby interfering with arithmetic learning.

The Rigidly Cumulative Nature of Arithmetic. Because each successive step in the learning of arithmetic depends on competence in all previous steps, the effect of failure or loss due to any reason is drastic. Thus, a child's absence or temporary emotional distress at the time when one process is being taught may create a pervading difficulty in his learning of all the subsequent processes.

Reading as a Factor in Arithmetic. Arithmetic disability, where it develops in later grades, may be due to inadequate skill in reading.

Treatment. Treatment of arithmetic disabilities involves the various methods applicable to treatment of other learning disturbances.

Spelling Disabilities. The rigidity and rote that are almost implicit in learning to spell are among the chief sources of trouble in this area. Again, the various dynamic factors which were said to be applicable to reading are found to operate here.

SPEECH DISTURBANCES

The development of meaningful speech begins toward the end of the first year of life. The most rapid progress in speech is characteristically made during the preschool years, when the child is experiencing a number of other critical developmental changes. Because communication is so largely dependent on vocalization, the development of speech patterns is inextricably interwoven with the development of interpersonal relationships; thus, speech difficulties may arise from tensions in the interpersonal field, in particular those occurring during the preschool years. In addition, some speech difficulties may result from organic factors such as malformation of the mouth or other components of the speech apparatus, or neurological impairments. It is estimated that some ten million people in the United States suffer from one or another form of speech impairment. The two forms of speech disorder discussed here are stuttering (stammering) and infantile speech.

Stuttering. Blocking of speech, repetition of initial syllables, or disturbances in speech rhythm are the principal forms of stuttering or stammering. Associated with the speech symptoms there may be facial contortions or grimaces, jerking of the head, and labored body movements. The amount of impairment in the speech of stutterers varies widely, from mere hesitation to prolonged and complete blockage of speech for minutes at a time. The degree of stuttering also varies with the nature of the situation in which the individual is speaking, typically being more extreme in situations of social pressure. For example, the stutterer may speak well when alone or with friends, but break down when required to speak to an older person or a superior or before a group. Conversely, stuttering may disappear when the stutterer, emotionally aroused because of excitement, enthusiasm, or hostility, loses his sense of self-consciousness and speaks without difficulty. Stutterers often may be able to sing or to engage in group reading without manifesting their impairment. It is a curious observation that some people who fail miserably when trying to speak normally and correctly have no trouble running through a monologue in dialect if they have any talent at all for performing.

CAUSATION. While the causes of stuttering are not fully understood, most specialists in the field are of the opinion that psychogenic factors are predominant. Evidence is present that a large number of stutterers come from families in which parents or other relatives also stutter. However, no convincing evidence of constitutional factors has been presented. One authority points to the neurological situation in which absence of clear-cut cerebral dominance may have created a predisposition to stuttering, but here, too, evidence is conflicting. Some clinical studies suggest that a forced change of handedness may precipitate a stuttering pattern. The best understanding of the stutterer comes from an explanation of some of the psychodynamic factors involved. These include:

Parental Anxiety over the Child's Speech. Most children in the early phases of speech development show hesitant and stammering speech. When the parent becomes overconcerned with such a speech pattern and strains already anxiety-ridden parent-child relationships, the result may be self-consciousness about speech and a continuing pattern of stammering in later years.

Blocked Aggression. Stringent parental interference with the normal needs of the child for assertive or aggressive expression may arouse such feelings of conflict as to affect the speech patterns. Since speech can so readily be used for the release of aggression, it is understandable that conflict in speech patterns might develop in the overinhibited child. In this connection, psychoanalysts point to the frequent association between stuttering and unconscious needs to use aggressive and even obscene language.

Feeding Problems. At least one study suggests that stuttering may be an aspect of an over-all disturbance in the oral stage of development. In this study, 80 per cent of the stutterers had a history of feeding difficulties, while such difficulties were present in the history of only 15 per cent of nonstutterers.

Other Factors. Stuttering as a reaction to emotional trauma may occur at any stage of speech development. Occasional instances of stuttering may be attributed to identification by the child with a stuttering parent, relative, or other adult. It must be said that any emotional distress experienced by the child during the development of speech may have its impact on adequate speech patterns. This is particularly true of stress occurring during the preschool period and of stresses which in one way or another the child relates to speech. Evidence that stuttering is most typically one symptom of a more general emotional instability is the fact that in the majority of stutterers other emotional problems are found.

TREATMENT. If a speech disorder such as stuttering is identified early, treatment consists of working with the parents and the environment to remove or change the pressures creating the difficulty. Speech disorders which have persisted for years are much more difficult to eradicate and require prolonged psychotherapy. Remedial training should be provided as an adjunct to psychotherapeutic effort. Under a comprehensive program of therapy and training, the prognosis for alleviating the speech disturbance is good.

Infantile Speech. Such speech patterns as lisping, baby talk, or extremely poor enunciation are included under this heading. Mild examples of these speech patterns are frequent in our society.

CAUSATION. If the speech problems are severe and persistent, they are indicative of unhealthy immaturity, traceable to one or another of the following factors: parents who unconsciously or consciously encourage their children to remain infantile by coddling; overprotection; sibling rivalry in which the child hopes to gain preferred treatment from the parent by remaining babyish; or even imitation of parents who use baby talk or have speech impediments themselves.

TREATMENT. Treatment of infantile speech consists essentially of those methods employed in the treatment of stuttering.

ENURESIS

Enuresis is involuntary urination during sleep, commonly referred to as "bedwetting" or "nocturnal enuresis." The term is actually inclusive of lapses of urinary control in the waking state ("diurnal enuresis"), but this is rarely seen. Studies during World War II among a group of 1,000 selectees showed that 16 per cent were enuretic beyond the age of five years and that 2.5 per cent did not gain control until the age of eighteen or later. Enuresis is more common among males than females.

Causation of Enuresis. In no more than 10 per cent of the cases studied could the causes of enuresis be demonstrated as organic. A study of the 90 per cent of cases in which psychological factors were important found that enuresis was the result of excessive emotional tension and was usually part of a syndrome which often included nail-biting, thumb-sucking, and temper tantrums. A circular type of reaction has been observed in which the bedwetting leads to feelings of shame or guilt, and these in turn intensify anxiety and tension, thus precipitating further bedwetting. A variety of psychodynamic interpretations of enuresis has been offered, among them:

—a specific expression of generalized anxiety;

—a displacement of sexual satisfaction frequently associated with repressed sexual fantasies;

—an expression of hostility toward parents or as a release of aggression;

—a persistence of immature attention-getting behavior patterns;

—inadequate habit training with attitudes of indifference and apathy on the part of the parents.

Treatment of Enuresis. The focus of treatment should be on the alleviation of the emotional tension underlying the difficulty rather than on the symptom itself. Extensive psychotherapy may be necessary. Many therapists suggest that no attention be directed to the enuretic incident itself. However, mechanical conditioning techniques or changes in regimen such as limitation of fluid intake in the evening and arousing the child during the night may be helpful in breaking the circularity of the pattern, thus providing the child with an opportunity to rebuild confidence. Such techniques must be used in an atmosphere of minimal parental pressure so that failure will not be felt as a new threat.

SLEEP DISTURBANCES

Sleep is relatively sensitive to any type of emotional disturbance which the individual may experience, and disturbances in the sleep pattern, especially in children, are the earliest indicators of increasing emotional tension. While habits of sleep vary widely from one individual to another, certain sleep phenomena are clearly recognizable as disturbances. Principal among them are somnambulism, nightmares and night terrors, narcolepsy, and insomnia.

Somnambulism. Although somnambulism (sleepwalking) may occur as a special symptom reaction, it is usually a symptom of a dissociative neurotic disorder (discussed in Chapter 8, page 111). Sleepwalking most often occurs for the first time during puberty and commonly disappears after a few episodes. Somnambulists are usually amnesic for the behavior that has occurred during the trance state. Sleepwalking activity may range from taking a few steps away from the bed and then awakening, to traveling some distance out of the house, and to performing complex activities.

CAUSATION. In general, somnambulism is (1) an attempt to resolve symbolically some conflict situation frequently connected with sexual fantasy and masturbation, or (2) an attempt in sleep to act out the content of dreams.

TREATMENT. Intensive psychotherapy is the treatment of choice, particularly in cases where severe emotional disturbances underlie the sleep disturbance. In severe cases of somnambulism, psychotherapeutic efforts are often hampered when other neurotic reactions (anxiety, hypochondria, etc.) arise in place of the sleepwalking occurrences.

Nightmares and Night Terrors. While they are similar, these two sleep disturbances are not identical. The *nightmare,* a relatively common disturbance in childhood, is a frightening dream which frequently awakens the child in an upset state. After the nightmare, the child can report the dream and usually is able to return to sleep after being comforted by the parents. *Night terrors* are fearful states arising during sleep, accompanied by screaming, sweating, thrashing about, crying, and even hallucinations. The individual rarely awakens spontaneously and even when partially awakened he does not recognize his surroundings and cannot be calmed for the duration of the attack, which may last from 15 to 30 minutes. After the attack the individual is amnesic for the entire experience.

CAUSATION. Sleep disturbances of the two foregoing types are usually associated with tension-producing experiences in the life pattern or the daily activities of the individual. They may occur irregularly in response to a specific disturbing event or may be recurrent, seemingly revolving about the particular conflict or emotional state.

TREATMENT. Some clinicians hold that for night terrors the principal cause is hypoglycemia—a condition of low blood sugar—and report success in treatment by an increased carbohydrate intake at the evening meal or just before bedtime.

Narcolepsy. Drowsiness during the day, frequently leading to sleep for minutes or even hours at a time, which cannot be explained as being due to lack of sleep during the night is referred to as narcolepsy.

CAUSATION. At one time thought only to be the result of some organic condition such as encephalitis, narcolepsy is now known to be also a response suggesting psychological maladjustment. It may be used unconsciously by the individual as a means of escape from unpleasant life discords. It is also found to occur in children whose home environment provides no stimulation, in which case it might be an expression of extreme boredom. Finally, it is seen in children of subnormal intelligence who do not have the capacity for finding interest in their environment.

Treatment. Where a persistent narcoleptic pattern occurs in an adult or the somnolence takes place in the midst of an ongoing activity, a serious emotional problem may underlie the sleep disturbance, and this usually requires extensive psychotherapy.

Insomnia. Probably the most widespread sleep disturbance is insomnia. It may appear on a sporadic basis as a reaction to immediate excitement or emotional disturbance or it may occur as a relatively persistent characteristic of the individual's sleeping pattern. Transitional bouts of insomnia are related to such physical conditions as extreme fatigue, changed sleeping accommodations and major diet changes as well as the excessive use of stimulants. Occasionally, drugs prescribed for other illnesses may lead to sleeplessness. Insomnia is most frequently thought of as an adult symptom but it is found in children where its persistence must be considered a concomitant of serious emotional distress. Occasional sleep disturbances in children may be expected as normal reaction to routine life excitement and stress.

Causation. Psychological factors producing insomnia are worry, fear, guilt, and anxious anticipation of coming events. Insomnia may occur as a simple symptom reaction or may be associated with such other psychiatric conditions as anxiety reaction, depression, and mania. In such cases the intensity of the insomnia will be related to the severity of the emotional disorder. The symptomatic development of insomnia seems to be related to personality characteristics as well as types of conflict. Coleman * in summarizing a series of studies states that insomnia is frequently associated with rigid conscience, and tendencies toward depression and self-punishment. He identifies the conflict between desire and moral restrictions as frequently leading to insomnia as a result of the feelings of guilt and fear of punishment that develop.

Treatment. Relief of the symptom of insomnia can be provided by a variety of medications. The problem, however, is twofold: if the underlying cause persists and medication must be used over

---

* After James C. Coleman, *Abnormal Psychology and Modern Life* (2nd ed.; Chicago: Scott, Foresman, 1956), p. 232.

a long period of time, increased dosages are found necessary; in addition, using sleeping pills becomes habitual and the act of taking medication then becomes a necessary condition for falling asleep. From a mental health point of view, the underlying psychodynamic cause of the insomnia should be identified and treatment directed toward its removal or alleviation. Frequently, psychotherapeutic effort (without being explicitly directed toward the symptom) is helpful in eliminating the insomnia.

"HABIT REACTIONS"

Under this heading are considered such troublesome reactions as tics, thumb-sucking, nail-biting, and lip-licking.

Tics. Tics are involuntary twitchings of small muscle groups, usually of the face, neck, and shoulders. Some common examples are spasmodic eye-blinking, jerking or twisting of the head, and shrugging of the shoulder. Tics occur most frequently in children during the grammar school years, are seen more often in boys than in girls, and have a higher incidence among bright than among dull children.

CAUSATION. Almost always the tics are symbolic manifestations of a specific emotional problem, which is chronic for the individual. They are frequently associated with either sexual or hostile impulses. Tics tend to occur when a high degree of stimulation is combined with severe restriction of motor activity. The tic serves as an indirect means of releasing pent-up tensions.

TREATMENT. Tics are most successfully treated through psychotherapeutic effort directed toward the underlying psychological problem. A tic occurring as a symptom of a compulsive or conversion neurotic reaction may be sufficiently severe to disable the patient. Under the foregoing condition the program of therapy must be based more extensively on pathological factors.

Thumb-Sucking, Nail-Biting, and Lip-Licking. The early years of childhood show a high incidence of such oral disturbances as thumb-sucking, nail-biting, and lip-licking. Nail-biting as a symptom of emotional tension tends to persist through the adolescent years with a high rate of incidence; some studies suggest that one out of five college students and draftees for military service have the habit.

CAUSATION. All these reactions are considered immature patterns which reflect dependent oral needs. Thumb-sucking may be a response to too early or abrupt weaning, to a feeling of neglect in the feeding situation, or to feelings of threat or rejection. Nail-biting has been interpreted as expressing a variety of emotional problems; one of the most common is a turning upon the self of hostile feelings toward others which cannot be expressed directly. As such it is often induced by a desire for rebellion against tyrannical authority figures. It may also occur as a tension-releasing device in the face of stressful or threatening situations. One significant source of stress inducing this habit is tension arising from repressed sexual needs, particularly during the adolescent period. Some psychoanalytic writers consider it to be a substitute form of masturbatory activity. Continuous licking of the lips could well be attributed to dehydration if it were not for the fact that the individual may persist in it to such a degree that it appears to afford an oral satisfaction which transcends an immediate organic need.

TREATMENT. There is general agreement that direct attack on these symptoms through the use of mechanical restraint, application of bitter-tasting preparations, or parental nagging, is undesirable because such methods tend to increase the tension. Apparent successes with these methods is illusory; the tensions find other means of symptomatic expression. While the conditions giving rise to the symptoms do not usually require extensive psychotherapy, some form of counseling will be helpful.

EXCESSIVE MASTURBATION

Self-stimulation of the genitals as a means of seeking sexual satisfaction is referred to as masturbation. About 90 per cent of males and 60 per cent of females are reported by Kinsey and others to have admitted to engaging in masturbatory behavior at some time or another in their lives. Self-stimulation of the genitals may be seen in the infant as a vague stimulation of an erogenous zone of the body, perhaps first discovered through natural exploration of the body. Later, during the preschool period, it may be manifested as a more sharply focused form of genital play. Ultimately, in adolescence, it may be carried to the point of release in orgasm. Occasional masturbatory behavior cannot be considered a symptom of mental or emotional abnormality, although it does present a moral problem for some individuals. The emotionally stable individual will alleviate his moral guilt according to the means his religion provides and need not develop abnormal anxiety. However, owing to widespread misinformation, wrong teaching, excessively rigid attitudes toward sex, and dire prophesies of the dreadful effects of masturbation (insanity, softening of the brain, mental deficiency, acne and other skin blemishes, and impotence), none of which are true, severe emotional conflicts have frequently been the consequence of masturbatory behavior. It is only in this connection that masturbation can be regarded as a cause of psychological disturbance. More often excessive masturbation is a *symptom* rather than a *cause* of emotional disturbance. Persistent masturbatory behavior is an expression of a basically immature adjustment to life.

Causation of Masturbation. More specifically, excessive masturbation may be understood as a reaction to feelings of inadequacy and emotional deprivation, the relief of which is sought in masturbatory activity. Another factor inducive to excessive masturbation is an underlying homosexuality which prevents the individual from developing normal heterosexual interests. Important in understanding the dynamics motivating such behavior are the fantasies accompanying it, the circumstances and manner of its practice, and the pattern of its occurrence. Bizarre accompaniments and excessive masturbation frequently suggest the possibility of a psychotic reaction.

Treatment of Excessive Masturbation. Because of its symptomatic nature, the problem of masturbation is best treated by a therapeutic program designed to resolve the underlying emotional difficulty. Frequently, however, where the concern over masturbation is particularly disturbing to the individual, briefer psychotherapy or counseling which affords accurate information, understanding, and support is helpful.

LYING, STEALING, TRUANCY

This triad of symptoms occurs frequently as a symptom reaction among children and young adolescents.

Causation of Lying, Stealing, Truancy. These reactions are usually expressive of hostility, negativism, and rebellion, which may be conscious or unconscious. They may occur as part of a juvenile pattern without necessarily indicating psychopathology in the individual. On the other hand, they may be danger signals indicating the development of a beginning sociopathic personality. When these symptoms express unconscious motivations relative to interpersonal relationships, particularly in the family, they may be indicative of neurosis.

Treatment of Lying, Stealing, Truancy. Because lying, stealing, and truancy are troublesome and threatening to adults, they are more apt to induce a punitive rather than an understanding approach by parents or school authorities than other symptoms of equivalent or more malignant psychological significance. As symptoms suggesting underlying emotional disturbance, they must be approached psychotherapeutically, with efforts directed to remove the cause rather than merely to punish the symptom.

11

SCHIZOPHRENIC REACTIONS *

Although schizophrenia is the most common form of psychosis, its fundamental nature is still not fully understood. The term covers such a broad range of symptoms that the appropriateness of classifying them under a single heading has been questioned. Most authorities agree, however, that the varieties of schizophrenia have enough in common to justify a common basic diagnosis. Involved in the etiology of schizophrenia are constitutional, neurological, emotional, social, and environmental factors.

The term "schizophrenia," introduced by EUGENE BLEULER (1857–1939) in 1911, means "split personality." This meaning cannot be applied literally to the disease as it is understood today. The personality of the schizophrenic should be regarded as disintegrating rather than splitting. Kraepelin's term *dementia praecox* ("insanity of youth"), formerly widely used (see page 8), has been discarded because experience has not supported the implication that this disorder has its onset in adolescence.

INCIDENCE

Schizophrenia accounts for one-fifth of all first admissions to mental hospitals in this country. In state hospitals about 50 per cent of the chronic patients have been diagnosed as schizophrenics. While the onset may occur in adolescence, most frequently the symptoms emerge in the age range from twenty to forty years of age; the average age of first admissions with schizophrenia is close to thirty-five years. In addition to the hospitalized population,

* Thus far Chapters 6 through 10 have each treated a different major category of abnormal behavior. Instead of presenting the psychoses in a single chapter, they are discussed in Chapters 11 through 14. Because the psychoses constitute a mental health problem of great magnitude and because of the wide range of material covered, such presentation is desirable from an instructional point of view. The student is referred to the Appendix for information concerning the position of these illnesses in the American Psychiatric Association classification system.

schizophrenics may be found among prostitutes, hobos, and isolated individuals in any population. The tendency to hospitalize schizophrenics is notably lower in rural areas.

ETIOLOGY (CAUSATION)

The etiology of schizophrenic reactions has been studied from many different viewpoints, yet it remains a highly controversial matter. Heredity, physical constitution, pathology of the nervous system, biochemical and physiological changes, and various psychogenic factors have, at one time or another, been presented by investigators as the chief determinants of the disorder. Such efforts have been extensive, but in general causation may be discussed on the basis of those causes which emphasize somatic factors and those which stress psychogenic factors. Most writers in the field of abnormal psychology, although aware of the probability of predisposing constitutional or physical factors, seek out psychodynamic and environmental factors to explain the development of the illness.

Hereditary Aspects. Despite the inaccuracies involved in using hospital records for statistical purposes, there is beginning to be general acceptance of the fact that schizophrenia is more prominent in certain family histories. The work of Kallmann in tracing family histories of schizophrenic patients has been especially influential. He reports that while 0.85 per cent of the general population become schizophrenic, 16.4 per cent of the children of parents one of whom is schizophrenic and 68.1 per cent of the children of two schizophrenic parents become schizophrenic. It must be realized, however, that this kind of statistical finding alone does not demonstrate predominantly hereditary foundations for schizophrenia, since it can be reasoned that schizophrenic parents do not provide the best environment for normal personality growth. Still, other findings of Kallmann tend to substantiate the existence of a genetic factor in this mental disorder. The figures in the accompanying table indicate that as the genetic relationship comes closer, the incidence of schizophrenia in relatives of schizophrenic patients increases.

The role of environment in schizophrenia is suggested by the different rates for identical twins raised together and for those reared apart. For the nonseparated identical twins, in 91.5 per cent of the cases in which one twin develops schizophrenia, the other will develop it. For twins reared apart, this figure drops to 77.6 per

INCIDENCE OF SCHIZOPHRENIA IN
RELATIVES OF SCHIZOPHRENIC PATIENTS *

Relationship	Incidence (Per cent)
Marital partners	2.1
Step-siblings	1.8
Half-siblings	7.0
Parents	9.2
Full siblings	14.3
Dizygotic twins	14.7
Monozygotic twins	85.8

* After Franz J. Kallmann, in A. H. Maslow and B. Mittelmann, *Principles of Abnormal Psychology* (New York: Harper, 1951), p. 119.

cent—though it must be admitted that this is a much higher figure than for any other genetic relationship.

Constitution as a Factor. Kretschmer reported a marked association between schizophrenia and the slender, fragile physique (asthenic type). Sheldon carried this work forward in greater detail; using the term "ectomorphic" to describe the same body type, he reported a high correlation between this physique and a temperament which makes the individual tense, overvigilant, sensitive, inhibited in action, and uncomfortable and awkward in social situations.

The reasoning of those who use the constitutional approach to explain schizophrenia is as follows: (1) Schizophrenics tend to have an ectomorphic (asthenic) physique. (2) Persons with an ectomorphic physique possess a tense, inhibited, oversensitive temperament. (3) Persons with the described temperament when faced with an environment hostile to warm and satisfying human relationships will tend to depend upon avoidant and withdrawing patterns of adjustment which may then carry them into schizophrenia. In reasoning thus, these investigators then relate the findings to heredity and state that it is the "inherited constitution" with its given temperamental reactions which provides the hereditary predisposition toward schizophrenia.

Both Kretschmer's and Sheldon's findings (see page 42) are still the subject of controversy among scientific workers. The theories growing out of their studies must be considered tentative.

Pathology of the Nervous System as a Factor. Attempts to correlate brain and nervous system pathology with schizophrenia have appeared often in the history of efforts to understand this disorder. However, when pathology findings have been reported in autopsied schizophrenic brains, it has not been possible to rule out other causes for the disease such as senile changes or secondary illnesses. In studies which have compared the brains of schizophrenics with those of normal persons, with other important factors held constant, it has been impossible to differentiate between groups on the basis of brain tissue. This is not to say that there is nothing wrong with or different about the schizophrenic brain. It is simply that techniques have not been developed which can uncover any brain pathology that would explain the disease.

Biochemical and Physiological Changes as Factors. Kraepelin, noting that the onset of schizophrenia was frequently associated with menstruation or childbirth, offered disordered secretions of the sex glands as a possible explanation. Although he later rejected this limited interpretation, he nevertheless continued to emphasize endocrine dysfunction as a possible cause. His thinking stimulated much research around the possibility that schizophrenics might suffer from a physiological or biochemical insufficiency produced by disordered functioning of the endocrine system. But such research has proved unusually complex and attempts to prove a close relationship between schizophrenia and endocrine dysfunction have been inconclusive.

Attempts have been made to explain schizophrenia as an outcome of *focal infection* and spectacular results have been reported from dental extractions, drainage, and surgical removal of infected parts. But the theory has not withstood the test of time and stronger proof, and interest in this approach to schizophrenia has waned markedly.

While it cannot be denied that schizophrenics as a group manifest impairment of bodily functioning, several investigators have pointed out that the physiological variation found in these patients may very likely be the result of their circumstances of living—prolonged or acute starvation, or dehydration resulting from sustained excitement. One study reports the following differences between schizophrenics and normal persons living under identical conditions:

1. The schizophrenics gave less adequate physiological responses to a variety of stimulating agents.

2. They showed a reduced response to thyroid medication, to autonomic stress, and to various other forms of stimulation which normally would produce physiological changes.

3. Their capacity to achieve a constant level of physiological functioning (homeostasis) was impaired.

These findings have been seen as a kind of physiologic withdrawal, a failure of the body to respond to stimulation which parallels the failure of the patient to respond emotionally. From this point of view, schizophrenia is said to result from a generalized failure of adaptation traceable to a basic defect in the maturational processes.

Psychogenic Factors. Freud recognized the role of the unconscious in schizophrenia, and two of his early papers described paranoid schizophrenia as a defense against unconscious homosexual wishes. Bleuler also emphasized psychological processes in the development of schizophrenia, laying stress on frustration and conflict. Adolf Meyer was the first to present schizophrenia as a reaction of the total personality in terms of social environment and personality organization. This concept has been most influential and has caused workers, instead of searching for first causes, to seek to determine the environmental conditions under which schizophrenia may develop. It is widely accepted today that the same kind of personal, social, and environmental factors which produce the neurosis also operate to prepare the groundwork for and to precipitate schizophrenia in those who are predisposed by heredity or constitution. Four kinds of psychological factors have been described: psychic trauma in infancy, childhood background, family relationships, and regressive patterns.

PSYCHIC TRAUMA IN INFANCY. One interpretation of the background of schizophrenia on a psychological basis assumes that the patient was exposed to a severe psychic shock in early infancy. This early trauma sensitized the individual to such a degree that he cannot tolerate later stress which might be accepted by others. As this stress mounts, he becomes so disturbed by it that he must seek refuge in complete withdrawal to an infantile world, which is incompatible with the world of reality but in which he can find the satisfaction that the real world does not afford.

CHILDHOOD BACKGROUND. Schizophrenia is seen as a developmental disorder having its roots in childhood. It is an extreme adjustment to a history marked by increasingly protective avoidance of human contacts, perhaps forced on the individual by the absence of secure and warm human relationships. Lack of interest in human contacts isolates the individual from the educational influences provided by social correction. He does not sufficiently expose his thinking to the social interaction that would adjust it to reality and give it structure and precision. His feelings and thoughts grow too much within himself. The end result is a failure to develop skill in role-playing and in shifting to different perspectives. The social environment is seen as an obstacle, and additional stress forces a progressive curtailing of interest in the world about him. The initial cause of this type of development must probably be sought in predispositions described above.

FAMILY RELATIONSHIPS. No one family pattern stands out in the childhood history of schizophrenics. Maternal overprotection is present in certain cases, but any factors in the family situation which serve to break relationships with people will have a harmful effect. Of particular significance in the development of schizophrenia are any events that lower the individual's self-esteem or challenge his adequacy. Frequently schizophrenia develops after a history of model behavior based on a fearful need to conform. It must be emphasized that neither family relationships nor esteem-shattering experience *alone* seem adequate to explain the development of schizophrenia.

REGRESSIVE PATTERNS. Psychoanalytic theories of schizophrenia emphasize an extensive pattern of regression, causing the individual to retreat to modes of thinking and behavior which are characteristic of the earliest years of life. In consequence the patient is dominated by basic, libidinal impulses which flood up from the unconscious. These are not subject to the laws of logic, time, or order. The splitting of emotion and intellect can be understood because at this early level of development these impulses have not yet become adequately differentiated. The schizophrenic pattern of regression can be precipitated by adolescent conflict or stress in meeting problems of maturity. To avoid his difficulties, the schizophrenic regresses to an infantile pattern. Many psychoanalysts follow Freud in emphasizing the strong unconscious homosexual wishes in schizophrenia and see the schizophrenic regression as a means of escaping what cannot be accepted at the conscious level.

CHARACTERISTIC SYMPTOMS

The symptoms most commonly seen among schizophrenics are: prepsychotic schizoid personality, emotional dulling, notable disorganization of thought processes, delusions and hallucinations, behavioral changes, and changes in speech.

Prepsychotic Schizoid Personality. Frequently, though not always, the person who develops schizophrenia will be revealed as one who previous to his breakdown exhibited a "shut-in" personality. Such "schizoid personalities," as they are called, show basic weaknesses in interpersonal relationships. They are poor mixers, seem incapable of forming warm friendships, and seem to lack capacity for appreciating the reactions of others. Their behavior tends to be highly individualistic, if not actually odd. Their thinking is complex, overabstract, and autistic. They frequently demonstrate an air of tenseness and urgency. Hostile feelings are usually present but the patient seems unable to express or accept them. The life history of nearly all schizophrenic individuals reveals this kind of behavior from early childhood.

Emotional Dulling. The schizophrenic characteristically shows an inability to experience genuine emotion. Apathy, aloofness, and dreaminess are his responses to situations which should arouse joy, fear, or anger. He seems unable to make contact with other persons. When emotional responses do occur, they are likely to be extreme and resemble a general state of excitement, even panic, rather than a specific emotional experience. Emotional responses are also undifferentiated and seem to run into one another, out of control, and yet apparently causing little concern in the patient.

Pathological emotional patterns found in schizophrenics include: *inappropriate affect,* such as discussing tragedy with a smile; *absence* or *blandness of affect,* as in expressing no feeling even when talking about the tragic; *disunity of affect,* as weeping and laughing at the same time; *rigidity of affect,* such as responding with a stereotyped emotional pattern regardless of variation of the emotional stimulus.

Disorganization of Thought Processes. Of equal importance with the emotional changes in the schizophrenic are the breakdown and disorganization of his thought processes. It becomes extremely difficult to follow his trend of thoughts, and, as a result, effective social communication becomes almost impossible for him. Close study of the responses of these patients to such tests as the Wechsler-Bellevue and the Rorschach has indicated that the specific weaknesses in the thought processes of schizophrenics are as follows: (1) confusing the concrete with the abstract; (2) condensing into one concept the aspects of several concepts; (3) establishing relationships among concepts where they do not exist; (4) using symbols extensively; (5) confusing the bar between the real and the fanciful; (6) using highly personal and subjective associations and explanations.

In part as a result of his erratic thinking, and in part because of his dominating emotional needs, the products of the schizophrenic's thought patterns are bizarre. His explanations of common phenomena are far-fetched and complicated. Frequently preoccupied with bodily function, he explains various physical sensations as being the result of complex and impossible causes (for example, he may associate an imagined odor from his mouth with foul thoughts). Mechanical devices are elaborated upon and applied in foolish and wholly impractical ways. The schizophrenic is often absorbed with unworkable inventions and hopelessly intricate plans.

Prevalence of such disorganized thought processes in the schizophrenic has raised the possibility that intellectual deterioration is a basic aspect of schizophrenia. Careful research, making use of psychological tests, however, has failed to demonstrate the consistent presence in schizophrenics of the kind of mental deterioration that is found, for example, in patients suffering from brain damage or paresis. The point remains controversial, with the final answer depending on the development of more refined investigative techniques. It is safe to say that much, if not all, of the schizophrenic's bizarre thinking results from the intrusion of subjective, emotionally toned needs into his thinking process, in such a manner that the patient is dominated by these subjective factors and finds it extremely difficult if not totally impossible to deal objectively with reality.

Delusions. The delusions commonly encountered in the thinking of the schizophrenic are false, irrational beliefs which are fixed in the patient's mind seemingly beyond any possibility of change. These irrationalities usually are expressed in (1) ideas of reference or of influence, and (2) delusions of persecution and grandeur. One of the earliest and most frequent signs of mental illness noticed by the patient's family is his tendency to attribute great significance to trivial events and his insistence that they refer to him in some special fashion. Such beginning ideas of reference then develop into persistent beliefs that people are talking about him, or laughing at him, or accusing him of immoral practices. Ideas of influence are manifested when the patient expresses the belief that someone is putting thoughts into his head, or directing his behavior, or causing him physical discomfort. The means which the patient describes for the perpetration of these influences may be hypnotic, electric, magnetic, or mystic. With delusions of persecution, the schizophrenic ascribes the troubling phenomena to enemies or to "persecutors." In milder forms the delusions are related in terms of "people being against him," but such delusions are often extensively elaborated into diabolical plots in which high officials or agencies of the government, even whole countries, are "out to get him." In delusions of grandeur the schizophrenic usually ascribes to himself some unusual or superior ability or identifies himself with some striking public figure, member of royalty, or historic or religious person.

Hallucinations. Also common symptoms of schizophrenia, hallucinations differ from delusions in that the hallucinating patient registers his experience with reality in a distorted, completely inaccurate fashion: hearing, feeling, smelling, or seeing things that are not present. (In contrast, a delusion is based upon misinterpretation of an experience that has been registered in the senses accurately in the first place.)

Auditory hallucinations are the type most commonly found. The voices or sounds reported by the patient may be someone calling him obscene names or commanding him to do things; at times he may claim that he is receiving "secret information" from "secret societies." *Gustatory* and *olfactory* hallucinations (taste and smell) are next in order of frequency. The patient complains of the curious taste of his food or reports peculiar odors emanating from his surroundings or his own body. In hallucinations of *touch* and *pain,* the patient experiences odd or painful sensations in various organs and he may associate these with sexual assault. *Visual* hallucinations occur as shifting scenes, objects changing shape, "fiery crosses," or animals.

Behavioral Changes. It is understandable that the schizophrenic, in responding to the phenomena described in the foregoing paragraphs, will exhibit a great variety of odd and exaggerated behavior. There are, however, particular reactions which seem to be characteristic of such patients: grimacing, stereotyped movements (such as rubbing the hands, brushing "things" away, pulling the hair, rigid and constrained posture, silly smiling), acting out the hallucinations he is experiencing (as in concentrated listening), assuming peculiar (often awkward and exhausting) positions for long periods of time—frequently the intrauterine position of the fetus.

Changes in Speech. Since the problem of communication is a basic one in schizophrenia, symptomatic changes in speech are always seen. They may range from mutism to a continuous flow of meaningless sentences and neologisms (words or phrases coined by the patient). Speech patterns of the schizophrenic include the following types of response: evasive and/or irrelevant answers; monosyllabic responses of "Yes" and "No"; a flat, monotonous quality of the voice; and "word salad" (a meaningless mixture of words and nonsense).

VARIETIES OF SCHIZOPHRENIA

The four principal and classic types of schizophrenic reaction are: simple, hebephrenic, catatonic, and paranoid. More recent experience with the study and diagnosis of schizophrenic reactions has led to the identification of five additional categories: acute undifferentiated type, chronic undifferentiated type, schizo-affective type, childhood type, and residual type. The classification rests entirely upon the symptom picture rather than upon possible etiology, in which differences have not been clearly established. There is, admittedly, much overlapping among the four principal groups, and occasionally the predominant symptoms change markedly for the same patient in the course of the illness, in which case a change of diagnosis is justified. Recently, the distinction has been drawn between process or true schizophrenia, and the reactive or benign schizophrenia.

Simple Schizophrenic Reaction. Of the schizophrenic reactions, the simple type presents the least bizarre behavioral picture. Many of these patients maintain relatively good contact with reality throughout the course of their illness. A large number of simple schizophrenics are able to get along outside mental hospitals, cared for by their families, adjusting marginally at some routine job, or perhaps lost among vagrants, prostitutes, or the criminal population.

The outstanding symptoms are a gradual narrowing and waning of interests, loss of ambition, emotional apathy, and withdrawal from social relations. Personal appearance is neglected, conversation is meager, and there is indifference to the opposite sex. The patient appears to be completely absorbed by his inner world of fantasy. Such persons when out of mental hospitals are considered eccentric by their neighbors. As a rule the simple schizophrenic loses all sense of responsibility and comes to lead a dependent, parasitic existence. Mental functioning may not be markedly impaired, but there is a lack of interest in any form of accomplishment. Close observation of such individuals often uncovers weak, distorted efforts to make contact with others, as a consequence of the pathetic need for love and affection which these patients experience. Usually, however, it is not possible to maintain any emotional contact with them.

Hebephrenic Reaction. Foolish behavior; incoherence of thought, speech, and action; and infantilism characterize the hebephrenic. It is this type of schizophrenic that probably gave rise to Kraepelin's term "dementia praecox," for in hebephrenics the breakdown occurs at an earlier age than in the other types, and the resulting disintegration is more severe than in the simple, catatonic, and paranoid types of schizophrenic. There is usually a history of "odd" behavior which may include overscrupulousness, preoccupation with religious and philosophical issues, or brooding over sexual problems, especially masturbation. A growing pattern of seclusiveness and dedication to fantasy leads up to the acute breakdown.

The hebephrenic engages in childish giggling; inappropriate, shallow laughter; and grimacing. His behavior is characterized by bizarre mannerisms—talking and gesturing to himself; alternating between weeping and laughing; talking gibberish. Hallucinations and delusions are prominent, in particular those involving sexual material. The patient may hear voices accusing him of perverse sexual practices; occasionally, he believes his "enemies" are after him. As the disease progresses the patient may engage in completely uninhibited and public sexual acts, or play with fecal matter or smear it on the walls or on his person. The hebephrenic can be pictured as a person so overwhelmed by life's stresses that he retreats to an infantile level of adjustment.

Catatonic Reaction. Although in many ways the behavior of the catatonic indicates a more complete withdrawal from reality, the chances for recovery are much better than for other types of schizophrenia. This is particularly true if the onset of the illness is acute, as it often is. However, the patient's history usually shows a typical pattern of gradual withdrawal and a degree of emotional apathy. In the catatonic reaction the patient alternates between a deeply stuporous state and excitement.

Stuporous State. In the stuporous state, the patient loses all animation, remaining motionless and in a stereotyped posture for hours, even days. He refuses food and shows no effort to control bowels or bladder. Extreme negativism is a characteristic reaction. A surprising feature is that even though apparently stuporous, the patient will take note of all that is going on around him and occasionally gives striking proof of this fact. Sometimes the negativism seems to be supplanted by a ready suggestibility, and the patient will imitate the behavior of others (*echopraxia*), carry out commands automatically, or repeat phrases in mechanical fashion (*echolalia*). In this phase, *cerea flexibilitas* (waxy flexibility) may be demonstrated as the patient maintains for some time any position into which his arm may be placed. Hallucinations and delusions occur in the stuporous state, and they may involve the patient in a conflict of cosmic significance (for example, the forces of Good and Evil may be experienced as at mortal combat in his body). The stereotyped posture and gestures are frequently related symbolically to the patient's fantasy experiences.

Excited State. In the state of excitement, which may come on suddenly and with no warning signs, the patient goes to the opposite extreme. He seems to be under great pressure of activity. He talks excitedly and incoherently, paces about, engages in uninhibited sexual behavior or viciously aggressive acts directed against himself or others. The phase of excitement may last hours, days, or occasionally weeks. Variations of the degree of stupor and excitement are commonly observed in the same patient.

Paranoid Reaction. The paranoid schizophrenic shows, in addition to the other characteristics of the schizophrenic reaction, ideas of reference and influence, and delusions of persecution and frequently of grandeur. The paranoid type of schizophrenia must be differentiated from true paranoia (described in Chapter 13, Other Psychotic Reactions). In the latter condition, the delusions but no other schizophrenic features are present.

The paranoid patient is characteristically moody, irritable, and suspicious. He gets into trouble with other people, accusing them of persecuting him. As his disease progresses, he cannot continue his work and his life becomes disorganized. He may not leave his home for fear of exposing himself to danger; his delusions may impel him toward violence; his speech may become excited and incoherent.

Paranoid patients should be hospitalized, but this is often difficult to accomplish. They resist treatment, and because the disease fluctuates, a severe psychotic episode may be followed by apparent social recovery, though with no insight into their illness. The patient will use this apparent recovery to avoid further hospitalization. Often, paranoid patients, because of their suspiciousness and evasiveness, put up a good "front" that hides the serious pathology that is present. In many cases the disease progresses and may result in a complete disorganization of the intellectual and emotional capacities.

Acute Undifferentiated Schizophrenic Reaction. This reaction includes early acute schizophrenic patterns such as confused thinking, perplexity, ideas of reference, and dissociative phenomena. There is also disturbed emotional response which may manifest itself in either excitement or depression. The reaction may develop without any evidence of a precipitating cause. Usually, however, a carefully taken history reveals some premonitory symptoms suggestive of the oncoming breakdown. Some of these patients recover in a matter of weeks, although there may be recurrences. Occasionally, this reaction marks the onset of one of the major schizophrenic reactions, which develops into a more classic form as the illness persists.

Chronic Undifferentiated Schizophrenic Reaction. A variety of chronic schizophrenic conditions which have been variously labeled as "latent," "incipient," and "prepsychotic" schizophrenic reactions is included here. The condition is a persistent state in which recognizable schizophrenic behavior is manifested, but not to the extent or in the form of the more severe schizophrenic patterns previously described. These patients show schizophrenic thought and affect beyond those of the schizoid personality. Very often the diagnosis of this state can be made accurately only with the help of carefully evaluated projective techniques, for example the Rorschach test. One of the diagnostic problems presented is the existence of a pseudoneurotic surface pattern which disguises the underlying schizophrenia.

Schizo-Affective Reaction. In this category are classified those patients who show both schizophrenic thought processes and affective reactions resembling the manic-depressive pattern. Thus, the patient may display manic excitement or severe depression. Analysis of the delusional content will usually indicate a quality of bizarreness and dissociation which clearly marks it as schizophrenia, as differentiated from manic-depressive reaction. Paranoid symptoms and disparity between emotional response and thought control are characteristic of the schizo-affective reaction. Many of these patients, as the disease progresses, develop a pattern of symptoms typical of the standard schizophrenic reaction types.

Childhood Schizophrenic Reaction. The existence of true schizophrenic reactions in children has been a matter of controversy. Official recognition has been given to this reaction type by its being listed in the diagnostic and statistical manual of the American Psychiatric Association (1952). Diagnosis of psychotic reaction in children must take into account the different criteria which apply to children in comparison with adults. In psychotic reactions of children the factor of arrest or failure of development of personality is more significant than the adult pattern of regression. The child's psychotic trends are less organized and more fragmentary, and are frequently associated with motor in-co-ordination and organic stigmata.

Bender, who has done the most extensive research on childhood schizophrenia, describes the condition as a "clinical entity occurring in childhood before the age of eleven years which reveals pathology in behavior at every level and in every area of integration or patterning within the functioning of the central nervous system, be it vegetative, motor, perceptual, intellectual, emotional, or social." * She considers the reaction a total personality defect with an essential biological substratum, probably some form of organic brain damage. Bender describes the symptoms under the following four headings:

(1) *Vasovegetative malfunctioning*—such as irregularities in body temperature, sleep, eating, perspiration, elimination, and growth.

(2) *Motor malfunctioning*—such as awkwardness, uneven motor development, and insecurity in achieving new motor patterns. (Bender particularly identifies head turning and whirling beyond

* Lauretta Bender, "Childhood Schizophrenia," *Nerv. Child.* (Vol. I, Spring 1942), pp. 138–140.

age six as almost pathognomonic of this illness.) Other characteristics are: extreme motor compliance and flexibility, overresponsiveness to any physical pressures in adjusting to postural position.

(3) *Perceptual unevenness and distortions*—such as extremely arrested perceptual motivation in some areas and accelerated development in others. In the same child there may exist grossly immature use of language with abnormal skills in drawing, painting, music, and so forth. Bender gave the example of the child who, in referring to himself, uses the infantile third person instead of "I" even though he has an advanced vocabulary.

(4) *Psychological disturbances*—Bender feels that the essential psychological disturbance is a problem of the relationship between the self and the rest of the world. She emphasizes the child's particular concern with problems of his identity, body image, and bodily functions. Interpersonal relations are of course damaged; orientation in time and space is inadequate.

Childhood autism, which may be a facet of the schizophrenic reaction does not in itself establish the diagnosis of childhood schizophrenia. Other symptoms which may be seen in the schizophrenic child are: profound withdrawal, apathy, happiness in isolation, and resistance to encroachment by others. Childhood schizophrenia must be considered a rare disease and the diagnosis must be made with the utmost care, only after excluding other pathological explanations. The *prognosis* for childhood schizophrenia is poor and an early erroneous diagnosis can handicap the treatment of other conditions for which it may be mistaken.

Residual Schizophrenic Reaction. This term is used to describe patients who have experienced a schizophrenic breakdown but have improved sufficiently to function in the community, showing, however, recognizable residual of thought, emotion, or behavior. The term is more useful for the keeping of statistical records than it is for understanding the behavior of the patient.

Process and Reactive Schizophrenia. The syndromes of process and reactive schizophrenia cut across the various diagnostic subtypes of schizophrenia and are based on prognostic and historical factors. The distinctions between the two types have been evolved out of numerous investigations of the differences between those schizophrenics who recover and those who do not.

Process schizophrenia develops gradually over a number of years. Symptoms are present early in life, increase in intensity as time goes on and emerge as a full-blown psychosis in adolescence or early adulthood. The early symptoms include a "shut-in" personality, failure in peer interactions and excessive fantasy living. When the psychosis becomes acute, the patient deteriorates and becomes what is often called a "burned out" schizophrenic. The patient is then chronically ill and chances of recovery are limited. The process schizophrenic shows a primitive and undifferentiated personality structure. Rorschach examinations of these patients reveal (1) marked perceptual immaturity and (2) organic signs that significantly differentiate the process schizophrenic groups from the reactive groups.

Reactive schizophrenia usually reveals in the patient adequate social development with some precipitating stress ushering in the psychotic reaction. The prognosis for recovery is generally good. The reactive schizophrenic has a better organized personality structure and his perceptual functioning is integrated. Herron, in a study of abstract ability in the process and reactive schizophrenics conducted at the St. Vincent's Hospital of the City of New York, concluded that the various subtypes of schizophrenia may be classified into process and reactive schizophrenia on the basis of history, his psychological test results indicate that the abstract ability of the process schizophrenic is significantly inferior to the abstract ability of the reactive schizophrenic. The major differences between the process and reactive schizophrenic lies in the prognosis and in the evidence of a progressively deteriorating adjustment pattern.

TREATMENT

Only within the past fifteen to twenty years has a positive treatment for schizophrenia been developed. Prior to that, prognosis was considered generally unfavorable. Even with bare hospital maintenance, however, about 30 per cent of the first admissions were discharged, some cured, others somewhat improved. The advent of the drug and shock therapies and the application of psychotherapy to schizophrenia have brought greater hopefulness to the prognosis.

Regardless of the kind of treatment used, favorable response is usually associated with the following circumstances: (1) early treatment (within eighteen months of the onset); (2) acute onset, in contrast to gradual and insidious onset; (3) definite precipitating circumstances, such as loss of job, broken love affair; (4) presence of insight, with a degree of understanding by the patient of his illness; and (5) a favorable environment to which the patient may return. In general, the catatonic type of schizophrenia offers a more hopeful prognosis than do the other types. Although there are some schizophrenics who can be treated at home, in the acute phase of the reaction most of them must at first be hospitalized.

Medical Treatment. Insulin shock therapy and later electro-shock therapy, which is more widely used today than insulin shock, have thus far proved to be the most effective medical treatment. Recovery and improvement rates for schizophrenics treated by this method are reported to range from 40 to 60 per cent of those so treated. A combined program of insulin shock and electroshock has been reported in some cases to be especially effective. Prefrontal lobotomy and other surgical techniques have been tried in chronic cases and on others not responding to the less drastic forms of treatment. While positive results have been reported, enthusiasm for psychosurgery is not widespread; it is felt that much more work is needed to evaluate the effectiveness and desirability of this approach. Many who use insulin or electric shock do so with the belief that it serves only to bring the patient into closer contact with reality so that proper psychotherapy can be attempted. Follow-up studies seem to indicate that without psychotherapy the positive effect of the shock therapies is only temporary.

Recent development of such drugs as the reserpines, the pheno-thyazenes, such as chlorpromazine, and other tranquilizers has markedly changed the treatment pattern for schizophrenia. Although it is too early to appraise the long-term impact of this form of drug treatment, it is certain that these drugs have provided an effective means of controlling symptoms, particularly for the actively dis-turbed schizophrenic. With their use earlier release to the commu-nity has been made possible. Those who must remain in hospitals are more manageable under this treatment and more amenable to other therapies. Because of the relative ease of administering these drugs, they are to some degree replacing the application of the prolonged insulin shock therapy. Medical treatment methods are discussed further in Chapter 19, under the heading Techniques of Somatotherapy.

Psychotherapy. For a small number of the total group of schizo-phrenics, psychoanalytic therapy has been provided. Workers such as Rosen and Fromm-Reichmann, using intensive and long-term psychoanalytic procedures, report promising results. The availability of such treatment is, at this time, far too limited to offer a realistic treatment approach.

INDIVIDUAL PSYCHOTHERAPY. Most often individual psychotherapy for the schizophrenic patient involves a dependent supportive relationship in which the principal treatment is reassurance and encouragement. Efforts must be made to reduce or eliminate the stress in the environment. The patient has to be helped in planning his activities. Direct interpretation of symptoms is avoided. Such individual psychotherapy is often supplemented by a marshaling of all hospital resources that may be used favorably in the treatment process (milieu therapy).

GROUP PSYCHOTHERAPY. Group psychotherapy has been adapted to the needs of the schizophrenic patient. Procedures of this sort are suitable for aiding the withdrawn patient and help to provide a secure environment in which he may learn skills in interpersonal relationships and test reality. Extensive use of group therapy in state hospitals has proved to be one way of meeting the severe shortage of trained therapists. Many staff personnel other than psychiatrists have been trained to conduct the group sessions with schizophrenic patients. The topics of these discussions range from ways of seeking employment upon release from the hospital to analysis of the dynamic factors involved in the illness. The latter type of discussion can be led only by highly trained professional personnel. (A fuller discussion of treatment techniques will be found in Chapter 19, The Therapeutic Process.)

12

AFFECTIVE REACTIONS
(MANIC-DEPRESSIVE PSYCHOSES)

In his major classification effort, Kraepelin (in 1899) drew together the excited, the elated, the melancholic, and the depressed states, and described them under a single diagnostic entity: manic-depressive psychosis. This disorder remains as the second major "functional" psychosis (the other being schizophrenia). Kraepelin recognized the complexity of the syndrome of manic-depressive psychosis, in particular the tendency of patients to mood swings, for it was a common observation that patients would make a spontaneous recovery from their excited and elated state, only to fall into a period of depression and melancholia. Today this group of psychotic reactions is described substantially as it was by Kraepelin, i.e., as reactions that are characterized by rapid mood changes, sudden onset, spontaneous recovery, and expectancy of recurrences. The official classification of the American Psychiatric Association terms them "affective reactions."

INCIDENCE

It has been estimated that one individual out of every two hundred in the general population may be expected to develop a manic-depressive psychosis in his lifetime. Manic-depressive patients make up about 8 per cent of the *first* admissions to mental hospitals, and from 10 to 15 per cent of all persons admitted or readmitted annually.

The average age at first admission is forty, but the spread is wide, for 25 per cent of manic-depressive first admissions are below thirty and another 25 per cent are above fifty. This reaction seems to occur at an earlier age in women; the sex ratio is 3:2. The specific reaction types are distributed as follows: depressive, 40 per cent; manic-reaction, 35 per cent; mixed or circular reaction, 25 per cent.

ETIOLOGY (CAUSATION)

Attempts to explain the causation of the manic-depressive psychoses have explored hereditary, constitutional, physiological, psychological, and cultural factors. Predisposing and precipitating factors have also been considered.

Hereditary Factors. Support for a hereditary interpretation of the etiology in manic-depressive psychoses has been sought in the fact that the incidence of these disorders is strikingly higher in the relatives of these patients than in the population at large. Whereas the expectancy for manic-depressive psychoses in the general population is 0.5 per cent, it will be seen in the table that follows that the rate is much higher in relatives of manic-depressive patients:

INCIDENCE OF MANIC-DEPRESSIVE PSYCHOSES
AMONG RELATIVES OF
MANIC-DEPRESSIVE PATIENTS *

Relationship to Patient	Expectancy Rate (Per cent)
Identical twins	70
Fraternal twins	16
Children	16
Parents	15
Sibling	13
Uncles and Aunts	5
Cousins	3
Nephews and Nieces	3

* After James D. Page, *Abnormal Psychology* (New York: McGraw-Hill, 1947), p. 263.

Interpretations of the foregoing figures must take into consideration that the factor of early environment has been left uncontrolled and for this reason it is impossible to disentangle entirely the hereditary and the environmental influences.

Constitutional Factors. Kretschmer, and more recently Sheldon, have related manic-depressive reactions to types of physiques. Kretschmer reported higher incidence of these disorders in the *pyknic* body type (short, stocky, thick-necked individuals). Sheldon has reported that both the mesomorphic and the endomorphic types are more susceptible to the development of affective reactions. The relationship between physique and manic-depressive reactions is not clear; determination of the extent of the influence of body type awaits further investigation.

Physiological Factors. Studies have been made of somatic changes accompanying the manic and depressive phases of this class of reactions. No important biological differences during the two modes were found which could not be explained by differences in activity level. Studies of physicochemical influences, especially in the form of a toxic factor, were first suggested by Kraepelin. Many such investigations have been undertaken, but none has produced convincing evidence that a toxin exists which is specific to the development of a manic-depressive reaction.

Psychological Factors. Parent-child relationships, prepsychotic personality traits, and the psychological reflections of environmental stress have all been identified as significant factors in the etiology of the manic-depressive psychoses. Frequently, these patients reveal excessively high moral goals and an early childhood history of extreme discipline. The examples which parents set in wide mood swings are thought to be contributory. The prepsychotic personality traits found in manic-depressive patients include ambition (to the extent of inordinate preoccupation with success); and a high degree of energy, extroversion, and sociability. In patients in whom the depressive phase is predominant one finds, in addition, anxiety, self-belittling trends, rigid conscience, and a notable tendency to repress hostility. Of striking significance is the high incidence of stressful life situations in the history of these patients—one study reports the presence of disturbing life problems dynamically related to the illness in almost 80 per cent of the cases.

In evaluating the etiological importance of physical versus psychological factors, Ewalt, Strecker, and Ebaugh * conclude, ". . . in more recent years, however, increasing evidence accumulates to support the belief that the psychologic pictures are much more persistent and recurrent and appear much the same in all cases, while the genetic, constitutional, and physiologic changes vary a great deal among patients. It is our opinion that the psychogenic factors with

* J. R. Ewalt et al., *Practical Clinical Psychiatry* (8th edition; New York: McGraw-Hill, 1957), p. 179.

genetic predisposition are basic and that the physical changes, when present, merely add to the ego load which the individual tries to carry."

Cultural Factors. Within the framework of the American culture, manic-depressive reactions tend to be evenly distributed among all socioeconomic levels. There are, however, significant differences in the incidence figures for this disease from one culture to another; for example, in New Zealand manic-depressive reactions occur two and one-half times as frequently as does the schizophrenic reaction, whereas the opposite is true of the picture in the United States. Among Kenya natives only manic reactions were observed to occur when the disease develops. The role of cultural factors in the etiology of the disease is not understood.

Predisposing and Precipitating Factors. It would seem reasonable to assume that the heredity of the individual can predispose him to breakdown in the direction of a manic-depressive reaction. This hereditary factor might function through genetic linkage with a particular type of constitution. However, the active development of the disease would depend upon early patterns of parent-child relationships and precipitating stresses in the life situation, for it must be granted that manic-depressive psychoses may develop under stress regardless of personality type or physique.

CHARACTERISTIC SYMPTOMS OF AFFECTIVE REACTIONS

Certain features are characteristic of the manic-depressive psychoses as a whole:

1. The onset is usually sudden; in only a small number of cases does the reaction develop gradually.

2. As a rule the reaction terminates in about six months, either spontaneously or in response to treatment.

3. Recurrences are to be expected, and the intervals between them may be as long as several years in duration.

4. There is no evidence of intellectual or emotional deterioration in these patients.

5. Mood swings constitute the single outstanding symptom.

6. Illusions, delusions, and hallucinations may be present, but they are not necessarily characteristic.

Three specific types of affective reaction have been recognized:

manic-depressive reaction, manic type; manic-depressive reaction, depressed type; and manic-depressive reaction, mixed or circular type.

Manic Type. The external manifestations of the manic phase of the manic-depressive reaction are:

Elation—the patient expresses a feeling of well-being, optimism, and good humor.

Extreme psychomotor activity—the patient is almost constantly in motion, constantly talking or shouting; this tendency is often referred to as "pressure of activity" or "pressure of speech."

Flight of ideas—the patient displays extreme distractibility and unstable thought processes which are reflected in his psychomotor activity and in the ideas which he expresses.

In the manic phase the patient shows irritability, anger, and abusive behavior when he is blocked. His delusions are typically of a grandiose nature, and when hallucinations are experienced they are associated with the delusional content. The heightened activity is accompanied by such physical changes as increased perspiration, rapid pulse, elevated blood pressure, stronger muscle tonus, and loss of sleep. Refusal to eat and dehydration produce physical debilitation.

Three subtypes of the manic phase of the manic-depressive reaction have been identified: *hypomania*, characterized by moderate elation, flightiness, and overactivity; *acute mania*, in which the symptoms are more intense and may be accompanied by delusions and hallucinations; and *delirious mania*, in which incoherence and disorientation are added to the other symptoms.

Depressed Type. The principal features of the depressed phase of the manic-depressive reaction are:

Feelings of sadness and hopelessness—the patient is indifferent to his surroundings; environmental stimulation, however strong, fails to rouse him from this state.

Psychomotor retardation—the patient performs even the simplest and least demanding acts with the greatest effort; his reaction time is very slow.

Difficulty in thinking—the patient seems unwilling or unable to grapple with the most elementary phenomena of the thought processes.

In addition, delusions and hallucinations may be present. The delusions most frequently grow out of feelings of worthlessness and guilt and take the form of "unpardonable sins" that have been committed. Hallucinations consist of voices calling the patient derogatory names. Various bodily reactions accompanying the depression include: decrease in gastrointestinal activity resulting in loss of appetite and constipation; reduction in blood pressure; cessation of menstruation; and sleeplessness. As a result, secondary physical ailments may develop.

Four subtypes are recognized in predominately depressed patients. The differences are principally a matter of severity of symptoms. The subtypes are: *masked* or *mild depression,* in which the symptoms of depression are frequently hidden behind preoccupation with physical symptoms; *simple retardation,* in which the patient is lethargic and seemingly incapable of carrying out routine responsibilities (he also experiences feelings of guilt and unworthiness, but there is no disturbance of consciousness or of intellectual functioning); *acute depression,* in which the symptoms are more intense and may include delusions and hallucinations; and *depressive stupor,* which is characterized by almost complete lack of response and a dangerous reduction in heart and circulatory action.

Mixed or Circular Type. Into this category are classified those patients who show either a marked mixture of the symptoms of both the manic and depressed types (mixed type) or a continuous alternation between the two other types (circular type).

CHARACTERISTIC SYMPTOMS OF PSYCHOTIC DEPRESSIVE REACTION

In this condition, which is not regarded as a type of manic-depressive psychosis or reaction, the patient is very depressed and shows evidence of a misinterpretation of reality. Delusions and hallucinations may be present. The disorder, although it resembles the depressed phase of the manic-depressive reaction, may be distinguished from it in that (1) there is no history of repeated depressions or severe mood swings and (2) it is usually associated with some environmental precipitating factor. The psychotic depressive reaction must also be differentiated from the reactive depression in that (1) psychotic depressive reaction is more severe and (2) the reality distortion is greater.

TREATMENT

A program for the treatment of a patient with a manic-depressive psychosis regardless of the type of reaction must include the following procedures: (1) protection of the patient from secondary developments which may be fatal (exhaustion, autointoxication, and infection); (2) precautions against attempts at suicide; (3) measures for making the patient accessible to psychotherapy. Only under such a basic program can a psychotherapeutic attack on the illness be launched. The treatment varies for the manic and the depressive phases, as follows:

Treatment of the Manic Reaction. Early treatment of a manic reaction must, of course, be directed toward controlling the behavior of the patient. In the milder cases, attempts are made to channel the heightened psychomotor activity into constructive outlets, as in the many forms of occupational or recreational therapy. Prolonged narcosis or hydrotherapy may be necessary in the most extreme cases, although immediate use of the new drugs (chlorpromazine, and other phenothyazine derivatives) will frequently produce a prompt cessation of symptoms. While electroconvulsive therapy is of greater effect in the depressive phase, it has also proved successful with manic patients in bringing about a remission of symptoms. These physical therapies, however, have not had any significant effect in the prevention of recurrences, nor in extending symptom-free intervals between attacks. To accomplish this goal, it is essential that psychotherapeutic procedures be initiated after the more acute symptoms of the disease have subsided. It is still true, however, that many patients apparently recover from a manic episode spontaneously, and this, added to the characteristic recurrences, has led to the belief that some element or elements of the environment may trigger the attacks; therefore, modification of the milieu to which the patient must return is an important part of any therapy for this condition.

Treatment of the Depressive Reaction. In view of the patient's unwillingness or inability to engage in any kind of psychomotor activity (sometimes to the extent of self-starvation), it is extremely important to see that he is adequately nourished and that his eliminatory functions are maintained. Electroconvulsive therapy is particularly effective in rousing the patient from his depression, thus alleviating his symptoms but without resolving the underlying conflicts. Recently, imipramine and monoamine oxidase inhibitors have been found to be effective in the treatment of depressive conditions.

Paradoxically, the program of shock treatment may turn out to be so successful that it produces a feeling of well-being as a result of which the patient will think that further treatment is unnecessary; he may remain entirely without insight into the true nature of his illness and may refuse to co-operate in a psychotherapeutic program.

Psychotherapy, in the sense of getting at the core of the problem, must be approached slowly. Early efforts in this area should be confined to conveying a feeling of kindness and understanding, with the therapist bringing up discussion of the milder difficulties and only gradually working toward major conflicts and frustrations.

13

OTHER PSYCHOTIC REACTIONS (INVOLUTIONAL REACTIONS, PARANOIA AND PARANOID STATES)

Although the most prevalent forms of functional psychotic reactions are the schizophrenic and affective reactions, there are two other categories of clinical importance: involutional reactions and paranoid reactions.

INVOLUTIONAL REACTIONS

The characteristic feature that differentiates the involutional psychotic state from the depressions seen in some manic-depressives is its occurrence in middle and late life, apparently as an accompaniment of the involutional (physiological) processes, such as the menopause in females. Another significant feature is the absence of any previous history of manic or depressive episodes. The principal form is known as *involutional melancholia;* another form is recognized as *involutional psychosis, paranoid type.*

Involutional Melancholia. Involutional melancholia is a depression of middle and later life which may be manifested in worry, guilt, anxiety, agitation, or paranoid and other delusional ideas. These reactions are often accompanied by gastrointestinal or other somatic complaints which may progress to delusions.

About 4 per cent of all first admissions to mental hospitals are diagnosed as involutional reactions. The disturbance is found more frequently in women than in men; it accounts for 7 per cent of female first admissions, and 2 per cent of male first admissions. The median age at admission is fifty-one for women, and fifty-five for men. A range from forty to sixty-five years covers 90 per cent of all first admissions with this psychotic reaction.

CAUSATION. Agreement on the causation of involutional reactions is lacking, though several theories have been offered. A list of theories follows.

1. Involutional melancholia and the menopausal syndrome occur

at the same time, but the biological factors play an aggravating role rather than a causative one. This is evident from the fact that no physiological changes have been observed in patients with involutional reactions that are not found in normal people during the climacteric.

2. Of primary psychological importance are the patient's reactions to his loss of social status and personal security, which may be dependent on physical vigor and are therefore threatened by the physical decline during the involutional period.

3. The involutional reaction is more likely to occur in persons having a certain constellation of personality traits (shyness, rigidity, frugality, overconscientiousness, and inhibition). Such persons usually have a compulsive sense of duty, a narrow range of interests, few friends, and overly strict moral principles.

4. Involutional melancholics usually show a history of failure or unsatisfactory achievement, with the feeling that life is "almost over" and there is no "second chance."

SYMPTOMS. While the onset of the disease is usually gradual, it may be precipitated suddenly by some distressing experience. The patient is depressed, expressing persistent fears concerning both his past and future. Hypochondriacal and nihilistic delusions may be present, and there is substantial danger of attempted suicide. Patients may have delusions of guilt over unpardonable sins and may blame themselves for the evils of the world. They are restless, anxious, sleepless, and have unprovoked spells of weeping. Their intellectual ability is not noticeably affected; questions unrelated to their symptomatic concerns are grasped easily.

TREATMENT. Hospitalization for persons experiencing an involutional psychotic reaction is advisable because of the danger of suicidal attempt. Electroconvulsive and metrazol shock have been effective in reducing the acute stage of the reaction. Psychotherapy is ineffective in the acute stage but may be used with profit after contact with the patient has been established through one of the convulsive therapies. Sex hormones are often administered to alleviate the stress of the physiological change.

PROGNOSIS. Between 30 and 40 per cent of these patients will show spontaneous improvement with routine care after a period varying from six or eight months to two or three years. Since the introduction of electroshock therapy, reports of early improvement in 70 to 90 per cent of cases have been published. The best results are achieved with patients whose prepsychotic personality was not warped, and when electroshock was accompanied by psychotherapy; in such cases marked improvement has been seen in four to six weeks. Following release from the hospital, psychotherapy should be continued to minimize the chance of recurrence of symptoms.

Involutional Psychosis; Paranoid Type. This special diagnostic label is applied to patients with involutional reactions in which depression and delusions of a paranoid nature are the principal features.

PARANOID REACTIONS

The term *paranoid reaction* refers to a class of disorders in which the main symptom picture is characterized by suspicion. In terms of personality disorganization, the reactions range from paranoia, wherein the personality structure remains relatively well organized, through paranoid states, wherein the personality loses some of its integration, to the severe disorganization manifested in cases of paranoid schizophrenia. Symptoms of a paranoid nature are found in many forms of mental disturbance.

Paranoia. Paranoia is a psychotic reaction in which there is good contact with reality except in the area of a well-systematized delusion. There is little or no intellectual deterioration. The elaboration of the delusion is logically constructed so that if the basic premise is granted all consequent thinking is reasonable. However, the basic premise is delusional, of a persecutory nature, with ideas of grandiosity sometimes involved. The personality remains relatively intact.

Although fewer than 2 per cent of first admissions to the state hospitals are diagnosed as true paranoia, it is highly probably that the actual incidence of the disorder is considerably higher, since many such persons have sufficiently keen judgment and control to be able to avoid hospitalization. Recent studies show approximately equal occurrence in both sexes.

CAUSATION. The cause of paranoia has not been definitely established. However, as in the case of other psychotic reactions, the beginnings of paranoia can be traced to early problems in interpersonal relationships. Of particular significance would seem to be parent-child relationships leading to the development of such traits as aloofness, suspiciousness, and resentment. In the paranoiac's history is frequently found evidence of strong feelings of inferiority following upon failures in major areas of adjustment. Almost invariably there exist problems in the heterosexual area which are often covered up by attitudes of prudishness and excessive inhibition. The general moral attitude is characterized by self-righteousness and rigidity. Paranoid symptoms are often reaction formations in response to feelings of guilt which cannot be accepted by the individual. There are two principal theories which attempt to explain the psychodynamics of the paranoid process: the psychoanalytic theory of Freud and Cameron's theory of the *pseudo-community*.

Psychoanalytic Theory of Paranoia. Freud suggested that the following pattern occurs in paranoia: *A.* "I love him"—but this is rejected because it is an expression of unconscious homosexual tendencies and is thus unacceptable. *B.* By a process of reaction formation, *A* changes to "I hate him"—but this, too, is rejected as unacceptable because of its aggressive content. Then *C,* the mechanism of projection converts *B* into "He hates me and is persecuting me."

While it is true that this pattern appears in many cases of paranoia, there does not seem to be sufficient evidence to postulate it as a universal cause of the disease.

Cameron's Theory of a "Pseudo-Community." The American psychiatrist, DR. NORMAN CAMERON (1896–   ), recognized the paranoid reaction as a product of reaction-sensitivity and projection. The individual who has not developed habits of confiding and sharing personal matters lives in a world of strangers with whom he cannot communicate and from whom he cannot obtain comfort or support. He is inadequate in role-taking and thus cannot appreciate another person's point of view. Deprived of this normal check on the accuracy of his own ideas, he is left in an anxious and uncertain state. To resolve the uncertainty, he organizes the persons and events about him into a "pseudo-community" which, while it can neither comfort nor reassure him, nevertheless satisfies his need to explain what is happening. In this manner, the false beliefs which he entertains are strengthened by the misinterpretation of the activity in his milieu and he dwells in a world of insulated ideas. As a result, what he perceives as a functionally integrated social group is only a pseudo-community—an organization of his own reactions based on a structure that holds no social validity.

Biological Factors. No specific evidence has been found of physical or biochemical pathology related to paranoia. Some studies have revealed that endocrine tumors observed at postmortem examinations occur in paranoiacs with ten times the frequency in normal persons and four times the frequency of nonparanoid psychotics.

SYMPTOMS. Well systematized, stable, slowly developing delusions of persecution and/or grandeur are the symptoms of paranoia. Apart from the delusional system, the behavior and thinking of these people are quite rational. They surpass other mental patients in intelligence and come from a better cultural background. In discussing their delusional material they refuse to consider even the possibilities of any explanation other than their own. This delusional system usually revolves about one theme, and in earlier writings there were subclassifications according to the theme content: erotic, jealous, or litiginous paranoia.

TREATMENT. Psychotherapy is of some value, but it must be carefully and skillfully handled. Good rapport with the therapist is indispensable and, when it is gained, gradual attempts should be made to let the patient become aware that his delusions are unfounded. Electrocoma is valuable in making the patient more accessible during psychotherapy.

In paranoid patients a condition known as "hospital insight" is apt to develop. They learn what symptoms and statements are considered favorable or unfavorable by the medical and nursing staff, and from this are able to pretend that their basic delusional beliefs no longer persist. Paranoiacs are especially talented at gaining release from the hospital in this way.

PROGNOSIS. The prognosis for long-standing disorders is not promising. Adequate psychotherapy in the early stages of the disorder produces the best results.

Paranoid States. Diagnosed under this term are patients whose delusions of persecution are transient and less well systematized, and who do not show the deterioration of the paranoid type of schizophrenia (see page 167). There are many nonpsychotic persons who harbor paranoid trends of thought and behavior. They may be hypersensitive, inflexible, aloof, suspicious, resentful of discipline, and may have an unrealistically high evaluation of themselves coupled with unreasonable goals. When they fail, they justify their failure by attributing to others motives of aggression. For the person whose behavior and attitudes are strongly colored by these traits, consideration should be given to early psychotherapy that may prevent the condition from taking on a chronic form.

14

ORGANIC PSYCHOSES

The greater portion of the official (APA) classification of mental disorders consists of a division entitled "Disorders Caused By or Associated with Impairment of Brain Tissue Function"; more than fifty clinical designations appear there (see Appendix). It is not to be inferred from the classification that the incidence of the various mental disorders follows this proportionate distribution. The majority of these organogenic clinical entities constitute the smaller segments of any institutional patient population. Of all the conditions listed in this category, only the patients suffering from senile psychoses and cerebral arteriosclerosis are numerically important in the total picture of mental illness. Combined, they make up about 20 per cent of first admissions to hospitals for mental illness.

The larger divisions of the APA classification are subdivided into acute and chronic disorders and, finally, within these subdivisions are shown the various specific conditions. While the classification is orderly and the best possible answer at present to a difficult problem in nomenclature and nosology, it is too encyclopedic for complete coverage in this Outline. The APA classification has therefore been condensed and adapted to the needs of the student of abnormal psychology. The terms used to designate the various sections of this chapter are in general those of the classification of mental disorders which was in use just prior to the adoption of the one shown in the Appendix. These sections are: Senile Psychoses; Psychoses Due to Disturbances of Circulation; Psychoses Due to Trauma; Psychoses Due to or Associated with Infection; Psychoses Due to Intoxication (including the alcohol psychoses and the psychoses due to drugs or other exogenous toxins); Psychoses Due to Disturbance of Metabolism, Growth, Nutrition, or Endocrine Function; Psychoses Due to New Growth; and Psychoses Due to Unknown or Hereditary Causes but Associated with Organic Change.

SENILE PSYCHOSES

A rather large proportion of psychiatric patients suffer mental disorders which are attributable to deterioration in the aged. Their number grows, as does that of the cerebral arteriosclerotics, as the median age of the population increases in response to medical and public health control of diseases which formerly held life expectancy at a lower figure. (The classification in the Appendix refers to these conditions as "chronic brain syndromes associated with senile brain disease.") Postmortem findings of the brain and nervous system in affected persons show marked destruction and alteration. Whether such changes are consequences of the normal aging process or due to pathological or infectious causes is still a matter of dispute. These changes apparently disturb the integration of the personality, and clinical experience with such patients reveals consistent, predictable patterns of abnormal behavior and attitude. About 9 per cent of first admissions to mental hospitals in the United States are assigned the diagnosis of senile psychosis. The mean age at admission is between seventy and seventy-five years of age.

Causation. None of the hypotheses advanced as to the cause of senile psychosis enjoys sufficient proof for universal acceptance. Among the explanations that have been offered are: innate lack of durability of the nerve cells in the brain, toxic and hereditary influences, chronic dietary deficiency (especially in vitamins and mineral elements), accumulated effects of emotional shock, and prolonged use of alcohol.

Characteristic Symptoms. In general, the behavior of senile psychotics is characterized by: reminiscences about their early life and self-centering in interests, combined with memory defect for recent events and easily aroused irritability. The presenting symptoms of the senile psychoses are differentiated as follows:

SIMPLE DETERIORATION. This form of senile psychosis is characterized by marked impairment of memory, defects of attention and concentration, misidentification of persons and places, and disturbance of time sense. Deterioration may progress to a state of vegetative existence.

PRESBYOPHRENIC TYPE. Though mental alertness and attentiveness are maintained in the presbyophrenic patient, and the patient is quite talkative, there are severe memory defects. The memory defects lead to confabulation in order to fill in the gaps (in this way resembling Korsakoff's syndrome, a form of alcoholic psychosis).

DELIRIOUS AND CONFUSED TYPE. The delirium and confusion are deep, and are often precipitated by some acute illness.

DEPRESSED AND AGITATED TYPE. Pronounced depression and persistent agitation mark the depressed and agitated senile patient. The condition is differentiated from involutional melancholia by a manifestation of memory defects.

PARANOID TYPE. Paranoid senile psychotics exhibit delusional trends of a persecutory or of an expansive nature. Differential diagnosis is difficult if memory defects have not developed.

Treatment and Prognosis. The most that can be done for the senile psychotic patient is to provide custodial care, with stress on an environmental setting as free as possible from sources of tension. As in the treatment of physical disease in persons of advanced age, the prognosis is unfavorable.

PSYCHOSES DUE TO DISTURBANCES OF CIRCULATION

The functioning of the brain depends so completely for its proper operation on an adequate supply of blood that disorders which alter the pattern of normal circulation may give rise to psychotic disturbances. The most prevalent of these disturbances are cerebral arteriosclerosis and cerebral embolism. In addition, there may be psychosis associated with some forms of heart disease.

Cerebral Arteriosclerosis. More than 11 per cent of the first admissions to mental hospitals in the United States are diagnosed as psychosis with cerebral arteriosclerosis. Because this disorder is usually an accompaniment of advancing years, it can be seen that along with the senile psychoses it poses a serious problem in needed hospital facilities owing to the gradual extension of the life span.

CAUSATION. A fairly consistent picture is seen clinically which, when medical examination reveals the presence of arteriosclerosis (hardening of the arteries), is diagnosed as cerebral arteriosclerosis. Agreement on the cause of hardening of the arteries (actually thickening of the artery walls) is lacking. Chronic anxiety and tension, inadequate rest, dietary factors (especially the metabolism of fats), all have been proposed as contributory factors.

SYMPTOMS. The onset of symptoms is usually sudden. Confusion and excitement ordinarily appear first. These are followed by defective concentration accompanied by impairment of memory which progresses from recent to remote events. Cerebral arteriosclerotics find it difficult to name objects; they respond with halting, confused attempts to describe their use. Such patients give vent to exaggerated emotional responses without adequate cause; depression and paranoid trends are common.

TREATMENT AND PROGNOSIS. Treatment is mainly custodial. Prognosis is generally unfavorable in view of the progressively deteriorative nature of the disease.

Cerebral Embolism. Cerebral embolism (obstruction of a blood vessel by a clot) brings about changes in circulation within the brain and may result in psychotic symptoms of a transitory character. Fewer than 1 per cent of admissions to mental hospitals are so diagnosed. Absorption of the clot leads to remission of symptoms.

Other Psychotic Symptoms Associated with Heart Disease. Psychotic symptoms are often encountered in patients with heart disease. In one category, "psychosis with cardiorenal disease," a syndrome is presented which includes delirium, memory impairment, and defective concentration; fearful hallucinations may be present.

PSYCHOSES DUE TO TRAUMA

In the physiological sense, "trauma" means injury or wound. The official APA classification recognizes both acute and chronic brain syndromes due to trauma. Psychotic reactions associated with injuries to parts of the body other than the brain are not included in this category.

Causation. The injury may have been sustained in a variety of circumstances: brain injury suffered at birth; brain injury from "gross force" (a blow on the head, for example); brain injury in the course of surgery or electrical shock; and brain injury following irradiation.

Symptoms. Symptoms of psychoses due to trauma include delirium, personality disorder, mental deterioration, and convulsive seizures.

DELIRIUM. The delirium following trauma is acute; it is usually noted immediately after the injury occurs, though some cases have shown a protracted, chronic delirium. There may be a superficial alertness, but persistent examination will uncover a marked disorientation, memory defect, and acute confabulation. Recovery from the delirium depends on the extent and severity of the brain damage.

PERSONALITY DISORDER. Personality disorder due to trauma is expressed in: changes in disposition, fatigability, and explosive emotional reactions; frequently, paranoid tendencies are manifested. Depending on the extent of brain damage, the prognosis ranges from complete recovery to a gradual and progressive deterioration requiring hospitalization.

MENTAL DETERIORATION. When the condition of mental deterioration exists, it takes on the form of gradually increasing mental enfeeblement which is often accompanied by a degeneration of moral judgment.

CONVULSIVE SEIZURES. These are not uncommon symptoms in cases of psychosis due to or associated with brain trauma.

Treatment and Prognosis. Since the symptoms of psychoses in this category result directly from head injury, the first aspect of treatment is necessarily of a medical nature. Depending upon the extent and location of brain damage, there may or may not be a permanent loss of psychological function. Where the possibility of recovery exists, rehabilitative and reeducative measures should be taken. Where the loss is of a permanent nature, psychotherapeutic endeavor should be directed to helping the patient adjust to his changed achievement level. In addition, the patient's emotional reactions to the injury frequently require supportive psychotherapy. Prognosis is chiefly dependent upon the nature and extent of the physical injury.

PSYCHOSES DUE TO OR ASSOCIATED WITH INFECTION

Damage or destruction of the tissue of the brain and nervous system by infectious microorganisms may cause psychotic reactions. The principal disorders in the area are: syphilitic infections (general paresis, juvenile paresis, and cerebral syphilis), encephalitis, Sydenham's chorea, and cerebrospinal meningitis.

Syphilitic Infections. Increased control of venereal disease has brought down the incidence of general paresis, juvenile paresis, and cerebral syphilis so that these conditions make up not more than 5 or 6 per cent of first admissions to mental institutions.

General Paresis. The physical and mental symptoms of general paresis are so clear-cut that they are not usually confused with those of other diseases. The course of the disorder is predictable and, if it remains untreated, both the mental and the physical changes become more pronounced as the disease progresses.

CAUSATION. The spirochetal (spiral) microorganism *Treponema pallidum* is the invading body in *all* syphilitic infections. In general paresis the infection attacks the brain and nervous system.

SYMPTOMS. There are both physical and mental reactions to the inroads of general paresis.

Physical Symptoms. Motor paralysis is progressive; the untreated patient will eventually become permanently bedridden. The earliest physical sign is a loss of the ability to perform the delicately controlled movements necessary for clear speech and consistent handwriting. In time, all movements become clumsy and slow. Laboratory tests of blood (Wassermann and Kahn) and spinal fluid (colloidal gold) confirm the diagnosis.

Mental Symptoms. Loss of judgment, leading to gradual loss of even everyday common sense and logic, is one of the psychological signs to appear. Profound memory defects occur, with marked loss of the sense of time. The patient is further beset with difficulty in calculating, general weakening of intellect, and a loss in the store of ideas. Behavioral changes result which often culminate in decreasing regard for propriety, sloppiness in dress and personal hygiene, impairment of ethical and moral values, and finally, disorientation as to time, place, and personal identity.

TREATMENT AND PROGNOSIS. The most effective treatment for general paresis is the method known as artificial hyperphyrexia (induction of fever), which was formerly accomplished by infecting the patient with malaria, but is now also carried out with diathermy (heat treatment) or inductothermy (treatment with electronics). Chemotherapy has been and still is being used, but with less favorable results; the drugs have included tryparsamide, arsphenamine, bismuth, mercury, and more recently penicillin. The prognosis of general paresis is generally poor; untreated general paretics usually die within two to three years of the emergence of symptoms. If therapy is begun before the brain damage is extensive, the patient may recover sufficiently to resume his premorbid way of living.

Juvenile Paresis. Juvenile paresis is a relatively small problem since of individuals infected with congenitally acquired syphilis only about 1 per cent develop general paresis.

CAUSATION. In juvenile paresis the fetus is infected prenatally with the spirochetal microorganism *Treponema pallidum*.

SYMPTOMS. Progressive mental and physical deterioration set in at about the age of ten following an early childhood free of symptoms. Most frequently noted are motor in-co-ordination and indistinct speech.

TREATMENT AND PROGNOSIS. Treatment of juvenile paresis is essentially the same as the treatment of general paresis. The prognosis for juvenile paresis is very unfavorable.

Cerebral Syphilis. Cases of cerebral syphilis account for about 1 per cent of all first admissions to state mental institutions.

CAUSATION. In cerebral syphilis the spirochete shows a preference for the blood vessels and meninges (linings) of the brain rather than the nerve tissue itself.

SYMPTOMS. The symptoms of this disorder are: (physical) severe headache, dizziness, disordered pupillary reaction, increased knee jerk; (mental) stupor, confusion, memory loss, irritability, and loss of the ability to sustain concentration.

TREATMENT AND PROGNOSIS. Chemical treatment with antisyphilitic drugs is used. Fever therapy is seldom employed for cerebral syphilis. As to prognosis, if the patient is young and the duration of the disease is short, there are favorable expectations of recovery or improvement. Otherwise, though the condition is not so debilitating as general paresis, the prognosis is poor.

Other Psychoses Due to or Associated with Infection. Included here are: encephalitis, Sydenham's chorea, and cerebrospinal meningitis.

Encephalitis. About 0.2 per cent of all first admissions to mental hospitals in the United States are diagnosed as psychosis with epidemic encephalitis.

CAUSATION. The disorder is believed to be caused by an ultramicroscopic virus.

SYMPTOMS. In the acute phase of this disease the patient is feverish and stuporous, with headache and disturbance of eye-movement reflexes. Serious residual symptoms are often seen. In children, behavior disorders of a restless and aggressive nature usually follow encephalitis.

TREATMENT AND PROGNOSIS. Adequate nursing care is about all that can be provided for the patient in the acute phase. For the various residual difficulties, only symptomatic treatment has been developed. Some special programs of reeducation of postencephalitic children have met with promising success. In general, the prognosis is unfavorable. About 75 per cent of the patients develop one or more residual symptoms, many of which are progressive in course.

Sydenham's Chorea (St. Vitus's Dance). This is an acute disorder of the nervous system. The disease is not uncommon in children; girls are affected more readily than boys.

CAUSATION. It is assumed that Sydenham's chorea is due to an infection of the cortex and the basal ganglia of the brain. The organism causing this condition is apparently closely related to that which is responsible for rheumatic fever.

SYMPTOMS. Involuntary, un-co-ordinated, jerky muscular movements are characteristic symptoms of Sydenham's chorea. Psychological changes appear in the form of restlessness, irritability, emotional outbursts, and quarrelsomeness. In severe cases, clouding of consciousness, hallucinations, and delirium may occur.

TREATMENT AND PROGNOSIS. Rest and quiet, with as much freedom from tension-producing stimuli as possible, constitute the treatment program. The prognosis is usually favorable; recovery occurs in about four months. Severe cases may last about a year.

Cerebrospinal Meningitis. Although cerebrospinal meningitis is a highly infectious disorder, no large-scale outbreaks have been reported in the United States. Fewer than 1 per cent of all first admissions to mental hospitals in the United States are diagnosed as cerebrospinal meningitis.

CAUSATION. As to causation, the microorganism *Diplococcus intracellularis* enters the body through the nasopharynx and attacks the meninges (linings) of the brain.

SYMPTOMS. The symptoms of cerebrospinal meningitis include: intense headache, delirium, stupor, impairment of memory, and acute concentration loss. As in the case of encephalitis, this disease leaves residual symptoms.

TREATMENT AND PROGNOSIS. Prompt intramuscular injection of antimeningococcus serum is the prescribed treatment. Sulfanilamide has also proved beneficial. Prognosis is very poor; the mental symptoms are almost always permanent.

PSYCHOSES DUE TO INTOXICATION

Toxins or poisons which enter the body through the blood stream and affect brain tissue often bring about psychotic reactions. When the reaction occurs in a person addicted to the use of either alcohol or drugs, the understanding of the condition is complicated by the strong suspicion that the addiction itself is a response to a personality maladjustment. Therefore, while certain behavior and attitudes may be regarded as symptoms of psychoses due to intoxication, alcoholism and drug addiction are also believed to be symptoms of a deeper-lying difficulty. Psychotic reaction to the inhalation of dust, fumes, gases, or other exogenous toxins can usually be regarded as situational or occupational.

Alcoholic Psychoses. At this point are discussed only those disorders in which long-continued or excessive intake of alcohol has resulted in serious damage to nerve tissue. Abnormal behavior associated with underlying personality disturbance, in which the individual develops an addiction to the use of alcohol, is described at length in Chapter 9, Personality Disorders.

Exact figures are not available on the incidence of the alcoholic psychoses because many patients suffering from these disorders are cared for at home or in private sanatoriums. Of all the first admissions to mental hospitals in the United States, 3 per cent are diagnosed as alcoholic psychosis. Another 6 per cent of the cases are diagnosed as "alcoholism," (the latter condition belonging within the types of cases discussed in Chapter 9).

CAUSATION. No single cause has been found for the various psychotic manifestations arising from the use of alcohol. In most cases excessive drinking is a symptom of an already existing, deeply-rooted personality disturbance. Even where it is determined that definite pathology exists, the alcohol which has precipitated the disorder is merely one factor in an extremely complex system of causation. The predisposing psychological or physiological factors, while they may be of equal importance, are less dramatic. Nutritional deficiency, especially of the B vitamins, appears to play a role in the profusive deterioration of some alcoholic patients.

CHARACTERISTIC SYMPTOMS. The main clinical types of alcoholic mental disease are: pathological intoxication, delirium tremens, Korsakoff's psychosis, and chronic alcoholic deterioration. The symptoms manifested by each of these follow.

Pathological Intoxication. Some individuals, upon taking even small amounts of alcohol, exhibit severe mental changes which seem to be pathological reactions to the alcohol itself. Rage, confusion, and excitement may occur with sudden onset. Acts of violence, including murder, rape, or arson, may be committed with complete amnesia on recovery.

Delirium Tremens. The symptom picture for delirium tremens consists of: visual and auditory hallucinations horrible or frightening in content; disorientation of time and place; anxiety; restlessness; inability to sleep or eat; tremors; general in-co-ordination; and sometimes convulsive seizures.

Korsakoff's Psychosis. The distinguishing symptom of this disorder is confabulation (filling in the gaps of memory with irrelevant or disconnected material), which serves to differentiate this reaction from the other alcoholic psychoses.

Acute Alcoholic Hallucinosis. This condition bears a close resemblance to both delirium tremens and schizophrenia. While the patient is not disoriented with respect to time and place, he experiences not only hallucinations in which he hears threats and accusations, but also delusions of persecution. The onset is usually sudden following a heavy drinking bout.

Chronic Alcoholic Deterioration. The excessive intake of alcohol over a long period of time may result in a thorough disintegration of the personality. Mental and physical abilities deteriorate along with a collapse of moral and ethical standards of behavior.

TREATMENT AND PROGNOSIS. Treatment of the presenting symptoms of an alcoholic psychosis is, of course, imperative. The chronically deteriorated alcoholic must be restored to physiological stability; nutritional deficiencies must be overcome in the patient suffering from Korsakoff's psychosis; the acutely hallucinating alcoholic and the delirium tremens patient must undergo a rigid program of rest, quiet, and withdrawal from alcohol. All these measures, however, serve only to remove the superficial evidences of an underlying personality difficulty. The person who abuses the use of alcohol is psychologically sick and cannot hope to improve or recover without treatment of the psychological basis for his illness.

The prognosis for any of the alcoholic psychoses is questionable, depending always on the degree of insight the patient brings to the therapeutic experience and his willingness to co-operate. For cases of chronic alcoholic deterioration, and for Korsakoff's psychosis, however, the prognosis is usually very poor. Not only is the damage to the brain often irreversible, but also the psychoses occur relatively late in life when patterns of behavior and attitudes are less amenable to reeducation.

Psychoses Due to Drugs or Other Exogenous Toxins. Psychotic reactions sometimes develop as manifestations of drug addiction or as a result of exposure to such toxins as dust, fumes, or gases.

The larger problem of drug addiction as a symptom of underlying personality disturbance is discussed in Chapter 9, Personality Disorders.

As to incidence, fewer than 1 per cent of first admissions to mental hospitals in the United States are diagnosed as psychoses due to drugs or exogenous toxins.

CAUSATION. Of the narcotic drugs, only morphine, heroin, cocaine, and marijuana are of importance in this context. Inhalation of dust or fumes from metals such as lead, arsenic, manganese, or mercury may cause poisoning and brain tissue damage. Except for lead poisoning, which is one of the oldest known occupational diseases, these disorders are rare. Carbon monoxide and other gases absorbed in large quantities may also result in psychotic reactions.

SYMPTOMS. The symptoms of these psychoses vary with the particular poison or toxin causing the reaction. Common poisons include metals, gases, and drugs.

For *metallic poisoning,* the symptom picture is one of restlessness, anxiety, and delirium. Hallucinations and delusions of persecution are also present. Intellectual or emotional defects of a permanent nature may result.

Carbon monoxide or other gases, if absorbed in large quantities, may induce psychotic symptoms as a result of brain toxicity. After initial unconsciousness, the victim may exhibit a confusion and aphasia (loss or impairment of language ability); apraxia (loss of specific habits, e.g., in shoe tieing) may appear. Severe damage due to gas poisoning may result in chronic mental enfeeblement.

Psychotic states caused by *drug poisoning* are expressed in such symptoms as visual and auditory hallucination, delusions of persecution, impaired judgment, apathy, and dullness.

TREATMENT AND PROGNOSIS. Psychosis due to the ingestion of *dust or fumes from metals* must be treated by ridding the body of the toxic substance. In lead poisoning measures are undertaken to control body calcium and thus eliminate lead from the tissues. Treatment of the patient suffering from psychosis due to *carbon monoxide poisoning* consists simply of care and observation following recovery of consciousness. The prognosis is usually favorable, with best progress made where loss of consciousness was of short duration. Psychoses due to *excessive use of narcotic drugs* require treatment similar to that for alcoholic psychoses: specific measures for elimination of the symptoms plus psychotherapy directed toward resolution of the patient's personality difficulties. The prognosis is only slightly hopeful.

PSYCHOSES DUE TO DISTURBANCES OF METABOLISM, GROWTH, NUTRITION, OR ENDOCRINE FUNCTION

In a relatively small number of patients psychotic disturbance occurs in association with disordered physiological functioning, with or without underlying personality disorder. The pathologic conditions most commonly seen are: Alzheimer's disease, glandular disorders, general physical exhaustion, pellagra, and pernicious anemia.

Alzheimer's Disease. Sometimes called "presenile psychosis," this disorder presents a syndrome of senile dementia appearing at a comparatively early age, sometimes before the age of fifty. The causes of this disease are unknown. Apraxia and aphasia are the distinctive symptoms. Also present are impairment of memory and judgment, incoherence in speech, disorientation, restlessness, and delirium and confusion. Marked atrophy of the brain takes place. There is no beneficial treatment known beyond custodial care. The prognosis is unfavorable.

Psychoses with Glandular Disorder. Psychotic reactions may be associated with disorders of the thyroid, the pituitary, and the adrenal cortex (Addison's disease); they may also accompany diabetes. Treatment of the glandular disturbance usually clears up the psychotic symptoms.

Psychoses with Exhaustion Delirium. Psychotic reactions may result from extreme physical exhaustion in the absence of infection or other pathology. Usually the physical exhaustion is combined with starvation. Symptoms include: insomnia, confusion, clouding of consciousness, vague fears, fleeting hallucinations, and delusions. Rest and proper food usually lead to a cessation of the mental symptoms.

Psychosis with Pellagra. Pellagra is a deficiency disease resulting from lack of vitamin B_2. A psychotic picture is seen in about 5 per cent of pellagra sufferers. The usual skin lesions and gastrointestinal disturbances are accompanied by delirium, confusion, memory impairment, and hallucinations. These mental symptoms clear up rapidly with proper diet and nursing care.

Psychosis with Pernicious Anemia. Roughly one-third of

patients with pernicious anemia manifest mental changes, which are thought to be due to defective nutrition of the brain cells arising from deficiency of red cells in the blood. The symptom picture varies with the personality of the patient. Correction of the hematic deficiency is imperative, and it may be combined with psychotherapy.

PSYCHOSES DUE TO NEW GROWTH

Tumors which grow in the brain may interfere directly with proper brain functioning. Tumors elsewhere in the body, through their general toxic effect, may bring about disordered brain functioning, but such cases are not common.

Statistics from mental hospitals show psychoses due to brain tumors to constitute only about 0.2 per cent of first admissions to mental hospitals in the United States. The incidence, however, is actually a good deal higher than that since a large number of such tumors are discovered at postmortem examinations in mental patients who had been diagnosed under other categories.

Causation. The reason for spontaneous appearance of new growths in the brain is as much in doubt as is the causation of all neoplasms.

Symptoms. The symptoms of brain tumors include both physiological and psychological signs. The physiological signs include: headache which is persistent and pulsating; vomiting which is unrelated to time of eating and is sometimes unaccompanied by nausea; and choked disk (inflammation of the optic nerve), in which cerebrospinal fluid is forced into the nerve causing impairment of vision if unrelieved. The psychological signs include stupor, depression, clouded consciousness, disorientation, and listlessness.

Treatment and Prognosis. Only surgical or radiological removal of the tumor will serve to relieve the patient of the physiological and psychological symptoms. Prognosis depends on the extent of damage caused by the tumor, its location, and the promptness with which treatment is instituted.

PSYCHOSES DUE TO UNKNOWN OR HEREDITARY CAUSES BUT ASSOCIATED WITH ORGANIC CHANGE

Some relatively rare psychotic disorders occur as a result of progressive degenerative changes in the nervous system for which the cause has not been discovered. Defects in psychomotor response, intellectual functioning, and emotional behavior are present, and occasionally hallucinations and delusions are noted.

Paralysis Agitans. This disease is also known as "shaking palsy" and Parkinson's disease. It is chronic, progressively degenerative, and most frequently appears in the ages between fifty and sixty.

CAUSATION. Causation is unknown.

SYMPTOMS. First to be observed are muscular rigidity and involuntary rhythmic tremors of hands and arms. The face takes on a masklike expression. The patient leans forward when walking and tends to pass from a walking to a running pace. The special senses and intellectual powers are unimpaired. Emotional apathy, indifference, and other psychological changes come about as the patient reacts to his affliction.

TREATMENT. Treatment of the physical symptoms is only supportive; psychotherapy has been used with moderate success to help patients to accept their condition.

Pick's Disease. A form of presenile dementia in which the patient's handling of the more complex social adjustments breaks down but his memory remains intact is known as Pick's disease.

CAUSATION. Causation is unknown.

SYMPTOMS. As the disease progresses, the patients gradually lose the ability to use their memory as an intellectual tool although the memory material is preserved. In severe cases violence and destructive tendencies are manifested.

TREATMENT. The only treatment is custodial care.

Huntington's Chorea. This is a chronic, progressive disease accompanied by mental deterioration and ending in dementia and death.

CAUSATION. This disorder is one of the very few conditions believed to be due to a hereditary factor; some investigators have expressed the opinion that it is transmitted directly as a Mendelian characteristic. Once the chain of heredity is broken by a person who does not contract this disorder, the offspring are not likely to develop Huntington's chorea.

SYMPTOMS. The choreic movements consist of jerky, irregular, squirming motions. Facial grimaces, accompanied by smacking of the tongue and lips and slow, inarticulate, agitated speech are further characteristics of this disorder. The patient's gait is bizarre and irregular. Memory and judgment are impaired and the patient is irritable and unable to maintain attention. He may fall into moods of depression, accompanied by suicidal tendencies.

TREATMENT AND PROGNOSIS. There is no known effective treatment. Once the course of the disease begins, it continues uninterrupted. The average age at the onset is thirty-five to forty years. The average length of life after onset is ten to fifteen years.

15

EPILEPSY AND RELATED STATES

Epilepsy is a recurrent disturbance in the chemicoelectrical activity of the brain which manifests itself in an aggregate of symptoms (symptom-complex), these being: impairment of consciousness, perturbation of the autonomic nervous system, convulsive movements, and psychic disorder. Perhaps because of its dramatic manifestations the disease has been recognized from earliest times; it was once known as the "sacred disease." The clinical recognition of epilepsy has been improved by development in electroencephalography; positive diagnosis can be established on the basis of the distinctive epileptiform brain waves. Through advances in chemotherapeutic measures, it has become possible to reduce the severity and frequency of seizures, which are the principal expressions of this illness.

For various reasons, and with varying degrees of evidence, such other conditions as migraine, fainting, vasovagal attacks, some forms of psychosis, and criminality have been related to epilepsy. In addition, a psychogenic form of epileptic seizure is sometimes seen.

EPILEPSY

Reports on the prevalence of epilepsy vary, depending on the inclusiveness of the definition applied. Furthermore, many cases of epilepsy are untreated and thus escape medical recording. Principally on the basis of rejections for military service and public health surveys, it has been estimated that some 700,000 persons in the United States or about 5 per 1,000 of the general population suffer from epilepsy. This disease accounts for about 2 per cent of first admissions to mental hospitals, but most epileptics remain outside these institutions. Many of them lead useful lives in business, industry, or the arts. Such eminent figures as Julius Caesar, Lord Byron, and Peter the Great suffered from this disorder. In spite of popular opinion to the contrary, mental deficiency is no more prevalent among epileptics than in the general population. More male epileptics are reported than females, but clinical evidence reveals no sex differences in the nature of the disorder. The onset of seizures is most frequent in the first two years of life and during adolescence.

Causation. As in the case of organic psychoses, epileptic reactions may be classified according to the factors causing them, thus: idiopathic, or essential epilepsy; epilepsy associated with birth injuries or postnatal head injuries; epilepsy resulting from toxic states; epilepsy produced by brain tumor; and psychogenic epileptic seizures.

Approaching the matter from the viewpoint of the general classes of factors which cause mental disorders, one may consider hereditary factors, environmental or biological factors, and psychological factors.

HEREDITARY FACTORS. Epilepsy occurs among the near relatives of epileptic patients about five times more frequently than in the general population. This pattern of relationship is higher among patients whose seizures occur early in life. Furthermore, brain waves typical of the epileptic patient during a seizure are found more often among relatives of such patients than in the general population. On the other hand, fewer than one-fifth of epileptic patients have a family history of epilepsy. The conclusion has been drawn by Lennox, a leading authority in the field, that epilepsy may be either genetic or acquired but its causation is most often of mixed origin. Heredity probably does no more than produce a predisposition toward seizure reactions which are actually brought on by various environmental (biological) conditions.

OTHER BIOLOGICAL FACTORS. Epileptic seizures may be produced, especially in predisposed persons, by intrauterine or birth injuries, asphyxia, excessive sedation, infections involving the brain, trauma, or brain tumors. When seizures are the result of brain injury, the "irritation theory" is offered in explanation: the seizure is said to be the direct result of stimulation or irritation within the cerebral cortex, which the injury has left hypersensitive to any stimulation. It is also maintained that the brain may be left predisposed to seizure reactions by irritative substances carried to the brain as a consequence of some metabolic disorder producing low levels of sugar, or by some endocrine disorder producing insufficient concentrations of calcium. One study reports a history of organic factors in 22 of 95 cases of epilepsy.

PSYCHOLOGICAL FACTORS. It is well known that emotional excitement can elicit a seizure in an already epileptic person. There is further speculation that epileptic convulsions are wholly the result of unconscious dynamic factors, in which the seizures function as tension-reducing mechanisms. However, the paucity of reports of successful psychotherapy with epileptic patients suggests the inadequacy of this theory.

Symptoms. The four principal symptoms of epilepsy (loss of consciousness, autonomic reactions, convulsive movements, and psychic disturbances) may occur with varying degrees of intensity from one individual to another and from one attack to another in the same individual. Epileptic seizures may occur in such mild form as not even to be recognized by the individual undergoing the attack.

Three forms of epileptic seizure are recognized: the grand mal, the petit mal, and the psychic-equivalent seizure (psychomotor attack). About 90 per cent of epileptic patients have grand mal attacks with or without other types; 50 per cent have grand mal seizures only; 8 per cent suffer only petit mal attacks; and 1 per cent suffer from psychic-equivalent (psychomotor) seizures.

GRAND MAL SEIZURE. In about half of these cases the attack is preceded by an *aura,* or warning, which may take the form of dizziness, physical discomfort, or a tingling or numbness in the extremities. The principal feature of the illness is violent muscular activity (convulsion) with loss of consciousness. An initial phase of rigidity (tonic phase) accompanied by suspended respiration gives way to one of jerky muscular reactions (clonic phase). Tongue-biting and evacuation of bowel and bladder may occur. The attack lasts a few minutes, after which consciousness is regained gradually. In severe cases headache, nausea, and depression may ensue. "Jacksonian" attacks are those in which the seizure begins in one of the extremities and spreads throughout the side of the body on which it originates. Frequency of the grand mal attack varies from patient to patient and from time to time, may occur without complete loss of consciousness. The variation in frequency ranges from one or two seizures in a year to several in the course of a single day. When the seizures occur in rapid, chain-like sequence, the condition is called *status epilepticus.*

PETIT MAL SEIZURE. Practically the only symptom of this type of epileptic reaction is a fleeting loss of consciousness lasting from a few seconds to a minute. There may be minor facial tic (twitching). The attack seems not to produce mental confusion, nor is mental deterioration associated with it. Petit mal seizures may occur frequently during a day. The onset is seen most often in adolescence, more frequently in girls than in boys.

PSYCHIC-EQUIVALENT (PSYCHOMOTOR) SEIZURE. This is the most complex of the epileptic reactions. While consciousness is lost, activity is maintained, with the patient capable of carrying out purposeful acts. The activity, however, is not subject to voluntary control or to direction by other persons, and it can take the form of destructive, even criminal, behavior. There is complete amnesia for the period of the seizure. Psychomotor attacks range from those lasting a few seconds to those which go on for several days. The convulsive feature of the grand mal attack is not present. Although sources list the incidence of this disorder as low, it is possible that other forms of disturbed behavior may actually be undiagnosed manifestations of this reaction.

Personality Structure in Epilepsy. Whether or not there is a distinctive epileptic personality is still a controversial matter. These patients have been described as extremely sensitive and egotistic persons, given to displays of temper tantrums and rages. From time to time, epileptics have been characterized as selfish and cruel, with tendencies toward antisocial and criminal behavior. The most careful researchers state, however, that the majority of epileptic patients show no evidence of a distinctive personality pattern or a consistent, predictable trend of behavior. One could point out that the undesirable traits found among epileptics are more satisfactorily explained on the basis of their social isolation. In other cases the behavior might be explained on the basis of associated brain conditions, reactions to drugs, or the results of mental deterioration.

Mental Retardation and Deterioration. The average I.Q. reported for various groups of epileptics is below average, ranging from 65 to 90. However, since many brain-damaged cases are included, the figures probably do not present a fair picture. Of a group of more than 1,600 clinical and private cases of essential epilepsy, 67 per cent were classified as mentally normal, 23 per cent slightly below normal, and 10 per cent mentally retarded.

Where mental deterioration is present, it is related to the type of attack, frequency of attack, and duration of the illness. Among the greater number of epileptics, mental deterioration does not take place.

Electroencephalographic Findings in Epilepsy. In approximately 85 per cent of the epileptic population, disturbances in the rhythm of the brain waves can be found. The disturbance, as revealed when the patient is not in a seizure state, produces bursts of waves of increased amplitude, coming with extremes of either speed or slowness. A key feature in diagnosing epilepsy are bursts of fast, "spiky" waves or alternating spikes and waves. In 15 per cent of the cases with no dysrhythmia, the seizures are rare. During actual seizures, petit mal attacks produce high amplitude waves and alternating spikes at a rate of three per second. Grand mal attacks produce a sharp increase in speed and amplitude of waves. In psychomotor attacks the pattern is one of high-amplitude waves, four to eight per second. Frequently, the changes in electroencephalographic findings are predictive of oncoming seizures. On the other hand, cortical dysrhythmia is found in twenty nonepileptics for each person with epilepsy. These include some cases of other abnormalities and those with a probable predisposition to epilepsy.

Treatment of Epilepsy. Although some psychotherapy should be provided to help the patient understand and accept his illness and to assist him in arranging environmental factors to minimize the effects of seizures, the principal treatment has been of a medical nature. The drugs phenobarbital and dilantin, and more recently mesantoin, have been found effective in reducing or eliminating the grand mal or psychomotor attacks in 90 per cent of cases. Tridione is used successfully for petit mal seizures. In order to be effective, medication must be continued throughout the life of the individual. Producing a state of acidosis by careful control of diet or bringing about dehydration has been helpful in reduction of seizures. At least one report claims control of attacks through electroshock convulsions. Reports of correcting epilepsy through psychotherapy are meager.

STATES RELATED TO EPILEPSY

Two reactions which may be confused with epilepsy are hysterical seizures and fainting attacks. In addition, it is thought that migraine may be related to epilepsy on a genetic basis.

Hysterical Seizures and Fainting. Persons suffering from a neurotic reaction may be given to attacks which resemble epileptic seizures. These may actually be hysterical attacks or simply persistent fainting (syncope). Electroencephalographic findings serve to differentiate the conditions. Brain wave patterns show no change during a hysterical seizure, and the patterns between seizures are likely to be quite normal. Further, the hysterical seizure seems to appear fortuitously when the patient is accompanied and can gain a secondary satisfaction from his display. The real epileptic patient may be seriously injured in his fall during an attack, but the neurotic person usually takes care not to hurt himself. However, persistent fainting that cannot be explained along physiological lines or as a neurotic reaction should be regarded with suspicion, and negative findings need not exclude epilepsy.

Migraine. The principal symptom of migraine is the incapacitating headache, usually accompanied by nausea, pallor, and other sympathetic reactions. Frequently, there are visual disturbances. The relationship to epilepsy is indicated by the high coincidence of epilepsy and migraine in the same persons, as well as the unusually high prevalence of migraine among the relatives of epileptics. Hereditary factors are said to be prominent in migraine. The symptoms of migraine are relieved promptly in most cases by the administration of ergotamine tartrate.

16

MENTAL DEFICIENCY

Retardation in the development of intelligence is known variously as mental deficiency, mental retardation, feeblemindedness, amentia (to distinguish it from dementia, a psychotic condition), and oligophrenia. The various types are differentiated in terms of either ultimate level of intellectual capacity attained or causative factors: for example, an idiot is an individual with an intelligence quotient below 25, and a cretin is one who suffers from improper functioning of the thyroid gland. Mental deficiency poses a major social problem because it requires special training facilities and procedures, and in some instances institutionalization is advisable.

INTELLIGENCE

Although there is general agreement among psychologists concerning the basic components of intelligence, their definitions vary as do the indices of intellectual level and the means for measurement.

Definitions of Intelligence. Numerous authorities in the field of mental deficiency have offered their definitions. Binet's conception of intelligence weighed judgment as the most important factor, though he also cited memory, reason, ability to compare, comprehension, use of number concepts, and knowledge of current events.

Stern defined intelligence as a *general capacity of an individual consciously to adjust his thinking to new requirements;* in other words, he stressed general mental adaptability to new problems and conditions of life.

Spearman has elaborated mathematical evidence that all intellectual abilities can be expressed as functions of two factors: one, a *general factor common to every ability,* and another, a *factor specific to any particular ability* and in each case different from that of all others. More recently a third-factor theory has been presented which allows for *group factors.*

Terman defines intelligence as *the ability to carry on abstract thinking.*

Wechsler states: "Intelligence is the aggregate or global capacity of the individual to *act purposefully,* to *think rationally,* and to *deal effectively with his environment.* It is global because it characterizes the individual's behavior as a whole; it is an aggregate because it is composed of elements or abilities which, though not entirely independent, are qualitatively differentiable."*

Measurement of Intelligence. Intelligence is indicated by three yardsticks: mental age, intelligence quotient, and percentile rank.

MENTAL AGE. Mental age refers to the mental ability characteristic of average children of a given chronological level. Thus, a child with a mental age of six is able to work at an intellectual level characteristic of the average six-year-old.

INTELLIGENCE QUOTIENT. Intelligence quotient is a measure of brightness in addition to mere level of ability. It is calculated according to the formula—

$$\frac{MA \times 100}{CA}$$

in which MA is the mental age and CA is the chronological age.

PERCENTILE RANK. Percentile rank is an expression of intelligence test scores in terms of relative standing in a designated population. It states the percentage of a population which a given score equals or exceeds; for example, a percentile rank of 70 indicates a score which equals or exceeds the scores made by 70 per cent of the population named.

Tests of Intelligence. Commonly used tests of intelligence are: the Revised Stanford-Binet Test of Intelligence; the Wechsler-Bellevue Scales (Form I, Form II, and WAIS): the Wechsler Intelligence Scale for Children; the Goodenough Drawing Test; and the Arthur Point Scale. (For fuller discussions of psychological tests, see Chapter 18, The Diagnostic Process.)

There are only slight differences of terminology in the most commonly employed scales of intelligence (the Terman revision of the Stanford-Binet and the Wechsler Scales), but the approach is from different statistical vantage points. The accompanying tables show how these two techniques handle the question of the distribution of intelligence in the general population. Terman bases his scale on ranges of intelligence (I.Q.); Wechsler adds the factor of percentage distribution of each of the levels. It must be noted that the I.Q.'s

* David Wechsler, *The Measurement of Adult Intelligence* (Baltimore: Williams & Wilkins, 1944), p. 3.

assigned to various levels vary slightly with the particular intelligence test scale used.

TERMAN'S CLASSIFICATION OF INTELLIGENCE *

Classification	I.Q. Range
Genius	Above 140
Very Superior	120–140
Superior	110–120
Normal, or Average	90–110
Dull	80– 90
Borderline	70– 80
Feebleminded: Moron	50– 70
Imbecile	25– 50
Idiot	Below 25

* After David Wechsler, *The Measurement of Adult Intelligence* (Baltimore: Williams & Wilkins, 1944), p. 37.

WECHSLER'S CLASSIFICATION OF INTELLIGENCE *

Classification	I.Q. Range	Per cent of Population
Very Superior	128 and over	2.2
Superior	120–127	6.7
Bright Normal	111–119	16.1
Average	91–110	50.0
Dull Normal	80– 90	16.1
Borderline	66– 79	6.7
Defective	65 and below	2.2

* *Ibid.*, p. 40.

CRITERIA OF MENTAL DEFICIENCY

A diagnosis of mental deficiency cannot be made on the basis of the I.Q. alone. The social, vocational, and emotional adjustment of the individual must be taken into account. In this sense, mental deficiency is regarded as an over-all inability to take care of oneself as a constructive, independent member of society. Dr. Edgar Doll has defined mental deficiency as *"a state of social incompetence*

*obtaining at maturity, resulting from developmental mental arrest
of constitutional, hereditary or acquired origin; the condition is
essentially incurable through treatment and unremediable through
training except as treatment and training instill habits which super-
ficially or temporarily compensate for the limitations of the person
so affected while under favorable circumstances and for more or
less limited periods of time."* *

A complete diagnosis of mental deficiency can be made only by
studying the individual from the medical, psychological, and socio-
logical points of view.

INCIDENCE OF MENTAL DEFICIENCY

Because the standards used to determine the existence of mental
deficiency vary, accurate estimates of the incidence of this condition
are difficult to make. The number of mentally deficient persons in
the United States has been given as from one and one-half to four
and one-half millions.

Some understanding of the scope of the problem of mental deficiency can, however, be obtained by referring to statistics based on
military rejections, school data, and institutional figures.

Military. In World War I, 0.5 per cent of the draftees were
recommended for discharge because of "mental inferiority" and 0.6
per cent were referred for special assignment for the same reason.
In addition, 0.9 per cent of men registered for the draft were either
found to be in institutions for the mentally retarded or were rejected
by the draft boards as mentally incompetent. In World War II 4.5
per cent of all men examined for selective service were rejected as
mentally defective. However, since complete screening procedures
were not developed until late in the war, it is probable that a considerable number of these cases were illiterate or psychotic.

School. The National Committee for Mental Hygiene has reported that 3.2 per cent of more than 50,000 school children tested
were mentally defective, and that an additional 3.7 per cent were
borderline cases. A survey of Baltimore schools indicated that 1.2
per cent of the school population were mentally deficient.

Institutions. More than 115,000 individuals are institutionalized
as mental defectives in public and private training schools and in
state and county hospitals in the United States.

* Edgar A. Doll, "The Essentials of an Inclusive Concept of Mental Deficiency,"
Amer. J. Ment. Def. (No. 46, 1941–42), p. 217.

GRADATIONS OF MENTAL DEFICIENCY

In the diagnosis of mental deficiency it is customary to specify the level of deficiency in accordance with the I.Q. level and the degree of social adjustment. The terms for these levels are: moron, imbecile, and idiot. It is generally agreed that 75 per cent of the mentally deficient are morons, 20 per cent imbeciles, and 5 per cent idiots.

Morons. Morons with I.Q.'s ranging from 51 to 69 show few physical abnormalities. With competent and sympathetic training they can achieve a fourth or fifth grade level and may be able to hold simple, routine jobs.

Imbeciles. Imbeciles with I.Q.'s ranging from 25 to 50 are awkward individuals, usually with some physical abnormality. They may achieve a social maturity that is characteristic of children four to nine years old. Imbeciles can learn to talk and thus communicate their basic needs, but usually cannot learn to read or write. They are able to protect themselves from ordinary dangers and to accomplish a few simple, concrete tasks. They can, though with difficulty, be taught to take care of their personal needs. Institutionalization may be advisable but it is not always essential.

Idiots. Idiots with I.Q.'s below 25 must be institutionalized. Their active developmental picture is one of severe retardation, with marked sensory and motor handicaps, physical anomalies, and a high susceptibility to disease. The idiot cannot learn to take care of his personal needs, nor can he protect himself from the most ordinary dangers.

CLINICAL TYPES OF MENTAL DEFICIENCY

From the clinical (and etiological) point of view, two types of mental deficiency are usually distinguished: (1) *primary* (endogenous) mental deficiency, in which the cause is principally hereditary; and (2) *secondary* or *acquired* (exogenous) mental deficiency, which results from brain pathology occurring after conception. Up to 40 per cent of all mental deficiency is of the primary type, the remaining 60 per cent being divided among the several subtypes of secondary mental deficiency. A third type of mental deficiency (for example, the idiot-savant) is categorized here under special types.

Primary Mental Deficiency. Three subtypes of primary mental deficiency are recognized: familial mental deficiency, amaurotic family idiocy, and phenylpyruvic oligophrenia. The latter is a rare condition.

FAMILIAL MENTAL DEFICIENCY. This is the "garden variety" of mental deficiency, the most prevalent diagnostic group of the primary type. Diagnosis rests on the presence of mental deficiency in the family and the absence of organic or environmental causes. Evidence for the hereditary causation of the disease is its tendency to high incidence in certain families. The parents of such children are usually below average intelligence. Recent studies indicate that many cases formerly diagnosed under this category actually resulted from prenatal anomalies due largely to oxygen deprivation during the development of the embryo.

AMAUROTIC FAMILY IDIOCY. Amaurotic family idiocy is a disease of the nervous system which results in mental degeneration after what has appeared to be normal growth. It is apparently transmitted as a Mendelian recessive characteristic. The onset can occur in infancy, childhood, or adolescence. Severe motor and sensory disorders accompany the mental deterioration. Death occurs soon after onset.

PHENYLPYRUVIC OLIGOPHRENIA. This hereditary condition of mental deficiency may develop from prenatal influences, birth trauma, or phenylpyruvic acid in the system. The presence of the acid in the urine is the main diagnostic sign. It is believed that the metabolic disturbance is genetically dependent on the effect of a simple recessive gene.

Secondary Mental Deficiency. Brain pathology producing mental deficiency may develop from prenatal influences, birth trauma, or early postnatal conditions.

MENTAL DEFICIENCY DUE TO PRENATAL INFLUENCES. The principal clinical types of mental deficiency resulting from prenatal influences are: mongolism, cretinism, microcephaly, macrocephaly, and hydrocephaly.

Mongolism. This type of deficiency constitutes the largest category in the "prenatal" group. It was so designated because the child's slanted eyes suggest the appearance of a Mongolian. These children are more likely to be imbeciles than idiots; they may achieve a maturity level of five years. Mongoloids are usually of affectionate disposition and seem to take special pleasure in aping the behavior of those about them. Although the cause of the condition is not certainly known, a pathological condition of the mother, probably glandular dysfunction, is most widely accepted as the etiological factor. No effective treatment is known. Life expectancy has been ten years, though the use of new antibiotics is helping to increase the life span.

Cretinism. Cretinism results from improper functioning of the thyroid gland. Most frequently it is due to lack of iodine in the mother's diet, though birth injury and certain diseases may also produce it in less severe forms. In response to improved nutritional practices in the diets of expectant mothers and as a result of early diagnosis, cretinism has been reduced to less than 5 per cent of the hospitalized mental defectives. Cretins have notable physical characteristics, such as dwarfed stature, thick eyelids, dry skin, abundant dark hair, and protruding abdomen. They may be either idiots or imbeciles. The personality of the cretin is flat, and he responds poorly to training. Thyroid medication, administered early in the course of the illness, can restore the individual to almost normal functioning. The prognosis is poor where the condition has existed for a long period prior to treatment.

Microcephaly ("Small Head"). In this condition the individual's skull is unusually small in circumference and conical in shape, with the forehead and chin markedly receding. Owing to the smallness of the cranial cavity, there is a limited development of cerebral tissue. The cause is not known, though meningitis or encephalitis during gestation is suspected. Microcephalics are usually idiots or imbeciles. They may develop simple motor skills but are restricted with regard to language development. Although microcephalics tend to be hyperactive, they are easily managed. Medical treatment is of no avail, and training is limited to developing the patient's ability to take care of his personal needs. The condition is rare.

Macrocephaly ("Enlarged Head"). This condition is caused by an outgrowth of the glia cells; these cells are only supporting structures and do not carry nerve impulses. Abnormal development of brain architecture results. The causes of the outgrowth are unknown and there is no successful treatment. This condition is also rare.

Hydrocephaly ("Water in the Head"). Hydrocephaly results from an obstruction in the ventricular system of the brain which causes an abnormal amount of cerebrospinal fluid to collect in the cranium. The result is damage to brain tissue with consequent enlargement of the head and mental deficiency. The face remains of normal size, but the skull above it has a bulging effect. The level of mental retardation varies with the amount of brain damage. The hydrocephalic is usually affectionate and even-tempered. Hydrocephaly has been successfully relieved by newly developed surgical techniques for reducing intracranial pressure, with the patients in some cases achieving normal development.

MENTAL DEFICIENCY DUE TO BIRTH TRAUMA. It is estimated that from 6 to 10 per cent of the institutionalized mental defectives are birth-injured; however, not all birth-injured children are feeble-minded. An additional 1.5 per cent suffer from mental deficiency due to injury occurring after birth. Accordingly, from 7.5 to 11.5 per cent of known mental defectives have conditions that were trauma-induced.

In birth trauma, the brain damage is caused by brain hemorrhage produced by difficult labor, accidents, or improper handling of the infant. It may also result from delayed breathing of the newborn, toxemias of pregnancy, premature separation of the placenta, or cord complications. Birth-injured children present a variety of symptoms and limitations in abilities, depending on the location and extent of the brain damage. The sensory defects and the extensive motor handicap make evaluation of intellectual level a challenging process, and each individual must be studied carefully to determine the degree of mental retardation, if any.

MENTAL DEFICIENCY DUE TO EARLY POSTNATAL CONDITIONS. Included here are head injury subsequent to birth and the infectious diseases of early childhood.

Head Injury. Head injury subsequent to birth causes mental deficiency much less frequently than is commonly believed; only 15 out of every 1,000 institutionalized mental defectives are diagnosed under this category. In such cases there is usually a definite personality disturbance and the mental impairment tends to be more selective than in other types of mental deficiency. These children tend to be restless, overstimulated, and easily fatigued. Their mental limitations produce perceptual disturbances and difficulties in abstract thinking. The brain damage, along with its consequent personality and intellectual changes, are thought to be irreversible. Such individuals must not, however, be regarded as typical mental defectives; they do show some learning ability, and their lowered mental performance may result from impaired sensory and motor faculties rather than from reduction of mental capacity.

Infectious Diseases. Infectious diseases in childhood which are significant in the etiology of mental deficiency are epidemic cerebro-spinal meningitis and epidemic encephalitis. In the case of the latter disorder, personality changes may also occur. Some recent studies have indicated that such common childhood diseases as whooping cough, measles, mumps, chicken pox, and influenza may produce brain changes leading to arrest of mental development. There is, however, no conclusive evidence that this occurs in any appreciable number of children.

MENTAL DEFICIENCY DUE TO UNCLASSIFIED CAUSES. A large number of cases of mental deficiency not falling into any of the afore-mentioned types are grouped together as unclassified mental deficiency. In most of these cases the suspected cause is infectious disease in the mother during pregnancy; such diseases include measles, typhoid fever, pneumonia, and syphilis. Other prenatal factors are uterine bleeding, acute trauma, and X-ray treatment of the mother during pregnancy.

Special Types. Two special types of mental defectives are those categorized under the terms pseudo-feeblemindedness and idiot-savant.

PSEUDO-FEEBLEMINDED TYPE. The pseudo-feebleminded are individuals who, reacting with extreme withdrawal in the face of fear, failure, or criticism, lose all interest in work and motivation for achievement. Such a person may respond to all demands with simple responses of "I don't know" or "It's too hard." Because the resulting pattern of behavior gives the impression of stupidity, the condition has been referred to as "pseudo-feeblemindedness." In reality, pseudo-feeblemindedness is an emotional disorder and does not produce mental retardation of the kind discussed in this chapter.

IDIOT-SAVANT TYPE. The idiot-savant presents a curious phenomenon of intellectual capacity. In spite of their apparently general dullness together with all the earmarks of mental defectiveness, these individuals possess exceptional, often striking, specific talents or aptitudes. An example of such accomplishments is the ability to identify the day of the week of any date in the past or future within a few seconds—always accurately. The idiot-savant has long been the object of curiosity in the field of mental deficiency. It is now felt, however, that these individuals are not truly mental defectives, rather that they are perhaps misdiagnosed schizophrenics of the simple type. In many cases the special talent, when investigated, has proved to be remarkable only because it stands out in contrast to the behavior of others in the social group. Furthermore, there are studies of mental defectives (not of the idiot type) who demonstrate remarkably complex neurotic reactions, special artistic talent, or mechanical skills. The achievement of the idiot-savant is based solely on memory, and he usually displays total lack of judgment, reasoning, and other controlled thought processes.

TREATMENT OF MENTAL DEFICIENCY

Although no specific cures for mental deficiency have yet been developed, except in a limited sense for certain types, therapeutic procedures designed to effect the highest level of adjustment for the individual have been tried. In all instances, early diagnosis is essential if treatment is to have the desired effect.

The Criterion of Trainability. Recent trends in treatment tend to separate the mentally deficient into three classes: the child who requires institutionalization, the child who is trainable in the home setting, and the child who is educable in special school programs designed for the mentally deficient individual.

THE CHILD WHO REQUIRES INSTITUTIONALIZATION. Where previously the mere fact of serious mental retardation had been considered grounds for institutionalization, recently more careful evaluation has been made of the possibility of training the child outside the institution. However, the child who along with low intelligence presents problems of physical care or medical treatment has of necessity to be institutionalized. Even in the absence of such special problems, the need for institutionalization may be indicated when parents are incapable of affording proper supervision or when the presence of the defective child creates a serious threat to the healthy emotional development of his brothers and sisters.

In institutions for the mentally deficient, efforts are made to capitalize on whatever motor and intellectual abilities the patient may have to bring him up to as high a level of adjustment as possible.

The decision to institutionalize a mentally defective child is a complex one, frequently arousing feelings of anxiety, uncertainty, and guilt in the parents. Although this decision is legally the responsibility of parents, they should avail themselves of the help and advice of specialists in the field. The optimum approach would be the use of a consultative team, including specialists in the fields of psychiatry, psychology, social work, and pediatrics.

THE CHILD WHO IS TRAINABLE IN THE HOME SETTING. A child in this category is one whose low I.Q. (50 or lower on the Terman Scale) might previously have resulted in institutionalization. Where such a child indicates any capacity for being trained in self-care and in rudimentary motor and social skills, he is today regarded as best cared for in the family setting with the professional assistance and guidance offered in special day care centers. Aside from providing special training for the child, these centers guide and counsel the parents in meeting the needs of the child. Children in this category will never become self-sufficient, but proper training can help them achieve a higher level of adjustment than was previously thought possible.

THE CHILD WHO IS EDUCABLE IN SPECIAL SCHOOL PROGRAMS. This child, with an I.Q. ranging from 50 to 70, is eligible for training in special classes within the regular school system. Ordinarily he may be taught basic skills such as reading simple signs, counting, and making change. The group experience in the school can provide satisfying emotional relationships for him. The more advanced of these children may be prepared for simple occupations and a modest degree of self-sufficiency.

Medical Procedures. In cretinism and hydrocephaly the treatments already mentioned (diet and surgery, respectively) have restored some individuals to normal development. Recently the inclusion of *glutamic acid* in the diet of long-standing cases of mental deficiency is claimed to have produced improvement in total personality functioning, with small but significant increases in the I.Q. and a general increase in alertness and efficiency. But the improvement of the individual can be maintained only through continued administration of the glutamic acid for life.

Work with Parents. Frequently the reactions of parents to a feebleminded child do much to handicap him in his efforts to achieve a satisfactory adjustment. They may refuse to acknowledge the child's limitations and dull his incentive for accomplishment by never displaying approval of what he *can* do. Subtly and fondly, or openly with rejection, they press the child to attain standards far beyond his level. Other parents pamper their mentally retarded children and keep them overdependent, thus blocking the development of even their limited capabilities. In such cases there is serious need of counseling help, which is available through social agencies concerned with mentally retarded children. Their guidance, based on professional understanding of the needs of the mentally deficient, can do much to reduce the effect of such faulty parental attitudes. Another valuable development is the voluntary parent association (an association of parents of mentally retarded children), which offers a source of understanding, consolation, and even a measure of optimism about what can be achieved with their retarded children. Groups of this kind are usually affiliated with and benefit from the national and state associations for the mentally retarded.

PREVENTION OF MENTAL DEFICIENCY

Because totally effective treatment of mental deficiency is not possible, for the present at least, much thought has been directed to its prevention. The majority of these efforts assume the inheritable nature of the condition, and thus the preventive measures urged are on the order of segregation or sterilization. But neither of these measures is notably effective. Much mental deficiency results from nonhereditary causes which cannot be identified prior to conception. Even in "hereditary" cases, the disease results from the action of recessive genes carried by parents who themselves are not mentally defective. Sterilization laws are on the statute books of twenty-seven states, but in over half of these no action has been undertaken. With so little positive improvement to recommend these eugenic measures, the social dangers of any program involving segregation or sterilization make them exceedingly unwise approaches to the problem.

Prevention today more aptly lies in increasing our knowledge of prenatal factors which may cause mental deficiency, and in encouraging prospective parents to seek early prenatal care.

17

SYMPTOMATOLOGY
IN MENTAL DISEASE

Abnormal behavior has traditionally been differentiated and classified in terms of symptoms. A symptom is a manifestation of disorder; it may be internally experienced (for example, the irrational fears in the neurotic) or externally observed (for example, profuse perspiration during anxiety, or the rigid posturing of the catatonic). Symptoms of mental disturbance are usually seen in a symptom-complex, or syndrome. It is the syndrome that serves to differentiate one disorder from another.

MEANING OF SYMPTOMS

Modern psychopathology holds that symptoms are meaningful in terms of the psychodynamic development of the patient's illness. This is in contrast to earlier thinking, which ascribed primary importance to the symptoms themselves and attempted to provide treatment for their alleviation or elimination. Because it is now widely appreciated that symptoms merely point to an underlying problem, clinical practice today emphasizes the need for understanding the basic causes of their development. The individual personality structure is believed to be of paramount importance because all psychological symptoms arise from the patient's inability to cope with inner feelings or external situations which embody acute or chronic stress. It is therefore generally agreed that there is greater benefit in formulating a treatment program based on an understanding of the patient's total personality than there is in attempting to classify his disorder within a rigid framework of disease entities and thereafter applying a therapeutic procedure thought to be "specific" for that type of disorder. When symptoms are especially disabling or painful, however, efforts may be directed toward treating the symptoms preliminary to deeper therapy.

ORGANOGENIC AND PSYCHOGENIC SYMPTOMS

Symptoms may be classified according to their origin as being either organogenic or psychogenic.

Organogenic Symptoms. In some mental disturbances the principal symptoms are those associated with tissue changes in the brain. These changes may be in response to exogenous factors such as an infection, a toxic agent, or an injury (trauma); examples are the syphilitic infection in general paresis, the alcohol in Korsakoff's syndrome, and a blow on the head. The changes may also be the consequence of endogenous deterioration or change in brain structure (for example, vascular changes in cerebral arteriosclerosis, new growth in brain tumor). Although persons suffering from this class of disorders report a great variety of internal experiences that are psychological in nature (euphoria in the general paretic, persecutory ideas in the senile psychotic), it is the organic symptoms, readily recognizable through simple observation or laboratory findings, that indicate the nature of the disease entity. The symptomatology of the various "organic" mental disturbances is discussed in detail in Chapter 14, Organic Psychoses.

In the organic psychoses, the particular coloring of symptoms is an expression of deep-set factors. Whether or not evidence of psychological disorder has preceded the development of the organic disease, the quality and degree of the symptomatic behavior will be related to the premorbid personality, and the unconscious stresses the patient is experiencing will be reflected during the course of his illness. Treatment must be directed toward more than mere symptom-removal; it must take into consideration not only the organic factors, but also the underlying psychological forces.

It should also be recognized that just as mental symptoms may occur as the result of organic difficulty, so physical symptoms may arise from either psychological or organic causes. This concept and the more common conditions associated with it are discussed in Chapter 7, Psychosomatic Disorders.

Psychogenic Symptoms. Psychogenic symptoms are generally expressions of the unconscious; accordingly, the patient is seldom aware of their origin or meaning. He is, however, aware of an underlying stress, and his symptoms are weapons for combating it. Psychogenic symptoms, therefore, do not "just happen"; they have a more purposive origin.

From psychogenic symptoms the patient derives two satisfactions or "gains": a primary gain and a secondary gain. The *primary gain* is the control of the anxiety and a reduction in the tension the patient is experiencing. The *secondary gain* results when the patient uses the symptoms to win needed sympathy, to avoid unpleasant tasks, or to control others. The last-named type of secondary gain is illustrated in the domineering and neurotic parent who delays or prevents the marriage of a son or daughter by a timely display of disabling but purely psychogenic symptoms.

While the foregoing separation of symptoms into the general categories of organogenic and psychogenic requires serious consideration, it is not useful in the practical clinical determination of the nature of the patient's disorder. Given symptoms may arise in one person as a result of organic factors, in another as a result of psychological factors. Symptoms, in the last analysis, are classified more usefully according to their special characteristic; these are termed as: cognitive, volitional, motor, emotional, and affectional.

SYMPTOMS OF DISORDERED COGNITION

Cognition is the mental process by which an individual becomes aware of and maintains contact with his internal and external environment. It is not correct to regard cognitive symptoms as separate entities; rather they are ways in which a person functions in relation to his surroundings. Thus, when the words "memory" and "attention" are used, in reality they mean "a person who is remembering," or "a person who is attending (paying attention)." The subprocesses of cognition are: sensation and perception, attention, memory, association, judgment, thought, and awareness (consciousness).

Disorders of Sensation and Perception. Sensation is the simple awareness of a stimulus. Perception is sensation *plus* meaning. Symptoms in this area are most often perceptual and involve a misinterpretation of the perceived reality. They may occur in any sense modality. Disorders that are due to malformation or dysfunction of the sensory organs themselves (for example, myopia, color blindness) are not symptoms of personality disturbances, though they may be a form of stress to the individual.

Two symptoms of disordered cognition which particularly require differentiation are illusions and hallucinations.

ILLUSIONS. An illusion is a false perception for which there is or has been a stimulus in external reality. The response is universal, predictable, and can be demonstrated experimentally. The misinterpretation is due to the operation of physical laws (as in the apparent convergence of railroad tracks at a distance or the appearance of a stick bending when it enters water), or predictable psychological confusion.

HALLUCINATIONS. Hallucinations, on the other hand, are false perceptions for which there is no stimulus in external reality (for example, voices heard when no one is speaking, a feeling that insects are crawling on the skin when none are present). The particular hallucination experienced by an individual is an entirely subjective phenomenon, unique for that individual. Persistent or recurrent hallucinations are characteristic symptoms of serious mental illness.

Falling between illusions and hallucinations is a type of perceptual error involving a distortion of some objective stimulus owing to the emotional "set" of the individual (for example, the shadow of a tree may be seen as a threatening person, or a shrill sound of the wind may be interpreted as a cry for help). These are usually due to transitory emotional states and are not necessarily indicative of serious mental disorder.

DISORDERS OF TACTILE SENSE AND SKIN SENSATION. Three symptoms of disordered cognition are closely allied because they are most commonly encountered in disturbances of the sense of touch. *Hyperesthesia* is the abnormal increase in sensitivity of a sensory process, most often seen in exaggerated sensitivity to heat, cold, pain, or touch. *Anesthesia* is the total absence of sensitivity of the skin's sensory organs. It may be generalized, over a large area of the body, or partial, as in loss of sensation in one hand or arm. When anesthesia is produced deliberately to eliminate pain in the course of surgery, the affected area is predictable on the basis of the known distribution of nerve fibers. When anesthesia is functional, the affected area may not coincide with the neural pathways which ordinarily produce anesthesia. *Paresthesias* are false or distorted sensations, usually of the sense of touch. Its most common forms are: *acroparesthesia,* a recurrent numbness of the extremities for which no apparent cause can be found; *astereognosis,* the inability to perceive accurately the form of a familiar object by touching it; and *phantom limb,* the phenomenon experienced by amputees, who even after an amputation feel sensations which they ascribe to the missing limb.

OTHER SYMPTOMS OF DISORDERED SENSATION OR PERCEPTION. *Syn-*

esthesia is a condition in which a stimulus appropriate to one sense organ is perceived in terms of another. It is not uncommon to have an individual report an auditory-visual fusion, in which he perceives a musical tone as a color. Sensations of color have also been reported to accompany sensations of other sense organs.

The sense of smell is subject to disturbance in two conditions: *Anosmia* is the partial or total absence of sensitivity to odor. *Hyperosmia* is exaggerated increase in this sensitivity.

The musculoskeletal system is not without its role in disorders of sensation and perception. *Hyperkinesthesis* is exaggerated sensitivity to bodily movement; it arises from a disturbed sense of movement. *Hypokinesthesis* is decreased sensitivity to bodily movement.

Disorders of Attention. Attention is the application and concentration of mental energy in a cognitive process. It may arise internally as an anticipatory or purposive set, or externally as the result of a given stimulus (loud noise, flashing light). Three disturbances of attention are mentioned here: *Distractibility* is the ready and rapid shifting of attention through a series of unimportant stimuli. *Aprosexia* is the inability to attend consistently, even for a brief period of time, to a given situation, regardless of its importance. *Hyperprosexia* is extremely concentrated attention resulting in a narrowing of the perceptual field.

Disorders of Memory. Memory is the mental process which includes the acquisition and retention of information and its subsequent recall and recognition. As in the case of many other cognitive disorders, these take on the form of exaggerated, reduced, and distorted sensitivity. *Hypermnesia* is a condition of exaggerated or heightened recall, in which the individual can describe past experiences to the minutest detail. *Amnesia,* or loss of memory, can be partial or complete, temporary or permanent. In *anterograde* amnesia the patient is unable to acquire and retain *new* information, though he can recall remote experience accurately. This condition may accompany stuporous, drugged, or confused states, which make learning impossible. In *retrograde* amnesia the individual is unable to recall or recognize events or information of which he was previously aware, though his capacity for remembering subsequent events (that is, subsequent to the appearance of the amnesia) is unimpaired. *Paramnesia* is a disorder of recognition in which an individual distorts familiar past memories. An example of this is the *déjà vu phenomenon,* a rather common experience in which one feels that what he is encountering here and now has been encountered before. This feeling may be very strong and convincing even when one is aware that the event and the surroundings are entirely new.

Disorders of Association. Association is the mental process through which a sense impression or memory image tends to elicit the recall of another image or concept which was previously related to it. The process implies the existence and operation of a connecting neural network, and clinical and experimental evidence in cases of brain damage tends to confirm this implication. An appreciation of the almost incomprehensible complexity and intricacy of the nerve structure in the brain points to the limitless potential that individuals have for establishing associations.

In normal mental life, associations occur continuously and in a reasonably ordered pattern. The pattern may be determined by several factors: current environmental circumstances, recent events, previous learning, expectancy or "set," habit patterns of the individual, and his needs and emotional history. The relationships of contiguity, similarity, and contrast assist in the process, as do primacy, recency, frequency, and intensity, all of which are fundamental to all learning.

SPECIFIC DISORDERS OF ASSOCIATION. Disorders of association are manifest in underactivity, overactivity, blocking, and distortion. Specific disorders of this class are: *retardation,* the occurrence of associations at a much slower rate than is normal; *dearth of ideas* (also called "poverty of ideas"), a deficiency in the number of available associations, as is seen for example in mental defectives; *perseveration,* persistent recurrence of a single association in which the individual seems to be incapable of shifting from the idea once he has expressed it; *blocking,* inability to form associations, ranging from a temporary situation produced by a strong emotional reaction to long-lasting blocking, as seen in severe mental disorder; *flight of ideas,* abnormally rapid flow of associations characterized by frequent shifts of topic; *incoherence,* a flow of apparently unconnected associations which may take on the form of "word salad"—a string of unrelated words or neologisms (newly coined words); and *aphasic disorders,* a group of symptoms which require special consideration and differentiation.

APHASIC DISORDERS. Aphasia is a generic term, first used in 1864, which describes partial or complete loss of the ability to use or understand language. It implies a break in the associative process owing to organic brain damage. The disorder assumes several forms, classified as: (1) predominantly *expressive* aphasias, in which defects in articulation and in the formation of words are the most prominent; (2) predominantly *receptive* aphasias, in which the defect is largely one of understanding spoken or written language; (3) *expressive-receptive* aphasias, in which language function is seriously impaired on both fronts; and (4) *amnesic* aphasias, in which the defect consists of an inability to evoke the names of objects, qualities, or concepts. The *incidence* of the foregoing, in the order given, is in the ratio of 4:3:2:1.

Three different approaches to an understanding of the aphasic disorders find acceptance among neurologists and psychologists working in this field: (1) The aphasias are a series of specific defects of language function, each the result of specifically located lesions in the cerebrum. (2) The aphasias are among the manifestations of a single basic change in the personality of patients with cerebral lesions. (3) The aphasias are symptomatic of a breakdown in the general process of symbol formation and expression. While the last-mentioned approach seems to be the most widely accepted, the fundamental nature of aphasic disorders has not yet been satisfactorily described.

Some of the specific symptoms in this aphasic group are:

Agnosia—inability to recognize the meaning associated with sensory stimulation; frequently the individual is restricted to recognition of objects through tactile sensation.

Agraphia—inability to write.

Alexia—inability to read.

Amimia—inability to imitate gestures.

Anarthria—inability to carry on articulate speech.

Aphonia—inability to produce prescribed sounds.

Autoagnosia—inability to recognize or identify parts of the body.

Disorders of Judgment. Judgment is the mental process through which perceptual experience is interpreted in broader terms. This is achieved by finding relationships in and drawing inferences from one's experiences—a process which leads to the formation of opinions and beliefs on the basis of which value systems are organized.

ERRORS IN JUDGMENT. The individual arrives at his judgments largely in terms of the entire pattern of his experiential background. As a consequence, the pattern of a person's judgments tends to be consistent. Errors in judgment are commonplace in everyday life and in themselves do not imply mental disorder.

DELUSIONS. The erroneous judgments which are symptomatic of mental illness are called delusions. A delusion is a fixed belief which cannot be justified on the basis of fact but which the individual persists in maintaining even in the face of efforts to dissuade him by appeals to reason. The presence of a delusion is a patent indicator of serious mental disorder (psychosis). Analysis of the content of a delusion can lead to an understanding of the dynamic factors causing the illness. It must, however, be recognized that "normal" people hold beliefs which are unsupportable in fact and which may approach the nature of delusions, but sooner or later such individuals recognize the true facts and their beliefs become less intensely maintained and less fixed than those of the mentally disordered person.

Delusions may be either systematized or unsystematized. *Systematized* delusions are woven into highly developed schemes which frequently have a surprising degree of plausibility; the delusional content is logically elaborated but the basic premise is false. *Unsystematized* delusions are hit-or-miss concoctions of disordered thinking which lack logic and consistency.

Delusions may also be classified according to their content. The delusional content manifested by the mentally disordered person usually has a predominant trend, as will be seen in the list that follows:

Delusions of grandeur—false beliefs through which the individual expands his own importance, the significance of his own qualities or actions, or the significance of the events or persons surrounding him, in a totally unrealistic fashion.

Depressive and self-accusatory delusions—unfounded beliefs of the individual that take on expression in accusations against himself for the commission of horrible crimes or the violation of moral codes. (The patient believes he has committed an unforgivable sin.)

Somatic or hypochondriacal delusions—distorted beliefs of a bizarre nature concerning bodily functioning or condition. (The patient believes he is "rotting away" or that his body is emitting foul odors.)

Nihilistic delusions—denial of the existence of the self or the world. (The patient says he is dead or that the world does not exist.)

Delusions of reference—false interpretations of conversation, gestures, and events as having direct reference to the individual himself; usually associated with delusions of persecution. (The term "ideas of reference" is frequently used to describe a similar phenomenon of less intensity.)

Delusions of influence—false beliefs of the individual that he is subject to influence by other persons or unseen forces.

Disorders of Thinking. In the process of thinking, present or past perceptual experiences are symbolically represented and integrated. The forms which thinking may take are: reasoning or problem-solving, reverie, and reminiscing. Capacity for thinking involves the processes of perception, association, and memory. Disorders of thinking are frequently seen in a wide variety of personality disturbances. The principal types of this class of cognitive disorder are:

Autistic thinking—disorder in the process of thinking which involves the failure to maintain the boundary between fact and fantasy. Thought processes are dominated by the individual's desires rather than by the limits of reality. Through autistic thinking the individual is often able to gratify his desires imaginatively at the expense of attempts to satisfy them realistically.

Confabulation—a thinking disorder in which the patient brings together irrelevant and unconnected ideas and events in an attempt to fill gaps created by memory losses.

Obsessive thinking—disordered thinking characterized by the constant recurrence of an idea which the individual himself recognizes as irrational but which he cannot disregard. Mildly obsessive thinking is occasionally encountered in the realm of normal mental experience, but it can ordinarily be minimized by concentration on other matters. Abnormal obsessions are most often morbid or odd in content and cannot be influenced or dispelled by appeals to logic. Obsessive thinking takes on the form of: *intellectual* obsessions, such as preoccupation with metaphysical ideas; *inhibitive* obsessions, consisting of exaggerated doubts or scruples; and *impulsive* obsessions, in which the individual is beset with thoughts of committing cruel or detestable acts, such as harming himself or someone dear to him or gratifying unacceptable sexual desires.

Disorders of Awareness. The mentally disturbed person may suffer impairment of his awareness of the environment in which he moves. The three principal forms of such symptoms of mental disorder are:

Delirium—general confusion accompanied by clouded sensorium, excitement, restlessness, and hallucinatory experiences.

Disorientation—tendency of the individual to lose track of spatial and temporal relationships and of his personal identity.

Stupor—a general lack of responsiveness to any stimulation; in its milder form it may be manifested only as a *clouding of consciousness*.

SYMPTOMS OF DISORDERED VOLITION

The majority of mental patients complain of or exhibit difficulties in making decisions and carrying out actions. Such "volitional" disorders are widely diversified in the manner of their expression in both the mental life and the behavior of the individual. Many psychology texts do not discuss this area, possibly because of the philosophical implications in the use of the term "will." The problems involving volition are, however, inescapable. A normal person feels able to control his behavior; in contrast, a frequent complaint of the mentally disturbed person is that he "cannot help" his thoughts and acts; in other words, he cannot control them. Voluntary action may be impaired by emotional disorders, cognitive disorders, organic brain damage, and lack of training or excessive training.

Symptoms seen in the mentally ill which may be regarded as disorders of volition are listed below.

Abulia—"weakness" of volition; inactivity resulting from inability to make decisions or initiate behavior. (A patient comes to a doorway and stands motionless for a long period of time, unable to make up his mind to pass through.)

Compulsion—a condition in which the individual feels driven to perform acts which are recognized as irrational or purposeless; occasional compulsive acts which do not interfere with the adjustive behavior of the individual are common and may be considered a normal occurrence. *Morbid compulsions* are contrary to the will of the subject; they interfere in a major way with his ability to meet the demands of everyday living. Some typical compulsions are: uncontrolled repetitive hand washing, counting, and ritualistic behavior in dressing and undressing. *Kleptomania* is compulsive stealing, frequently of articles that have symbolic rather than practical value to the individual. *Pyromania,* compulsive fire-setting, is regarded as a symbolic form of sexual gratification.

Negativism—inability to act upon suggestion, frequently resulting in action opposite to that suggested.

Rigidity—lack of flexibility in deciding to alter one's behavior. (An extreme form is *stereotypy,* in which the individual repeats mechanically some gesture or movement already in progress.)

SYMPTOMS OF MOTOR DISORDER

Motor behavior is behavior involving muscular movement. Skeletal muscles, which produce movements of the body frame and the limbs, are referred to as *striate* (i.e., striped) muscles; those which activate the viscera, the internal organs of the body, are called *smooth* muscles. The latter are not normally under voluntary control, and the individual has little awareness of their activity.

Because it is responsive to the environment, motor behavior is one of the avenues through which human beings express certain aspects of personality. Disorders of motor behavior can arise as symptoms of physical or emotional disturbance and are thus differentiated as *organic* or *functional.* Motor symptoms are broadly grouped in three categories: hyperactivity, hypoactivity, and disordered activity.

Hyperactivity. An abnormally high level of muscular activity is seen in two principal types of symptoms: *motor restlessness,* in which there is overactivity of all forms of muscular responses, with movements speeded up and intensity of response heightened (ranging from the restlessness of a nervous child to the manic activity of a psychotic patient); and *hypertonicity,* wherein muscular tension is heightened even when the body is not in motion (ranging from the transient tension associated with normal emotional response to the persistent and chronic tensions seen in some types of organic brain damage).

Hypoactivity. The level of muscular activity may be considerably reduced. The three principal symptoms of this kind are: *motor retardation,* in which over-all activity is reduced (from the listlessness associated with gloom to the stuporous state of a severely depressed person); *atonicity,* in which the muscles are in a state of subnormal tonus or contraction (which may involve the whole body or particular muscle groups); and *paralysis,* or complete loss of function of a muscle or muscle group.

Disordered Activity. A large number of symptoms of motor disorder are neither hyperactive nor hypoactive in nature, but rather maladjustive, in that they do not suitably meet environmental demands. The chief symptoms of disordered motor activity listed alphabetically are:

Apraxia—inability to manipulate objects in a purposive manner.

Ataxia—in-co-ordination in the movements of the limbs or in posture, usually associated with a neurological disorder.

Athetosis—tentacle-like movements which are continuous, diffuse, and often painful.

Choreiform movements—widespread, jerky, irregular, involuntary movements seen most often in children and associated with Sydenham's chorea (St. Vitus's dance), a disease resulting from brain infection, often following rheumatic heart disease.

Convulsions—continuous, violent spasms widely distributed over the body and usually accompanied by a loss of consciousness. They may begin in a limited area and spread, or they may be generalized from the very beginning. A *Jacksonian convulsion* is one limited to a specific muscle group. Like spasms, convulsions may be tonic or clonic in nature. The convulsion most widely encountered is the *grand mal* attack of the epileptic patient, but convulsions also arise from many other conditions.

Spasm—involuntary contraction of muscle or group of muscles. In *tonic spasm* the contraction is continuous for a period of time; contractions which come intermittently are *clonic spasms*. Spasms believed to be functional in origin are distinguished from other types and are called *tics;* some tics frequently observed are: eye-blinking, twitching of shoulders, sniffling, and clearing the throat.

Tremors—slight rhythmic, involuntary contractions of muscle fibers. They are described as slow or fast, coarse or fine, regular or irregular. Symptoms may occur in two forms: the *intention tremor,* which occurs only when a voluntary movement is attempted, and the *passive tremor,* which is present even though no attempt at motion is being made.

SYMPTOMS OF DISORDERED EMOTION AND AFFECTION

There is probably no form of behavior, however prosaic, which does not involve some element of emotional or affective response. Under appropriate circumstances emotion may be strong and yet be considered entirely normal. It therefore becomes necessary to establish criteria which will help to differentiate a "normal" from an "abnormal" emotional response. Among commonly accepted criteria indicating normal emotion are: (1) predictability and appropriateness, the emotion being usual, expected, and relevant to the stimulus situation; (2) duration, the emotion being neither continued for an undue length of time, nor shut off too abruptly, considering the nature and importance of the precipitating circumstances; and (3) intensity, the emotion expressed being neither too weak nor too strong in relation to the situation.

Abnormal Emotional Patterns. Uncontrolled emotional intensity becomes critical when the potential for injuring ones self or others exists. Emotional patterns which are considered abnormal because they do not meet one or another of the foregoing criteria are:

Affect which is inappropriate—a symptom of disordered emotion in which there is noteworthy discrepancy between the nature of the emotion expressed and the situation which aroused it, as when one laughs at a time of tragedy. Inappropriateness of emotion is generally characteristic of psychotic behavior, though a transitory occurrence of it need not be regarded as evidence of personality disorder.

Affect which is excessively rigid—a persistent maintenance of a given mood despite the occurrence of stimuli that usually evoke a different emotional response.

Ambivalence—simultaneous existence of opposite feelings toward the same person or object. This is one of the key concepts of psychoanalytic theory, which holds that ambivalence characterizes many of our deeper feelings.

Anxiety—a state of tension associated with apprehension, worry, feelings of guilt, sense of insecurity, and need for reassurance. Anxiety is largely an anticipatory response, the dynamic precipitating factor being unconscious. Without some degree of anxiety that is in accord with reality, an individual would be without concern for future events which is so essential to his protection. Morbid anxiety, however, overwhelms the individual and leads to paralysis of decision and action. It is typically accompanied by a host of psychosomatic symptoms, such as profuse perspiration, difficulty in breathing, gastric disturbances (for example, peptic ulcers), and rapid heart beat. Anxiety is a core symptom of all psychopathological conditions.

Apathy—a symptom characterized by marked reduction in or complete absence of emotional response in situations which may be expected to arouse emotions.

Depression—a mood characterized by feelings of dejection and gloom. It is frequently associated with motor retardation, feelings of worthlessness or guilt, and dread of impending disaster. Depressions may be mild or deep; in their extreme manifestation they may lead to attempts at suicide.

Elation—feelings of intense and excessive well-being. The extreme form of inappropriate elation, *euphoria,* is usually a symptom of a psychosis.

Emotional lability—a symptom in which the patient exhibits extreme instability and variability of emotional response. One frequently seen form is the *mood swing,* in which the individual passes rapidly from one extreme of emotion to another.

Unreasonable guilt feelings—guilt feelings are emotional responses in which the person expresses the feeling of blameworthiness regarding an act, desire, idea, or impulse which is contrary to his own ethical standards, and which has not been expiated. These complex responses may not only appear in consciousness as observable symptoms but also may reside in the unconscious where they operate as causes of other symptoms, such as anxiety, compulsion, obsession, and phobias.

All feelings of guilt are derived from the superego and/or the conscience. Although many authors use the terms interchangeably, superego may be distinguished from conscience as follows: The *superego* is a set of attitudes derived from internalized social values which are used by the individual to evaluate his own behavior. It is affective, irrational, largely unconscious, and the source of emotional guilt which may be neurotic or pathological. The superego is adopted by the child from parental sanctions without reflection upon, or insight into, the meaning of his own experience. *Conscience,* on the other hand, involves intellectual judgment concerning right and wrong; it is conscious and self-reflective, and is the source of normal moral guilt (e.g., a normal reaction to sin in the theological sense). Conformance to the demands of the superego represents a childish and dependent mode of behavior; responses to the dictates of conscience represents a mature evaluation of realistic duties and responsibilities.

In the normal sense, guilt feelings constitute a means of controlling one's behavior so that one meets the duties and responsibilities of everyday living. Even in the normal experiencing of guilt there will be variations in the intensity of the feeling.

Regarded as pathological are those guilt feelings which arise from unconscious wishes or impulses and which are usually disproportionate to the consciously experienced situation. Such pathological feelings of guilt are unreasonable and beyond the control and insight of the individual; paradoxically, these symptoms of unconscious turmoil do serve the function of helping the individual maintain a kind of pathological equilibrium. The need for punishment found in many emotionally disturbed patients is derived from pathological feelings of guilt. Feelings of guilt also serve as balancing forces for unconscious hostility and unacceptable sexual urges.

Irritability—the tendency to overrespond to situations with varying degrees of anger or impatience. This may range from chronic complaining, through frequent expressions of annoyance at trivial incidents, to the explosive violence of the temper tantrum.

Disorders of Affection. The normal need for love and affection may be distorted in several ways; the individual may be unable to give or receive love, or he may be overdemanding and indiscriminate in his love relationships. These may result from basically unconscious feelings of hostility, anxiety, or insecurity, which are usually lifelong patterns set in early childhood. Another distortion in the expression of affection is jealousy. Although occasional jealousy may be related to the intensity of the love feelings, persistent jealous reactions are pathological and indicative of marked insecurity and ambivalence in the love relationship.

18

THE DIAGNOSTIC PROCESS

The scientific approach to an understanding of the nature of an individual's disordered behavior requires thoroughgoing and objective study before a conclusion is reached or a decision for action (treatment) is made. Diagnosis in clinical psychology and psychiatry is notably different from that in the case of many somatic disorders, wherein the appearance of abnormal chemical characteristics in blood or urine, the isolation of a microorganism in the feces, or even the mere observation of manifest symptoms such as fever, flushed complexion, immobility of a limb, or bowel upset will often point directly and unmistakably to the existing disorder. The ideal diagnosis of disordered behavior must take into account *the whole person,* with full realization of the continuing interaction between soma and psyche, or body and mind. This is frequently a tedious, time-consuming process, constituting a distinct challenge to the diagnostician's powers of description and interpretation.

Nor can diagnosis be an end in itself; expertly done, it combines a statement of the dynamic and etiological factors and an estimate of the prognosis, along with the usual identification of the patient's condition in terms of one of the accepted clinical entities. So comprehensive an approach requires the combined efforts of physician, psychologist, social worker, and psychiatrist operating as a team.

THE INTERDISCIPLINARY APPROACH

The mentally disturbed patient is studied through individual and family interviews, psychological examination, laboratory reports, school records, and social investigations—in a word, whatever will contribute to a complete picture of the background of the disturbance.

The *physician* conducts physical and neurological examinations in order to identify the organic factors which may be of etiological importance to the patient's disordered state. Examples of such factors are: a severe and protracted illness in childhood, an injury to the brain or spinal cord, persistent intestinal upset, headache, blurred vision, glandular imbalance.

The *psychologist* conducts interviews with the patient, administers and summarizes the results of a battery of psychological tests which assist him in evaluating the individual's abilities and personality dynamics.

The *psychiatric social worker,* through the techniques of the interview and the field visit, prepares a life history of the patient which includes his developmental record, school accomplishment, social and marital adjustments, work experience, economic status, and other related factors.

The *psychiatrist* studies the mental status of the patient in relation to all other findings.

While the trend today is toward the establishment of a diagnosis through an interdisciplinary approach, the ultimate responsibility for pinpointing the diagnosis and for setting up the treatment program rests with the psychiatrist.

THE DIAGNOSTIC PROCEDURES

The specific procedures employed in the diagnosis of behavior and personality disorders are: the medical and neurological examinations, the case history, the psychological examination (which emphasizes psychological testing procedures), and the psychiatric examination.

The Medical Examination. Although this examination may be conducted by the psychiatrist, in actual practice it is almost always done by another physician. A general medical history is taken and the functioning of the various organ systems of the body is investigated by both direct examination and laboratory studies, to discount the presence of any physical conditions having a bearing on the presenting problem—the personality disorder. Among the phenomena commonly studied are the metabolic and endocrine functions, cardiac activity, blood and urine chemistry, and gastrointestinal and genitourinary function.

The Neurological Examination. This may be done as part of the medical study, but it may be done by a neurologist if the behavior disorder suggests the possibility of disturbance of the brain or the spinal cord; this would be true, for example, if brain damage (from injury or infection) were suspected. Some of the procedures used in the neurological examination follow.

Tests of reflex mechanisms. There are several tests which serve to establish whether the central and autonomic nervous systems are functioning normally. Examples are the *knee-jerk test* and the *Babinski test* (response of the great toe to the stroking of the under side of the foot).

Electroencephalography. The EEG (electroencephalogram) records the changes in the electrical potential of the brain. Patterns of brain waves are studied by combinations of electrodes placed on different areas of the scalp. Epileptics show abnormal wave patterns that are specifically diagnostic of epilepsy. Brain wave patterns are also used to help diagnose brain tumors. Abnormalities have been observed in other mental disorders, but they are not sufficiently specific to be of diagnostic value.

Ventriculography. Also called *pneumoencephalography,* this test serves to determine the presence of structural changes in the brain by means of an X ray of that organ after air has been injected into the ventricles.

X ray of the spine and skull. Anomalies of structure, injury, or neoplasm may be discovered by roentgenography.

Biochemical analysis of the cerebrospinal fluid. The cerebrospinal fluid is studied to discover possible infectious organisms and to determine abnormalities of the fluid chemistry.

The Case History. The case history is usually obtained by the psychiatric social worker from the patient or a close relative. A typical case includes the following data.

1. Identifying data (name, address, age).
2. Statement of the presenting problem (symptoms, complaints).
3. Health history (illnesses, serious disease, surgical operations).
4. Developmental history (course of growth in infancy and childhood, maturation).
5. Family history (description of the family constellation, its health history and interpersonal relationships).
6. Educational history (school and college progress).
7. Work history (record of occupations, length of service, general occupational adjustment).
8. Patient's interpersonal relationships (patient's attitude and behavior toward others in various aspects of his life experience).
9. Psychosexual history (sexual habits and attitudes of patient).
10. Marital history (statement of marital status and description of marital adjustment).

11. Special personal habits and interests (talents, skills, hobbies).

12. Personality traits (description of mannerisms, reactions, moods, and emotional patterns of the patient).

The Psychological Examination. The psychological examination is conducted by the clinical psychologist. Although he also uses the interview technique, his principal function in the diagnostic team is the administration and interpretation of a battery of psychological tests which may vary in content from one type of diagnostic problem to another. It is the psychologist's responsibility to select the test battery to be employed with the particular patient. He may include tests of intelligence, aptitude, special function, interest, and personality. The personality tests constitute the significant core of the typical test battery.

INTELLIGENCE TESTS. In clinical practice intelligence tests are used to gauge the patient's mental ability, to distinguish between his potential and his functioning level, and to aid in the process of differential diagnosis. Group tests of intelligence are used, but rarely in the clinical setting. The principal individual tests are the Wechsler-Bellevue Intelligence Scales and the 1937 Revision of the Stanford-Binet Intelligence Scale (recently revised and now available as the 1960 L-M Revision). Where a language handicap exists, intelligence is measured by one of the nonverbal performance scales.

Since their publication in 1939, the *Wechsler-Bellevue Intelligence Scales Form I and Form II* have been the preferred instrument for evaluating the intelligence of patients in the adolescent and adult age range. The scales comprise five verbal subtests (information, comprehension, digit-span, arithmetic, and similarities) and five performance subtests (picture completion, picture arrangement, object assembly, block design, and digit symbol substitution). An additional vocabulary subtest may be included. A revision designated the Wechsler Adult Intelligence Scale (WAIS) was published in 1955 and a scale for children (WISC) in 1949. The Wechsler scales afford much material for qualitative diagnostic evaluation and they give a highly valid quantitative measure of mental capacity.

TESTS OF SPECIAL FUNCTION, APTITUDE, AND INTEREST. For some special diagnostic problems, the *Goldstein-Scheerer* or the *Hanfmann-Kasnin* tests may be used. These tests reveal weaknesses in concept formation and abstract thinking and are useful in work with patients in whom brain damage is suspected, as well as with schizophrenics. Other useful tests of special function are the *Bender*

Visual Motor Gestalt, the *Porteus Mazes,* and the *Lowenfeld Mosaics* tests. Tests measuring various *aptitudes* may be used in cases where vocational adjustment is indicated to be a problem. Tests of *interest,* such as the *Strong Vocational Interest Inventory* or the *Kuder Preference Record,* are similarly useful.

PERSONALITY TESTS. Without question the major contribution of the clinical psychologist in the diagnostic process is his skill in the administration and interpretation of various personality tests. These may be grouped into projective techniques and personality inventories. Although the latter are occasionally used for clinical work, most psychologists have found the projective techniques more sensitive and of greater diagnostic value.

Projective Techniques. Under this heading is grouped a large number of methods for the development of insight into the functioning of the personality. These methods have in common the following characteristics: (1) They evaluate the total personality instead of merely providing scores on a series of discrete traits. (2) The stimulus situations that are used call forth a broad range of individual responses so that a pattern of responses uniquely characteristic of the individual under study will be revealed. (3) The subject is asked to respond to, interpret, or complete a relatively unstructured stimulus (for example, an ink-blot). In doing so he projects his conscious and unconscious needs, wishes, and fears. These projections provide the raw data for analysis by the clinical psychologist. (4) The individual's behavior (beyond his verbal responses) is noted and interpreted under relatively standardized conditions.

The most widely used projective techniques are the *Rorschach Examination,* the *Thematic Apperception Test* (*TAT*), the *Draw-a-Person Test,* the *Make-a-Picture Story Test* (*MAPS*), the *Sentence Completion Test,* and the *Word Association Test.*

The Rorschach Examination, devised by the Swiss psychiatrist HERMAN RORSCHACH (1884–1922), and published in 1921, is the most widely used projective technique for testing the personality of adults and children. It consists of ten ink-blots presented to the subject in a standardized sequence for his interpretation and association. His responses are analyzed on the basis of his use of form, color, texture, movement, content, conventionality, originality, and speed of response. Normative data are available in psychological literature, but the validity of the test interpretation is largely dependent on the skill and sensitivity of the clinician. While the Rorschach test is an aid in diagnostic classification, its principal value is to shed light on the structure and dynamics of the personality. The test reveals such aspects of the personality as contact with reality, richness of mental life, defense mechanisms, anxiety, depression, and other aspects of interpersonal adjustment. The Rorschach Examination also lends itself to a qualitative evaluation of the patient's behavior in the test situation. As is the case with all psychological tests, it is most valuable when used as a part of a battery of tests.

The Thematic Apperception Test (TAT), devised by Morgan and Murray in 1935, consists of a series of pictures of somewhat indefinite content. These are presented to the subject with instructions to make up a story for each picture. The stories are then analyzed according to the predominant themes, mood, or emotions attributed to the characters in each story. The underlying hypothesis is that by a process of identification, which may be unconscious, the patient projects his own drives and conflicts. This test has greater value for uncovering personality dynamics than it has for establishing diagnostic classification. The patterns it reveals are more likely to be related to the life experience of the individual than are those uncovered in the Rorschach. The pictures are also used to stimulate association in therapeutic sessions. For use with children, a variation, the *Children's Apperception Test (CAT)*, has been developed.

The technique used in the TAT lends itself to the development of a special series of pictures for particular diagnostic purposes (for example, prediction of delinquency, or measurement of prejudice).

The Draw-a-Person Test requires that the patient draw a person as well as he can. Upon completion of the first drawing, he is asked to draw a person of the opposite sex. The analysis takes into consideration such factors as size and placement of figures, relationships between the male and female figures, type of lines, distortions, omissions, erasures, and bizarre treatment of various parts of the human figure. The basic assumption is that the drawing represents the patient's body image, and that attitudes, impulses, and conflicts are reflected in his drawing. Problems in psychosexual adjustment are frequently revealed by this technique. The drawings must be interpreted with caution and require a high level of clinical skill. One of the values of this test is its brevity and the ease of administration. A variant of this test is the House-Tree-Person (HTP) drawing test.

The Make-a-Picture Story Test (MAPS) consists of a large number of cut-out figures and various backdrops. The patient is asked to select figures and arrange them before a selected backdrop. He is then asked to tell a story about the arrangement he has made. It is assumed that the patient will select, arrange, and tell stories about the figures in accordance with his own conscious and unconscious needs and feelings.

The Sentence Completion Test consists of a series of incomplete sentences which the subject is asked to complete with his first spontaneous associations. The content of the stimulus phrases is arranged to elicit reactions to principal conflict areas. The hypothesis underlying the technique is that in completing the sentences the patient will reveal his own attitudes toward the areas touched upon. Although standard sentence completion forms are available, interpretation is largely dependent on the ingenuity and clinical skill of the examiner.

The Word Association Test, probably the oldest of all projective techniques, was originally described by Carl Jung. Since his time psychiatrists and psychologists have used lists of words to elicit spontaneous associations from their patients with a view to uncovering conflict areas. Diagnostic indicators of conflict are said to be characterized by lengthy reaction time, odd or bizarre associations, stammering, or other signs of tension. Clinicians vary in the way in which they analyze the association processes revealed by the test.

Other projective techniques include: *The Szondi Test,* which utilizes a series of portraits of psychiatric patients, which the subject is asked to arrange according to preference. His choices are said to reveal material of diagnostic value. *The Rosenzweig Picture Frustration Test* utilizes a series of action pictures in which the patient is required to identify with one of the figures and express his verbalization of the described frustrating situation. Rosenzweig provides normative data on the basis of which various ways of handling aggression may be determined.

Handwriting analysis is another projective method in which detailed, painstaking study is made of the patient's handwriting on the assumption that it is an expression of personality.

Play techniques, although principally used as a therapeutic vehicle for children, may also be used in the diagnostic process. Dolls, puppets, and playhouses are utilized to elicit emotional attitudes and conflicts.

Art analysis utilizes finger painting or more formal means of art expression to reveal patterns of emotional reaction in both adults and children.

Personality Inventories. In these objective, standardized tests, the patient is required to answer specific questions about his own behavior or attitudes. The patient's responses are usually restricted to indicating whether or not a given statement is pertinent or not. Some of the tests are relatively simple, calling for only a "Yes" or "No" response; others require comparisons and selections among several items. Generally speaking, personality inventories have a limited application in clinical practice; they are used mainly with groups, for purposes of preliminary screenings.

Although there are numerous published inventories, the *Minnesota Multiphasic Personality Inventory* (*MMPI*) is the preferred test of this type. It consists of 550 items which have been gathered from the case records of patients having various psychiatric disorders. The degree to which the subject's answers correspond to items normally found in particular types of psychiatric history suggests his tendencies in that direction. Scores are expressed in psychiatric terms and provide measures of tendencies toward the following types of disorders: hypochondriasis, depression, hysteria, psychopathic deviation, paranoia, psychasthenia, schizophrenia, and hypomania. The test also purports to measure masculinity-femininity and sociability. Extensive research has been done with this test, and it stands alone among the inventories with respect to its usefulness in clinical practice.

The Psychiatric Examination. The psychiatric examination utilizes an interview with the patient to observe and evaluate significant aspects of his behavior. Exaggerations, distortions, and the absence of expected responses or the presence of abnormal responses are recorded. The traditional psychiatric examination includes statements on the following.

Appearance and General Behavior. This statement usually describes general health and appearance, habits of dress, personal habits, speech, moods, and sociability.

Attitude and Behavior during the Interview. This statement describes the patient's attitude toward the interviewer (expressive movements as revealed by manner, voice and posture, facial expressions, and motor activity).

Stream of Mental Activity. The data recorded here concern verbal productivity, spontaneity of stream of thought, distractibility, language deviations, and reaction time.

Emotional Reactions. These are related to the patient's general activity, his mental trend or thought content. Generally, the emotional reactions observed by the interviewer and what the patient says about his feelings are recorded. Thus, the interviewer may note whether the emotional reactions are appropriate or not, whether the patient is composed, suspicious, depressed, indifferent, angry, elated, etc.

Mental Trends. The statement with regard to mental trend or thought content describes persecutory trends, hypochondriacal ideas, ideas of unreality, nihilistic ideas, depressive trends, and grandiose ideas or hallucinatory experiences.

Sensorium, Mental Grasp, and Capacity. This statement estimates the patient's intellectual capacities and resources. The estimate is based on the patient's responses to questions that measure his orientation as to time, place, and person, his memory for the remote and recent past, his powers of retention and immediate recall, his abilities in counting, calculation, and writing, and his school and general knowledge.

Summary of Psychiatric Examination. The main findings are summarized and a statement is made concerning the patient's intellectual capacities, evenness of performance, deteriorative trends, and self-evaluation.

19

THE THERAPEUTIC PROCESS

While there is general agreement on the objectives to be sought in treating mental disorder and illness, the procedures employed to achieve these objectives vary according to the professional discipline of the therapist and the school of psychological thought in which he was trained. The principal types of therapy will, however, fall into two classes: *psychotherapy* and *somatotherapy*. Along with these, use is made of supplemental measures—occupational therapy, physiotherapy, recreational therapy—which are properly understood as *therapeutic adjuncts*.

GOALS OF THERAPY

In the field of mental illness, therapy of any type (be it psychotherapeutic or somatotherapeutic) is directed toward promoting a more effective relationship between the individual and his environment and producing in him an inner sense of security and well-being. It must be emphasized that the goal of therapy in any individual case will depend on certain more or less fixed factors (diagnostic findings and the personal history of the patient) and other, extraneous factors which will be brought to bear upon the patient outside the therapeutic experience (family, social, and economic situations). Even within single diagnostic entities, patients bring to therapy varying capacities for setting up satisfactory relationships, and the goal must be set accordingly. Therapeutic goals are described as being either short-range or long-range.

Short-Range Goals. Although the therapy may be directed toward cure, it frequently becomes necessary to set up and accept a more limited goal. In a given case, for example, the realistic goal of the therapist may be simply to maintain the patient's present level of adjustment, and thus protect him from the inroads of a more serious illness; in another case the therapist may find grounds for expecting some improvement in the patient's adjustment, but not enough to hope for resolution of all the patient's problems. The short-range goals, therefore, are directed toward the elimination or amelioration of the patient's symptoms, adjustment of the individual to immediate environmental demands, and release of the patient's pent-up emotions in a controlled setting.

Long-Range Goals. Long-range goals include: development of insight, resolution or modification of the causes of the patient's distress, and development of the patient's concept of himself based on a realistic appraisal of his worth, his potential, and his limitations. When these long-range goals have been attained, one can look forward to such desired end results as increased efficiency, more effective interpersonal adjustment, and a more realistic life pattern, with a consequent improved inner sense of security and well-being.

THE TECHNIQUES OF PSYCHOTHERAPY

From the term "psychotherapy" it can be inferred that techniques of this class are basically psychological in nature. All psychotherapeutic procedures involve a personal interaction between therapist and patient, the essence of which is an alteration of the patient's learning process in contrast to the physiochemical conditioning that characterizes somatotherapies (see page 255). Through talks with the therapist, or in the course of a hypnotic or narcoleptic state, the patient's life experiences and his reactions to them are explored, and interpretations are made. But the therapist is more than an interviewer; his role is a dynamic one, for the patient reacts to him as well as to his own problems, and in this role the therapist is able to foster the unlearning of maladaptive habits of emotional response and the learning of new, healthful habit patterns.

The principal forms of psychotherapy are: psychoanalysis, psychobiological therapy (also called distributive analysis and synthesis), directive psychotherapy, nondirective counseling, hypnotherapy, narcosynthesis, play therapy, group therapy and psychodrama.

Psychoanalysis. The framework of psychoanalytic therapy was developed by Sigmund Freud over a period of years in the course of his private practice as a physician. This framework continues to provide the basis for all forms of psychoanalytic treatment, though the various schools of psychoanalysis differ in the emphasis that is placed on one or more of the methods.

ESSENTIAL METHODS OF PSYCHOANALYTIC THERAPY. The four essential methods and mechanisms of all psychoanalytic therapy are: (1) systematic utilization of free association, (2) dream analysis, (3) the transference neurosis, and (4) interpretation and reeducation, with the goal of resolving the principal emotional problems of childhood. By these methods, the patient's repressed unconscious material is brought to the level of awareness, is explored, and is interpreted in relation to his symptoms, his concept of self (ego), and his relationships with others.

Free Association. Following preliminary interviews during which a case history is obtained and a working diagnosis established, the patient is encouraged to relax by reclining on a couch, with the therapist in the background. He is then instructed to report to the therapist anything and everything that comes to his mind without censorship of any sort. In the early psychoanalytic sessions, the patient may experience great difficulty in achieving this free association; one or more sessions may pass in which he produces nothing which is suitable for the therapist's analysis and interpretation. As the therapeutic relation proceeds, however, the ability to associate freely is developed and this enables the patient to express ideas and feelings which have been repressed, some for a period of many years. The rapidity with which this ability is developed is related to the degree of resistance to therapy displayed by the patient. Nor does free association always proceed evenly or in chronological sequence; it may be interrupted by blocking, withholding of associations, and purposive production of irrelevant and distracting material.

The associations, as ultimately produced by the patient and recorded by the analyst, gradually form a mosaic of ideas and feelings which, while they seem to be incoherent, illogical, and faulty in time sequence, are nevertheless emotionally related. Equipped with his knowledge of the patient's life history and his observation of the patient throughout the therapeutic experience, the analyst recognizes the dynamic meaning of these associations and from time to time guides the patient toward particularly meaningful areas of thought and feeling. The chief virtue of this method is its "ventilating" effect, referred to as "catharsis."

Dream Analysis. Dream analysis is often a fruitful method of psychotherapy. Following the lead of JOSEPH BREUER (1842–1925), Freud perceived that in the dreams reported by his patients lay clues to significant unconscious material. The method has since persisted as a standard practice among psychoanalysts. During a therapeutic session the analyst asks the patient to report his dreams.

The difficulty of recalling the details of a dream is well known, but a patient who has been under analysis for some time and has gained the ability to free-associate readily will also have developed a facility in dream recall. The content thus revealed by the patient, along with the substance of the underlying problems which the dream suggests, are then employed by the therapist as stimuli for further associations. (Dream analysis may be conceived as a form of free association, but in the Freudian concept the dream is so highly organized a form of mental activity that it merits special listing.)

According to Freud, dreams have both a manifest and a latent content. The dream images and their apparent meanings are the *manifest content;* the unconscious, conflictive material, for which the dream images are symbolic substitutes, is the *latent content.* Both levels have importance in the treatment process. The manifest content of dreams is often determined by immediate environmental circumstances and recent or remote life events. The symbols chosen to express the unconscious (latent) meaning of the dream may be universal or accidental. *Universal symbols* are those which have a generally accepted meaning for a given cultural group (such as phallic symbols); *accidental symbols* are those having a special meaning in terms of the life experiences of the individual relating the dream.

Two mental mechanisms characterize the manner in which a person works out a conflict or other problem in his dream. Through *condensation* a single composite image of the manifest content may stand for a number of ideas or feelings. In the mechanism of *displacement,* affect which is in reality associated with one aspect of the dream is expressed in relationship to another aspect. These two mechanisms bring about a *distortion* of the dream content, believed by Freud to be an unconscious device to disguise unacceptable thoughts and feelings and thus protect the ego against a sense of guilt.

The mode of dream interpretation and its application in psychotherapy differ among analytic therapists, depending on the school of psychoanalysis in which they are grounded, but the fundamentals are by and large the same.

Transference Neurosis. A transference neurosis exists when the patient transfers to the therapist the emotions which have been repressed since early childhood. In the treatment experience, such transferred emotions usually emerge as mild manifestations directed toward the analyst. As the therapeutic procedure continues these emotions grow in intensity and duration. In the eyes of the patient, the therapist assumes the role of a stern parent (or other person who stood in this relation to the patient in childhood). This is an extremely valuable instrument for the therapist in his probing of the patient's unconscious because it encourages the patient to relive the emotional experiences of his early years. Referred to as *abreaction,* the patient's response to this mechanism is the most critical phase of the psychoanalysis.

The transference neurosis may lead to attachment to, dependency on, and even love for the therapist (positive transference); or it may give rise to resentment, impatience, and often violent antagonism toward the therapist (negative transference). The latter reaction brings about a severe, though usually temporary, disruption of the therapeutic process. The anxieties aroused by the transference neurosis are among the unpleasant features of psychoanalytic therapy, and if they are not successfully resolved they may be harmful to the patient, in view of their "out-of-the-frying-pan-into-the-fire" effect. It should be noted that a *counter-transference* from a therapist to a patient may develop. To guard against this the therapist must in his own attitudes remain as aloof as possible and must avoid being thrown into the morass of the patient's turmoil.

Interpretation. Interpretation is essential throughout the course of a psychoanalysis; the therapist must be continually alert to opportunities to decipher and interpret the dynamic meaning of free associations, dreams, and the behavior of the patient. He pays particular attention to any feelings that are expressed by the patient and seeks to ferret out the relationship between these feelings and the nature of the material being discussed.

The interpretations offered by the analyst fall into two categories: those which call the patient's attention to the emotions he is expressing (the dynamic significance of which are then explained); and those which help the patient to recognize the defenses he employs to keep threatening or unpleasant feelings repressed.

The analyst must have a keen *sense of timing.* He must be extremely careful to pick the opportune and appropriate time to share his interpretations with the patient. The employment of these repeated interpretations, called the "working through," constitute the essential phase of psychoanalytic therapy. The unveiling of an interpretation at a point when the patient is unprepared to accept it and profit by it can be valueless or even dangerous.

Because interpretation is so critical a matter, the analyst must be completely aware of his own defense mechanisms and drives; otherwise he will fall into the trap of interpreting the patient's dynamic feelings and thoughts in terms of his own life experiences and underlying problems. This is one of the reasons why psychoanalysts are required to undergo a personal analysis.

GOALS OF PSYCHOANALYTIC THERAPY. When the methods employed by psychoanalytic therapy begin to develop in the patient a new insight into the forces of his personality, then the psychoanalytic process is on the road to creating a successful adjustment of the patient to his environment.

Psychobiological Therapy. As an outgrowth of the development of his psychobiological approach to personality, ADOLF MEYER (1886–1950) advocated what has been called a "common-sense" approach to psychotherapy. This therapeutic technique, also known as "distributive analysis and synthesis," considers the total personality in its environmental setting.

ESSENTIAL METHODS OF PSYCHOBIOLOGICAL THERAPY. The analyst using the psychobiological technique may, in the course of the treatment experience, have recourse to reassurance, hypnosis, catharsis (free association), abreaction, and interpretation. The Meyerian approach to therapy was one of the first to insist that *all* the patient's problems (conscious as well as unconscious) must be identified, their causes traced in the life history (distributive analysis), and the patient encouraged to work out solutions under the guiding hand of the therapist (synthesis).

The Life Chart. The therapy begins with the patient's statement of his specific complaints. These are traced historically to their developmental origins, and their special significance to the patient is sought. In the process, the therapist with the patient's help, seeks to develop a *life chart*. Examination of this chart helps the therapist to understand the patient's symptoms in relation to his total personality organization.

The Life History. During the therapeutic sessions, the therapist encourages the patient to discuss all phases of his life history spontaneously; he does not insist that everything be told him. As therapy proceeds, forgotten or neglected materials are brought out and fitted into the total framework. In this way, the causes of the problem behavior become apparent to the patient and he is urged to work out his own solutions.

GOALS OF PSYCHOBIOLOGICAL THERAPY. In a more or less unobtrusive way, the techniques of psychobiological therapy attempt to provide for the patient guidance along the lines of sound principles of mental health. Successful life experiences are evaluated, and the patient's assets are used as the basis for building a more effective life adjustment.

Directive Psychotherapy.
The term "directive psychotherapy" was popularized by F. C. THORNE (1909–   ) in a series of publications in which he recommended more active participation by the therapist than that advocated by the Rogerian school of nondirective counseling (see following section).

ESSENTIAL METHODS OF DIRECTIVE PSYCHOTHERAPY. The methods Thorne described in his directive approach have had a long history in psychotherapeutic practice. These methods are reeducation, persuasion, and direct suggestion.

Reeducation. The foremost advocate of reeducation was Alfred Adler, who viewed the therapist as a teacher whose role was to point out to the patient his maladaptive patterns of behavior and to reeducate the patient toward more effective learning procedures. In the reeducation technique, a definite effort is made to quicken the tempo of treatment. The therapy's success lies in the warmth of the relationship developed between the therapist and patient during the treatment period. Its principal danger is that premature interpretations may be made, thus arousing anxieties and resistances. Other proponents of the reeducation method have been Austin Riggs in this country and Déjèrine in Europe.

Persuasion. An even more active form of directive psychotherapy is persuasion, in which the patient is specifically directed to take certain steps toward the solution of his problem. The effectiveness of the method lies in selecting as the therapy progresses those steps which the patient can carry out.

Suggestion. Suggestion is one of the older practices in psychotherapy and is largely directed toward the relief or elimination of symptoms. It involves the therapist's open or indirect statement to the effect that the patient is getting better or that he is improving. Suggestion has been largely used in relationship with hypnosis. The prescribing of placebos (harmless and ineffectual medication used widely in general medical practice) is a form of suggestion therapy.

GOALS OF DIRECTIVE PSYCHOTHERAPY. The therapist, in his use of the directive methods, endeavors to guide and persuade the patient to the point where he will adopt healthier patterns of adjustment. It is generally accepted that the methods employed by directive therapists are more effective in the treatment of minor maladjustments.

Nondirective Counseling. Also referred to as "client-centered therapy," this technique was originally described by CARL ROGERS (1902–   ) in 1942. Since then, there has been a widespread acceptance of many Rogerian principles of therapy. However, the more rigorous application of his techniques has been mainly confined to the counseling of college students and other young adults with simple adjustment problems.

ESSENTIAL METHODS OF NONDIRECTIVE COUNSELING. Rogers describes the process of nondirective counseling as based on six conditions which are to be met by the therapist. He states that the patient will respond if: (1) the counselor respects the client's responsibility for his own behavior; (2) the counselor recognizes that the client has within himself a strong drive moving him toward maturity and independence and utilizes this force rather than his own efforts; (3) a warm and permissive atmosphere is created, allowing the patient to express or not to express whatever he wishes; (4) simple limits are set on behavior, but not attitudes (for example, the client may express his desire to extend the session beyond the agreed time limit, but the therapist abides by the original schedule); (5) the therapist restricts his activities to indicating his understanding and acceptance of the emotions being expressed by the client, which he may do by sensitively reflecting back and clarifying the client's feelings; and (6) the therapist avoids questioning, probing, blaming, interpreting, advising, suggesting, persuading, and reassuring.

GOALS OF NONDIRECTIVE COUNSELING. During the first session the counselor lays the pattern for the relationship by setting time limits and describing his own nondirective role. Since the client usually expects and wants more active support from the therapist, this "structuring" may have to be repeated. The client usually attempts to break this down by asking for advice or reassurance. Rogers states, however, that if the therapist meets the six major conditions, the client will accept his role and assume responsibility for working through his own problems. Ultimately, the client, through exploring his own attitudes and actions, both negative and positive, will come to a fuller realization of his motivations and a more complete accept-ance of himself. On this basis he will begin to set new, more realistic goals which are more satisfying for him. As the therapy comes to a conclusion, he will begin to make plans for the attainment of these goals.

Hypnotherapy. Hypnotic methods have been in use for almost two hundred years, although the psychological nature of the process was not understood by its early users. Even today, despite wide-spread interest and study, there is still much that is unknown.

ESSENTIAL METHODS OF HYPNOTHERAPY. The essential techniques and uses of hypnotherapy include the hypnotic state, direct sug-gestion, and finally, hypnoanalysis.

The Hypnotic State. The essential condition leading to a state of hypnosis is repetitive stimulation with continued suggestions to relax or sleep. This stimulation may produce responses of varying intensity ranging from a state of mild relaxation (with an ame-nability to suggestion) to deep trance. In deep trance states, the patient, upon suggestion, can experience hallucinations and anes-thesias and has more complete control over some of the autonomic functions of the body. The principal value of hypnosis for therapy is that materials long thought to be forgotten or repressed are readily brought to consciousness.

Direct Suggestion. The simplest (and earliest) use of hypnosis is the elimination of symptoms by direct suggestion. Hypnosis of this sort is used currently to restore memory in amnesia, to eliminate particularly disabling symptoms in hysterical reactions, and at times to aid in differentiating organic from hysterical symptoms.

Hypnoanalysis. A recently developed intensive use of hypnosis is hypnoanalysis, which combines the analytic process with hypnotic techniques. This combination accelerates the process of therapy chiefly through its effect in helping to overcome resistance and bring to consciousness significant repressed materials.

USES OF HYPNOTHERAPY. Merely bringing the repressed materials to the conscious level in the hypnotic state is not enough to effect a cure. Once this condition has occurred, however, the material be-comes more readily available in the nonhypnotic state and so can effectively be used in developing interpretation and insight. Abreac-tion (see page 248) can be facilitated by causing the patient to regress to the ages at which critical emotional experiences occurred. The technique may be used to induce dreams, which may then be subject to analysis. Hypnosis may be used with most of the other psycho-therapeutic techniques. It has been employed recently in medical and dental practice to induce relaxation and control pain. One short-coming of hypnotic methods is the lack of adequate responsiveness of many patients. Amateur use of hypnosis must be considered dangerous.

Narcosynthesis. Also called *narcoanalysis,* this type of treatment depends on the use of drugs to induce a state of relaxation and increased suggestibility.

ESSENTIAL METHODS OF NARCOSYNTHESIS. Two drugs frequently used are sodium amytal and sodium pentothal, either of which is administered by slow intravenous injections until adequate relaxation is achieved.

USES OF NARCOSYNTHESIS. The use of narcosynthesis came into prominence during World War II as a means of treating cases of combat fatigue. During the narcotically induced trance the soldier was encouraged to relive his traumatic experiences; in doing so with the help of the therapist, he gradually became desensitized and was able to tolerate those experiences in consciousness. In civilian prac-tice, the use of narcosynthesis is limited largely to transient person-ality disorders and to the treatment of such symptoms as amnesia, hysterical paralysis, and other conversion symptoms. The use of these drugs is also helpful in some problems of differential diag-nosis.

Play Therapy. Because children find it difficult or impossible to verbalize their conflicts, in play therapy they are encouraged to engage in free play in which conflict can be more adequately expressed.

ESSENTIAL METHODS OF PLAY THERAPY. Various media for free play are offered such as dolls, puppets, miniature household furni-ture, clay, sand, water, finger paints, and other toys. Through the manipulation of these objects and the verbalizations which accom-pany the play, the child unwittingly reveals to the therapist his feelings of frustration, hostility, or fearfulness.

USES OF PLAY THERAPY. The free play activities provide a thera-peutic release of emotional tensions in a controlled setting. The play with dolls is particularly helpful in understanding the dynamic relationships in the family as the child experiences them, and it frequently allows the child to express unconscious aggressions. Play with creative materials such as clay and finger paints is useful in diagnosis as well as in providing release of tension for the patient. The creative materials are also used with adults.

Group Therapy. Because of the large ratio of patients to therapists, psychotherapists have resorted to the treatment of patients in groups. The dynamic factor evolving from the group situation itself brings into play new factors which some practitioners consider an advantage over individual therapy.

ESSENTIAL METHODS OF GROUP THERAPY. In practice, group therapy has as many variations as individual therapy. The earliest forms of group therapy were largely didactic with the group leader lecturing, persuading, and directing. With the new developments in this field, the group leader has come to serve the same function for the group as does the individual therapist for his patient. He encourages expression, examines motives, offers interpretations, and gradually elicits participation of the individual members of the group in this function. As currently practiced, the essential features of group therapy include the following:

1. The group is selectively screened to achieve some degree of homogeneity and congeniality. The factors considered are age range, sex distribution, diagnosis, general personality characteristics, and prognosis. The controlling consideration and the weight given to any of these factors in selecting patients depend upon the therapist. Groups are usually small, the optimum number ranging from six to ten. Most groups meet once or twice a week for several months or longer.

2. Varying practices exist in the use of group therapy in its relation to individual therapy. Thus, some therapists will select and prepare a patient for group therapy only after a course of individual therapy; others will maintain the patient in individual and group therapy concurrently; some will enter the patient directly into the group setting without individual therapy.

3. The therapist attempts to create a permissive atmosphere which encourages spontaneity of expression. In the beginning, patients relate their own symptoms and problems. Gradually, they embark upon discussions of significant emotional experiences in their outside life, and, eventually, they evaluate and comment upon the experiences of other members.

4. In the group situation conformance to a rigid pattern of participation is not required. Thus, patients can participate in their own manner, at their own pace, and with varying degrees of resistance.

Uses of Group Therapy. Participation in such a group experience tends to break down the patient's feelings of isolation and the uniqueness of his illness, thereby allaying his anxieties and encouraging him to discuss more fully his inner feelings. As in individual therapy, the patient's participation in group therapy provides for him a release of tension and the abreactive experience of reliving a number of emotionally charged incidents. In some of the more intensive forms of group therapy, analysis of the transference relationships developed in the group is also provided.

A particular advantage of group therapy is that it affords an opportunity for a social experience in which the patients may test their own growth in intersocial relations and the therapist may observe the patient's progress.

Psychodrama. A variant form of group therapy, developed by J. L. MORENO (1892–   ), is psychodrama, in which the patient is encouraged to act out before an audience and in unrehearsed fashion a role of emotional significance.

Essential Methods of Psychodrama. As developed and practiced by Moreno, a highly theatrical setting is used. This places the acting-out in the realm of fantasy and, thus, the patient feels free to express deeply rooted attitudes and intense motivations. As the role is developed, the realistic implications of his dramatic behavior become apparent. The skill of the therapist in recognizing and interpreting the dynamics that are revealed facilitates the therapeutic process.

Uses of Psychodrama. In the acting-out of his inner conflicts, the patient is able to achieve some release and may develop new insights which enable him to modify his real life role.

Role-playing. Role-playing is a variant of psychodrama which dispenses with the theatrical props and is widely used to stimulate discussion and develop new perceptions in a variety of group situations such as classrooms, human relations programs in business and industry, and training conferences.

THE TECHNIQUES OF SOMATOTHERAPY

Although a number of medical agents and techniques have been used over the past twenty years with a certain measure of success in the treatment of the more severe mental disorders, no full understanding of why they work has been reached. Medical research on these procedures suggest that they be used with extreme care and only for particular types of mental illness since the total impact of these approaches on the patient is not yet fully known. The principal medical approaches may be classified as chemical, electrical, and surgical.

Chemical Methods. Chemical methods involve the alteration of bodily function by the introduction of some chemical agent. The principal chemical methods are: insulin shock therapy, metrazol therapy, chemical narcosis, the use of tranquilizing agents, and the induction of fever. Research on the use of other chemical agents has been widespread and is continuing with attention being given to the effects of carbon dioxide, vitamins, and hormones (such as sex steroids, ACTH, cortisone) and other products which influence the biochemistry of the nervous and glandular systems. Research is also being carried on to investigate the production of abnormal mental states in normal individuals by such chemical agents as d-lysergic acid with the hope of a clearer understanding of the metabolic changes involved in the disease process.

INSULIN SHOCK THERAPY (also called *insulin coma* therapy). M. J. SAKEL (1900–1958) announced in 1933 the results of a study of insulin therapy in various mental conditions. He used insulin in the treatment of morphine addiction. The occasional unintended deep comas produced by the insulin were noted to have beneficial effects on personality. This suggested to him the possibility of using it for other mental disturbances, especially schizophrenia.

Since the introduction of insulin shock therapy to this country, it has remained one of the important forms of somatotherapy for schizophrenics. The procedure is to give the patient increasing doses of insulin on almost a daily basis until the dosage required to produce a state of shock is established. The insulin lowers the blood sugar, producing a state of severe hypoglycemia with coma and at times convulsions. At first, the patient reactions are weakness, profuse perspiration, sleepiness, mild muscular twitching, spasms, and grunting. Gradually, over a three- or four-hour period, he slips into a progressively deepening state of coma. (In some patients the transition stage is accompanied by a convulsive reaction, although this result is not intended.) The patient is permitted to remain comatose for a period varying from a few minutes to one hour. The coma is terminated by the administration of sugar orally, or by nasal tube, or intravenously. Although Sakel himself gave treatments six times a week for a total of twenty to fifty treatments, modern psychiatric practice has introduced many variations in this pattern. Since considerable physical stress is experienced in the treatment, patients with a history of heart weakness, tuberculosis, and severe arteriosclerosis are usually excluded from such therapy.

The psychiatric consensus is that the introduction of insulin shock represents an important advance in the treatment of schizophrenia. Recovery or improvement rates after insulin shock as reported in psychiatric literature vary considerably. However, it is safe to estimate that from 60 to 70 per cent so treated recover or show improvement. Further research is necessary to determine the types of schizophrenic patient most responsive to insulin treatment, the duration of improvement or cure reported, and the extent of other effects on the functioning of the patient. There are indications that when insulin shock treatment is accompanied by psychotherapy the recovery rate is higher. Many psychiatrists feel that the principal role of such forms of somatotherapy as insulin shock and tranquilizing drugs is to make the patient accessible to psychotherapy.

METRAZOL SHOCK THERAPY. On the basis of his clinical observations, VON MEDUNA (1896–   ) assumed there was an antagonism between epilepsy and schizophrenia and theorized that the production of convulsive seizures in schizophrenic patients might have beneficial results. After experimenting with camphor as a convulsant, he turned to metrazol because it reliably produced an immediate convulsion following intravenous injection. Because of the violence of the convulsive seizure, definite precautions must be taken to protect the patient against physical damage such as fractures, dislocations, strangulation, and tongue bite. A course of treatment usually extends from 4 to 15 weeks, during which time 12 to 30 seizures are induced. Metrazol treatment has been largely replaced by electric shock treatment.

CHEMICAL NARCOSIS. The induction of prolonged sleep by means of sodium amytal or other sedatives as a means of treating mental disturbances was first described in 1922. It was widely used in World War II to provide an opportunity for rest and recuperation for soldiers disturbed by combat conditions. It must be looked upon as merely an adjunct to other forms of therapy and is used principally to keep the patient comfortable until he becomes accessible to psychotherapy.

TRANQUILIZERS. Since 1953, two drugs, chlorpromazine and reserpine, have been given considerable attention because of their notable effect on the behavior of the mentally disturbed. Both drugs apparently work in some way to counteract or subdue the physiological factors attendant on anxiety, and both have been found to produce a tranquilizing effect in patients suffering from many types of disturbances. Early reports of their use were highly optimistic. As further evaluation has continued, however, a more cautious view has been taken. The drugs undoubtedly serve to make the hospital care, especially of severely disturbed patients, a less difficult problem. As a result of their use it is possible to return a great number of patients to their homes. They are also in widespread use in office practice for the relief of anxiety and tension in nonhospitalized patients. The drugs are of most benefit in calming excited or agitated patients but are ill-advised in depressive cases because of danger of suicide. Known undesirable side effects, such as jaundice and convulsions demand caution in their prescription. As with the other forms of somatotherapy, chlorpromazine and reserpine cannot be looked upon as cures in themselves but rather as valuable adjuncts in caring for the anxious, agitated, or disturbed patient. New tranquilizing drugs are being developed regularly.

FEVER THERAPY. Before the development and use of antibiotics for the control of infectious diseases, several organic psychoses of infectious origin, particularly general paresis, were best controlled by the induction of a high fever in the patient. The principal means of accomplishing this was by inoculating patients with malaria. Later, electrical or mechanical methods were found more adequate in producing a controlled level of fever. Since then, these methods have been displaced by use of antibiotics.

Electrical Methods. Passing electric current through the brain in controlled amounts has been found to produce effects somewhat similar to those produced by chemical agents. The strength, duration, and phase of the current can be controlled by the physician to produce either a convulsive seizure, narcosis, or a coma.

ELECTRIC SHOCK TREATMENT. The inducement of convulsive seizures by electric shock was first described by CERLETTI and BINI in 1938. It has considerably displaced metrazol treatment because it is easier to administer, affords greater control, and does not seem to produce as much anxiety in the patient. Electric shock is induced by passing an electric current through the cortex by means of two electrodes placed on opposite sides of the head. The amount of current used varies from patient to patient. The shock produces unconsciousness immediately and the patient experiences no pain. The convulsive seizure usually lasts no longer than one minute. Usually the patient remains stuporous after the convulsion for about an hour. Modern practice has refined the treatment by use of sedatives and muscle relaxants before the application of electrodes.

Electric shock is usually administered two or three times a week, although special circumstances may cause a change in this pattern. The patient's reaction to treatment and his rate of improvement determine the duration of treatment. Usually, however, one course of treatment consists of ten to twelve shocks. Clinical practice indicates that patients for whom such treatment will be beneficial tend to respond with some improvement after the first few convulsions. For many patients only four or five shock treatments are sufficient to produce the desired improvement. Electric shock treatment is most helpful in the treatment of depressed patients, with some sources reporting a recovery rate of 90 per cent. Used in combination with insulin shock for schizophrenic patients, the recovery rate varies with the type of schizophrenia. One undesirable effect of electric shock treatment is the impairment of memory, which initially may be severe but in most cases lessens with the passage of time.

ELECTRONARCOSIS. This form of treatment is characterized by a sustained loss of consciousness during which the patient experiences mild convulsive movements. After a 30 second shock at 250 milliamperes, current is reduced and maintained for seven minutes. These treatments may extend over a period of ten to fourteen days. The period of narcosis seems to make the patient more amenable to a discussion of his mental conflicts, and the period during which he is recovering consciousness may be used for psychotherapy. The results of this recently developed form of somatotherapy are promising but final conclusions cannot be drawn.

ELECTROCOMA. The induction of coma by electric current differs from electronarcosis in that it uses a different form of electric current and apparently causes less damage to the brain. A very weak electric current of complex phase structure (3 to 10 milliamperes) induces a series of mildly clonic movements. This current is applied for a period of time which averages 12 minutes. The patient is mentally clear as soon as the treatment is terminated, and there is no known memory impairment. This is the most recent adaptation of electrical techniques in the treatment of mental patients and shows promise in the treatment of paranoid delusional states.

Surgical Methods. Based on observations of personality changes consequent to brain injuries and operations for removal of frontal lobe tumors, E. MONIZ, a Portuguese neuropsychiatrist, in 1936 used brain surgery to treat functionally psychotic patients. Since then, research using psychosurgical techniques on a wide variety of mental illnesses has been reported with mixed results. After an enthusiastic reception in the early years of its use, a much more cautious attitude toward psychosurgery has developed. Almost all therapists today consider psychosurgery as a possibility only after all other forms of therapy have been carefully used without result and after a sufficient lapse of time. Since the brain damage is irreversible, there will always be some loss of function. In general, patients who have undergone psychosurgery show any or all of the following characteristics: emotional flatness, poor judgment, loss of spontaneity, aggressiveness, impaired attention and concentration, and a general loss of the finer sensibilities. In current practice, psychosurgery is used principally for the alleviation of intractable pain. A discussion of the various methods of psychosurgery follows.

PREFRONTAL LOBOTOMY. Moniz's operation, prefrontal lobotomy, consisted of severing the neural pathways between the frontal lobes and the thalamus by means of an instrument introduced through holes cut on either side of the skull. Since Moniz's work several variations of surgical techniques have been introduced.

TRANSORBITAL LOBOTOMY. Transorbital lobotomy, introduced by WALTER FREEMAN (1895–   ), and JAMES W. WATTS (1904–   ), the outstanding exponents of psychosurgery in the United States, varies from the prefrontal lobotomy in its procedure of entering the brain. In this method, a sharp, slender instrument is inserted between the eye ball and the eye lid through the transorbital bone into the brain.

TOPECTOMY. Another variation of the prefrontal lobotomy, is the topectomy, developed by LAWRENCE POOLE, which consists of opening the skull and excising or removing specific areas of the frontal cortex.

THALAMOTOMY. In another procedure, thalamotomy, destruction of brain tissue is accomplished by a searing electric current introduced by an electric needle passed through the skull opening.

ULTRASONIC IRRADIATION. A recently developed technique is the use of ultrasonic irradiation, in which high frequency sound waves are used to destroy specific subcortical tissue.

The widespread study of postoperative behavior following the aforementioned methods of psychosurgery has led to an increased understanding of the function of the frontal lobes in emotion and judgment.

THERAPEUTIC ADJUNCTS

Supplementary to the basic psychological and medical treatments is a variety of resources upon which the therapist can draw to aid the patient in his progress toward mental health. Some of the more frequently used aids are: physical therapy, occupational therapy, recreational therapy, bibliotherapy, music therapy, milieu therapy, and environmental therapy.

Physical Therapy. Physical therapy is the use of various procedures such as heat, massage, and exercise. Continuous baths and sprays, once used widely (and called "hydrotherapy") are now used less frequently in the therapeutic program of most mental hospitals.

Occupational Therapy. Occupational therapy is the involvement of the patient in such manual activities as weaving, woodworking, leatherwork and beadwork, ceramics, and other arts and crafts. Such activities are beneficial in providing physical exercise as well as a wholesome use of time during the period of hospitalization. A more basic aim of occupational therapy is to draw the patient out of himself and give him an opportunity for gradual renewal of his contact with reality. In well-integrated treatment programs, occupational activities are used in psychodiagnosis and serve as a measure of progress in treatment.

Recreational Therapy. Recreational therapy employs such activities as: athletic events, dances, parties, entertainments, and plays. Such measures are of value in providing a normal social life during hospitalization and in preparing the individual for a return to society on his release. In many cases, teaching the patient to participate in social gatherings constitutes an important phase of his rehabilitation.

Bibliotherapy. Bibliotherapy is a program of directed readings designed to enhance the patient's understanding of himself, to provide a broader range of emotional experience, and to widen his cultural horizons. Such reading is usually under the general direction of the patient's therapist.

Music Therapy. Music therapy is a means of providing a pleasant environmental setting for the mentally ill. The therapeutic aspect of music has been recognized since the days of the ancient Greeks. Modern research suggests the possibility of many more specific applications of the various musical forms in the treatment of mental illness. The tranquilizing effects of quiet music on excited patients and, conversely, the energizing effects of military music and strong rhythms on depressed patients have been recognized. The relationship between musical patterns and specific mental illnesses is being studied, but has not yet been documented.

Milieu Therapy. Also known as "total push" therapy, milieu therapy is an attempt to integrate all of the patient's daily activities with the therapeutic process. This is achieved by enlisting the co-operation and participation of all staff personnel—professional and nonprofessional. The planning of all the activities of the patient can be accomplished only in an institutional setting.

Environmental (Social) Therapy. Environmental or social therapy is a program which attempts to modify the patient's home and work environment, and thus reduce stress. This may be done through such means as involving relatives in therapy, arranging for more adequate living facilities, working toward material rehabilitation, and providing opportunities for healthy social experiences. Environmental therapy is conducted by the social service department.

THE THERAPEUTIC PROCESS: SOME CONCLUSIONS

In its early history, abnormal psychology was dominated by problems of diagnosis and classification. Only in the past fifty years has any systematic attempt at treatment been offered. While Freud and his associates and disciples had been experimenting in psychotherapy in the early 1900's, not until the last two decades has a semblance of scientific validity been provided for these methods. The principal somatotherapies began their history in the 1930's. Prior to that time, little more than custodial care was available for the vast numbers of the mentally ill. It is understandable, therefore, that there are so many unresolved problems in treating mental disease. Among these problems are: (1) the inability to provide a complete rationale for the various forms of somatotherapy, (2) the uncertainty of criteria indicating the patient's potential response to the various forms of therapy, (3) the inability to select with assurance the specific form of treatment for a particular mental disorder, and (4) the still evolving relationships among the disciplines involved in the therapeutic process.

On the other hand, progress is being made in attacking these problems. Research is being directed toward the establishment of adequate prognostic criteria. The extreme theoretical positions of various schools of therapy are being modified and a common core of therapeutic practice is emerging. The increasing awareness of the wisdom of early treatment for the mentally disturbed in the community (through outpatient clinics and private practitioners) is a hopeful sign in the direction of solving the complex problem of mental illness.

20

MENTAL HYGIENE

The treatment of mental illness is usually a long, arduous, and costly task, constituting a heavy burden on the public health resources of the community, state, and nation. As a consequence, consistent, well-planned efforts to maintain mental health and prevent mental breakdown must be recognized as an investment of considerable personal, social, and economic value. Efforts in this direction were first formally termed "mental hygiene" by Adolf Meyer and Clifford Beers and promoted by the formation in 1909 of the National Committee for Mental Hygiene. Later, state governments established separate departments of mental hygiene or mental health, and in more recent years the federal government has set up, as a part of the National Institutes of Health, an Institute for Mental Health.

Mental hygiene, as defined by the American Psychiatric Association, consists of "measures to reduce the incidence of mental illness through prevention and early treatment, and to promote mental health." Mental hygiene activities fall into two broad categories, namely, those designed to *prevent the development of mental illness or facilitate its early recognition,* and those designed to *restore to mental health the emotionally or mentally disturbed.* In the furtherance of the first of these activities, attention is directed particularly toward education of the public; the second type of activities strives for recruitment and training of personnel, improvement and expansion of treatment facilities, and promotion of essential research.

A SOUND PROGRAM OF MENTAL HYGIENE

A sound program designed to promote wholesome mental adjustment and prevent mental breakdown should include: (1) wide-ranging efforts at public education, (2) development of carefully set up procedures for the recognition of early symptoms of mental disturbance and their treatment, and (3) promotion of community facilities to assist the individual in developing his powers of creative self-expression and in making effective and enjoyable use of his leisure time.

Public Education. An educational program for mental hygiene should have two primary objectives: to correct the many widespread misconceptions about mental illness and to furnish mental hygiene facts for families. In the pursuit of such a program, extensive use should be made of training programs in schools, community organizations, and industry, and of education through the mass media of television and radio, magazines, and newspapers.

CORRECTION OF MISCONCEPTIONS. Unfortunately, mental illness has been stigmatized in the lay mind and has become enshrouded in many popular misconceptions. The strongest obstacle to public education in matters of mental health has been the persistence of attitudes of fear, revulsion, and mystery toward the subject. These attitudes, arising out of several misconceptions of the nature of mental disorder, are the most significant factors that deter people from seeking treatment for the early symptoms of mental illness. It is also these attitudes which force physicians to use the euphemistic term "nerves" and "nervous breakdown" even when they are discussing the condition of a patently emotionally disturbed patient with the patient himself or his family. Few people will reject the suggestion that they undergo a routine physical examination, but the mere mention that consultation with a psychiatrist or psychologist would be of benefit is too often cause for a flare of temper, the expression of resentment, or a self-righteous statement that "there is nothing wrong with my mind." Some of the more common misconceptions which continue to hamper efforts at an effective mental hygiene program include the following:

1. *"Mental illness is inherited."* Mental illness is not passed from parent to child as are many physical characteristics. Recent evidence has indicated that there may be a genetic or constitutional factor which renders some people more vulnerable to certain stresses, the reaction to which may take the form of mental illness. Kallmann's table, seen on page 158, shows that the development of mental illness from a given hereditary pattern is not inevitable.

2. *"Mental illness is incurable."* Under the best treatment conditions, as many as 80 per cent of those admitted for mental hospital care are returned to the community as either "improved" or "cured." Under merely routine hospital conditions, partial or complete recovery occurs in 40 per cent of patients and, with advances being made

in the various therapeutic areas, this picture is progressively improving.

3. *"Mental illness attacks without warning."* Mental illness never occurs suddenly in an otherwise healthy individual, and no single life crisis is ever the complete and only cause of mental breakdown. The seeds of mental disorder are usually present long before the illness becomes manifest to a trained observer, who is then in a position to take appropriate corrective measures. Dramatic incidents, such as the death of a loved one or sudden economic reverses, which may be the occasion for the onset of obvious symptoms of mental illness, are precipitating factors rather than direct causes.

4. *"Mental illness is a disgrace."* Mental illness is the result of natural causes, just as other human illnesses. No stigma should be attached to a disorder of the mind, nor should it be considered a disgrace to the family name, nor should the individual patient be blamed for becoming mentally disturbed. Such unfortunate attitudes are probably a residue of former fanciful ideas which attributed the cause of mental illness to evil spirits, demons, or evil behavior.

5. *"Mental illness is a single disease."* Mental illness is not a single disease entity. There are many and varied forms of mental disorder. There is no more convincing evidence of this than the official classification (see Appendix).

6. *"Sex is the cause of all mental illness."* The occurrence of abnormal sexual behavior is usually a symptom rather than the cause of deep-lying and complex personality maladjustment. Sex is a strong and persistent human drive, and its frustration can be a source of intense conflict and stress. The misconception that sex is the basis of all mental illness is a generalization derived from the observation of the sexual behavior of some disturbed patients. Where sexual activity *is* causally involved, it is the guilt and anxiety consequent to the behavior, rather than the sexual activity itself, that are the principal causes of the difficulty.

FURNISHING MENTAL HYGIENE FACTS FOR FAMILIES. Throughout this volume, the authors have underscored the influence of the early personal history of the individual in the development of personality and in the causation of mental disorder. It is generally agreed that a proper family atmosphere and satisfactory parent-child relationships are essential for the development of a healthy personality. In the family setting the child learns his worth as a person, evolves a sense of belongingness, and lays the foundation for the attitudes with which he will respond to the world around him in later life. It is, therefore, the responsibility of the family, in particular the parents, to surround the child with a mentally healthy atmosphere, in which he can learn to know and accept reality, feel secure from abnormal fear, and find normal gratification for his basic emotional needs of love and affection.

A sound program of mental health education should embrace all the approaches through which current useful information can be transmitted to parents. Such approaches include lectures and workshops with parent-teacher groups, instructional films, pamphlets, and brochures for distribution by both private and public agencies. The use of such mass media of communication as radio, television, magazines, and newspapers, in trained hands, can do much good.

Recognition and Treatment of Early Symptoms. The axiom "An ounce of prevention is worth a pound of cure" is at least as valid in the field of mental health as elsewhere. Because the hope of cure and the speed with which it is accomplished depend heavily on early treatment, recognition of the beginning signs of mental illness is especially critical. One of the tasks of a mental hygiene program must be the dissemination of information which will assist in the identification of early symptoms. When this kind of information is publicized, it must be phrased in understandable language and in a nonthreatening manner.

SOME EARLY SYMPTOMS OF MENTAL DISTURBANCE. Just as serious physical illness may be manifest through such early symptoms as elevated temperature, cough, or headache, so also may mental illness be preceded by premonitory signs which are noticeable deviations from the individual's normal patterns of behavior. Some of these deviations are: excessive irritability, disturbances in sleep or appetite, unwarranted preoccupation with one's health, persistence of physical symptoms which seemingly cannot be explained on an organic basis, loss of interest in activities or responsibilities that have previously been of concern to the individual, withdrawal tendencies, hypersensitivity in response to criticism, and the expression of exaggerated, unfounded suspicions.

TREATMENT: MENTAL HYGIENE SERVICES. Regardless of the degree of success that is achieved in awakening the public to the need for recognizing the early symptoms of mental illness, there remains the necessity for agencies staffed by specially trained personnel who can offer guidance in solving an individual's or a family's particular problems, be they marital, vocational, or of another nature. Such services can provide assistance in minor adjustment difficulties, and, as the number of people using such facilities increases, the long-range needs for more drastic forms of treatment should diminish. To accomplish such an objective, it is necessary that mental health agencies be provided in more abundant fashion and that a continuous effort be made to inform people about the availability of community mental health resources. Information of this type can be provided through published directories of social agencies, which are frequently referred to by clergy, teachers, doctors, and others who are called upon to advise those in need of help.

Programs for the Effective Use of Leisure Time. The effective and enjoyable use of leisure time and the opportunity for creative expression can be bulwarks against the development of emotional illness. In contemporary society the family is often unable or unwilling to provide adequate resources for such activities or is not aware of the need; and therefore the community must be depended upon to establish such programs.

With the increase in leisure time that has been made possible by technological advances, the significance of leisure time programs has become greater. Thus, the Boy Scout and Girl Scout movements, settlement houses, school recreation programs, church-sponsored recreational groups, industrial athletic activities, and adult education programs all have significant contributions to make to sound mental health. Their mental hygiene value lies in the opportunity they offer for participative or creative activity. It is through this that they can counteract the growing dependency on passive forms of recreation such as television and motion pictures. Unfortunately, only a small percentage of the population of communities in which such programs exist support and participate in them. Further, owing to a frequent lack of over-all community planning and integration there is a loss of maximum benefit.

RESTORATION TO MENTAL HEALTH

The principal facilities for restoring the mentally ill to a state of mental health are: public mental hospitals, private mental hospitals, outpatient psychiatric services, and convalescent centers.

Public Mental Hospitals. Historically, the heaviest burden in the care and treatment of the mentally ill has been carried by the publicly financed hospitals. Recent figures indicate that 97.8 per cent of the hospitalized mentally ill have sought help at a public hospital center. The need to protect the community from disturbed patients and the prohibitive cost of the long-term custodial care formerly necessary for the mentally ill largely account for this fact. The principal public facilities are state hospitals (by far the most widely used facilities); federal hospitals (maintained by the Public Health Service and the Veterans Administration); and municipal hospitals. The last named generally serve as "observation" hospitals, with patients in need of extended care and treatment being passed on to state or federal hospitals.

STATE MENTAL HOSPITALS. About 85 per cent of the hospitalized mentally ill are in state institutions. There is a wide variation in the extent to which the states provide the benefits of adequate treatment; in many areas the institutions serve mainly to protect the community from violent patients and suicidal patients from themselves. While the average cost per day per patient in 1956 was $3.26, the range was $1.84 to $5.51. Until very recently, limited budgets for mental health facilities resulted in inadequate buildings, low salaries, and staff shortages at all levels. For this reason, treatment in state hospitals has long been stigmatized and often subjected to derogatory journalistic treatment. State hospitals have only about 56 per cent of the total number of beds needed to provide patients with good care and few of them meet the standards set up by the American Psychiatric Association. However, vigorous efforts are now under way to obtain adequate budgets and competent personnel so that more effective treatment can be provided. For this reason it can be safely stated that patients being currently admitted to state mental hospitals have a good chance of receiving effective treatment and so can expect an earlier return to society. An encouraging note was heard early in 1958, when one state reported that for the first time in history its resident patient population (1957) was lower than in the previous year. The National Association for Mental Health in 1956 reported that in one state where the expenditure per patient per day rose from under one dollar (!) to almost four dollars in a seven-year period, there was a 700 per cent increase in the number of patients discharged within six months after admission.

FEDERAL MENTAL HOSPITALS. The work of the state hospital is supplemented by hospitals of the United States Public Health Service and the Veterans Administration. Veterans Administration hospitals provide services for approximately 10 per cent of hospitalized mental patients. In the year 1956 there were 60,000 neuropsychiatric patients in Veterans Administration hospitals, with a waiting list of more than 16,000. The daily expenditure per patient in these hospitals in 1956 was nine dollars, which is almost three times the state hospital average. The Veterans Administration mental health program was considerably expanded after World War II to offer psychiatric care and treatment to veterans. Incidental to its own growth, it gave impetus to the entire field of public hospital care.

The United States Public Health Service maintains a total of 2,421 psychiatric beds in general hospitals and the two specialized psychiatric facilities for the care and treatment of narcotic addicts, located in Lexington, Kentucky, and Fort Worth, Texas. Although the Public Health Service cares for only a small number of the total mentally ill population, its influence reaches far beyond this through its high standards of treatment and its intensive training and research programs. It also provides extensive consultation services to community mental health organizations.

MUNICIPAL HOSPITALS. Most large cities maintain psychiatric services in connection with their general hospitals. These serve the purpose of providing emergency care for acutely disturbed patients, observation and preliminary diagnosis, and short-term treatment. The avenue of admission to most state hospitals is through these municipal facilities. The most widely known of these is New York City's Bellevue Hospital.

Private Mental Hospitals. There are about 370 psychiatric hospitals, most of them owned and operated as a private business although under state licensing and control. In addition to these, there are private general hospitals that offer psychiatric care. Generally, private psychiatric hospital care is so costly as to be beyond the means of the vast majority of the mentally ill. Only 2.2 per cent of the hospitalized mentally ill at any given time are in private institutions. However, 23 per cent of all admissions enter such hospitals. This apparent discrepancy is accounted for by a rapid turnover among private hospital patients. The rapid turnover is due to one of several of the following factors: (1) the acute nature of the disorder (e.g., alcoholic states); (2) the higher rate of recovery resulting from earlier and thorough diagnosis, intensive treatment, and favorable staff-patient ratios; and (3) the expense of maintaining a patient in a private hospital for a long period of time.

A small number of private hospitals are given over to the exclusive study and treatment of emotionally disturbed children. These residential treatment centers are exploring new procedures in the overall treatment, education, and understanding of the child. Because of their work, impact on the field of mental hygiene is greater than indicated by their numbers. One of the experimental approaches is the development of a foster home placement program, which features the careful selection of foster parents in terms of the psychological needs of the child. Such placement is usually after an intensive program of treatment at the residential center.

Outpatient Services (Mental Hygiene Clinics). There are more than 2,100 outpatient psychiatric clinics in the United States, varying in patient capacity, quality of services rendered, and types of problems treated. Many of the clinics operate on a part-time basis and their fees are adjusted to the means of the patient. Since 1946, and as a result of the impetus given to psychiatric work after World War II, the number of clinics has increased by 60 per cent.* Many of the clinics are a part of the outpatient department of general hospitals; others are sponsored by family welfare agencies, churches, and universities. The National Mental Health Act of 1946 made it possible for federal and other public funds to be used for local health services. More than 400 clinics are using such funds. An extensive network of psychiatric clinics has been established as part of the Veterans Administration program for psychiatrically disabled veterans. In addition, the United States Public Health Service has aided the movement by making available grants for research, training, and increases in staff. Despite the rapid growth in recent years, the National Committee against Mental Illness estimated in 1957 that the nation still possesses less than 81 per cent of the full-time clinics needed. Almost all mental health clinics have waiting lists involving delays of three months to a year. The outpatient clinic provides treatment for the neurotic adult and child, the milder forms of psychotic reaction, marital and family difficulties, and other behavior problems. Some clinics also provide aftercare for patients discharged from mental hospitals. All clinics are established to provide care only for those unable to afford private psychiatric treatment.

Convalescent Centers. One of the most important phases of treatment is the reintroduction of the hospitalized patient to his

* George S. Stevenson, *Mental Health Planning for Social Action* (New York: McGraw-Hill, 1956), p. 167.

home and to his community. This problem is being solved by the development of various convalescent centers, which soften the impact of the patient's return to the community and also maintain therapeutic support. At this time convalescent centers are few in number and largely experimental in nature. The direction of their development points to the establishment of three kinds of facilities: day-night hospitals, half way houses, and rehabilitation centers. The *day-night hospital* provides an opportunity for the patient to work during the day and return to the haven of the hospital in the evening, or to spend his days in the therapeutic atmosphere of the hospital while returning to his family group at night. The *half way house* is a nonmedical resource designed to provide sheltered leisure time and social activity for the recently hospitalized mental patient. The Fountain House of New York City is an example of this type of convalescent center. The *rehabilitation center* focuses largely upon preparing the individual for useful employment through a program of aptitude testing and vocational training.

ADMISSION PROCEDURES

Provisions for admitting a patient to a mental hospital vary widely according to state laws. There are three basic methods of admission: voluntary admission, medical certification, and legal commitment.

Voluntary Admission. The most desirable form of admission is the one in which the patient himself is aware of his need for treatment and accepts hospitalization. He is required to sign a request for admission and in some states must agree to stay a stipulated minimum length of time.

Medical Certification. When a patient is too ill to recognize his need for hospitalization or refuses to accept it, medical certification may be necessary in order to gain his admission. In this procedure, two physicians, who need not be psychiatrists, certify that they have recently examined the patient and that he is in need of hospitalization.

Legal Commitment. Under some circumstances or as required in some states, it may be necessary to arrange that a judge, after brief examination of the patient, legally commit him to a mental hospital. In some states, at the judge's discretion, or at the request of the patient, his family, or friends, a jury trial may be held to determine his sanity and the consequent need for commitment. The procedure of commitment becomes complex since both legal and medical concepts are involved. On the one hand, the legal procedures are designed to protect the community against a potentially dangerous patient; on the other hand, they are designed to protect the individual against the loss of his basic rights by forcible commitment. The patient's admission may be further complicated by ambivalent attitudes of his relatives toward hospitalization.

ORGANIZED MENTAL HYGIENE ACTIVITIES

Beginning with the formation of the National Committee for Mental Hygiene in 1909 there has been a steady, albeit slow increase and spread of formally organized efforts to promote mental health. The committee attained national status in 1919 and in 1930 sponsored the first International Congress of Mental Health (in Washington, D.C.). World War II dramatized the problems of the mentally ill and highlighted the need for further organized attack on the problem of mental illness.

International Organizations. The three principal international organizations in the field of mental hygiene are the World Health Organization (WHO), the United Nations Educational, Scientific and Cultural Organization (UNESCO), and the World Federation for Mental Health (WFMH).

WORLD HEALTH ORGANIZATION (WHO). This organization functions as a clearing house for mental health information and practices to all member states of the United Nations. Studies have been conducted under its auspices on alcoholism, community mental hygiene facilities, mental hospital accommodations, treatment of crime and delinquency, child adoption, and psychiatric legislation. The organization's emphasis is on preventing mental illness.

UNITED NATIONS EDUCATIONAL, SCIENTIFIC AND CULTURAL ORGANIZATION (UNESCO). This is an agency of the United Nations whose function is to stimulate an intercultural exchange of information in many areas. Its social science department has conducted a number of outstanding studies in international tensions and the causes of war, which have implications for mental health practice.

WORLD FEDERATION FOR MENTAL HEALTH (WFMH). The Federation, set up in 1948, at a joint meeting of the International Committee for Mental Hygiene and the British Association for Mental Health, is a group of nongovernmental mental health agencies. It helps to develop mental health activities of underdeveloped countries and gathers information on mental health throughout the world for the two United Nations organizations. Approximately fifty countries hold membership in this group.

National Organizations in the United States. Extensive organized mental health efforts in the United States were stimulated in 1946 with the passage of the National Mental Health Act. The principal groups functioning in this field are the National Institute for Mental Health (NIMH), the National Association for Mental Health, and the National Committee against Mental Illness.

THE NATIONAL INSTITUTE FOR MENTAL HEALTH (NIMH). The National Mental Health Act of 1946 reorganized the mental health activities of the government and set up NIMH as an agency of the United States Public Health Service. This institute sets training standards, provides grants for research, and aids in the development of community mental health programs. It functions through a number of regional mental health authorities. It compiles statistics on the incidence of mental illness, maintains a mental health study center for evaluating treatment methods and procedures, and periodically publishes educational and research reports.

NATIONAL ASSOCIATION FOR MENTAL HEALTH. This organization resulted from the merger of the National Committee for Mental Hygiene, the National Mental Health Foundation, and the Psychiatric Foundation. It is a private nonprofit organization which sponsors research, improvement of standards in training, and the development of mental health facilities. With the National Institute it co-sponsors Mental Health Week annually.

NATIONAL COMMITTEE AGAINST MENTAL ILLNESS. At a national governor's conference on mental health in 1954, a ten point "Bill of Rights" for the mentally ill was adopted. To promote these principles through a program of public education and to exchange information on mental health problems, the National Committee against Mental Illness (formerly National Mental Health Committee) was organized. Its emphasis is on research and the encouragement of early treatment.

State and Community Activities. State mental hygiene programs, usually administered by the Department of Mental Hygiene, vary greatly in quality and scope. In addition to maintaining the state hospital programs, state mental health leaders, with the assistance of federal funds, are promoting the development of mental hygiene clinics and local mental health education programs. State mental health activities are supplemented by efforts of many private agencies at the community level.

MENTAL HEALTH PERSONNEL

A major mental hygiene problem today is that of maintaining adequate numbers of competently trained personnel to work in the field. The principal categories of mental health personnel are psychiatrists, psychologists, social workers, psychiatric nurses, occupational and recreational therapists, psychiatric aides, and volunteer workers.

Psychiatrists. In 1956 there were 9,295 psychiatrists enrolled as members of the American Psychiatric Association, and of this number 2,700 were listed as administrators, superintendents, or commissioners. The Council of State Governments in 1953 estimated a shortage of 10,000 to 20,000 additional psychiatrists. To meet the personnel requirements set by the American Psychiatric Association, it is estimated that almost 4,000 psychiatrists are needed in our state mental hospitals alone.

Psychologists. There are about 15,000 members in the American Psychological Association, and of this number approximately 2,000 are trained as clinical psychologists. It is estimated that about 10,000 more are needed. To meet the minimum standards of the American Psychiatric Association, about 1,500 psychologists are needed for the state hospital system alone.

Psychiatric Social Workers. Although there were more than 1,300 psychiatric social workers employed in state hospitals in 1955, it is estimated that at least 2,500 more were needed. These figures do not take into account the personnel shortages in outpatient clinics and private agencies.

Psychiatric Nurses. The shortage of graduate nurses in psychiatric hospitals ranks among the most acute of personnel problems. Of more than 25,000 needed, there are only about 6,200 actively employed in state mental hospitals.

Psychiatric Aides. Minimum requirements call for an increase of 37 per cent more in the number of competently trained psychiatric aides.

Other Personnel. Comparable shortages exist in the numbers of other types of personnel, such as occupational therapists, recreational therapists, and volunteer workers.

Efforts to meet these personnel needs include the grant-in-aid program of the National Institute for Mental Health, local state government programs, and educational programs designed to attract high calibre personnel into this field of professional service.

RECENT DEVELOPMENTS

In 1961, a report was released by the Joint Commission on Mental Illness and Health. This group, comprised of representatives from 38 professional and government agencies, had been commissioned by Congress in 1955 to study federal, state, and local programs of care and research in the field of mental illness. The report revealed that four-fifths of the nation's state mental hospitals still provided only custodial care rather than actual treatment for their patients. Drastic reforms and changes were recommended. Some of the most important recommendations are the following:

1. That a widespread program of public education be implemented in order to erase misconceptions, dissolve prejudices, and provide an attitude of understanding toward the emotionally or mentally ill.

2. That the amounts spent by all levels of government for mental health services be doubled in the next five years and tripled in the next ten years. This would bring the total expenditures to three billion dollars a year by the end of this period.

3. That institutions for the mentally ill be reduced to smaller units with intensive treatment programs. These would be supplemented by community clinics, psychiatric care programs, and emergency clinics in general hospitals. Existing hospitals with more than 1,000 beds should be converted to institutions for the care of all chronic diseases, including psychiatric illness.

4. That the entrance of qualified personnel into the mental health fields be encouraged by scholarships, loans, and other economic incentives.

5. That basic research in the area of mental illness be increased.

6. That the concept of treatment be redefined to include the paramedical disciplines such as clinical psychology and psychiatric social work, as well as a number of the nonmedical disciplines concerned with the care of the mentally ill.

APPENDIX

OFFICIAL CLASSIFICATION OF THE AMERICAN PSYCHIATRIC ASSOCIATION

NOTE TO THE READER ON THE CLASSIFICATION
IN THIS OUTLINE

In general the authors of this Outline have followed the official APA classification; where APA terms differ from traditionally used terms, both the old and the new terms are shown in chapter titles and section headings. Sequence of chapters in this Outline moves, essentially, from the less serious to the more serious disorders. Chapter 6 discusses transient situational personality disorders, which are largely reactions to immediate situations and which have few if any lasting effects. Chapter 7, in discussing psychosomatic disorders (psychophysiologic disorders), deals with more lasting reactions in which the personality upset is largely limited to some physical malfunctioning. A broader type of pathological reaction, the psychoneurotic reaction, is described in Chapter 8. Personality disorders, traditionally called "character" disorders, are examined in Chapter 9; these disorders grow out of a basic weakness in the development of the personality structure, a situation which is not encountered in the psychoneuroses. Special symptom reactions, particularly those occurring in childhood, are taken up in Chapter 10. The more serious and debilitating disorders are discussed in Chapters 11 through 16. (The principal departure from the APA classification occurs in the arrangement of the "acute and chronic brain disorders." The organic psychoses are grouped together in Chapter 14. Epilepsy and related seizure disorders are given special attention in Chapter 15. Finally, mental deficiency, a topic which has merited much psychological effort over the years, is presented in Chapter 16.)

DISORDERS CAUSED BY OR ASSOCIATED WITH IMPAIRMENT OF BRAIN TISSUE FUNCTION

Acute Brain Disorders *

Disorders Due to or Associated with:

Infection

    Acute brain syndrome associated with intracranial infection

    Acute brain syndrome associated with systemic infection

Intoxication

    Acute brain syndrome, drug or poison intoxication

    Acute brain syndrome, alcohol intoxication

      Acute hallucinosis

      Delirium tremens

Trauma

    Acute brain syndrome associated with trauma

Circulatory Disturbance

    Acute brain syndrome associated with circulatory disturbance

Innervation or Psychic Control

    Acute brain syndrome associated with convulsive disorders

Disturbances of Metabolism, Growth, or Nutrition

    Acute brain syndrome associated with metabolic disturbance

New Growth

    Acute brain syndrome associated with disease of unknown or uncertain cause

Unknown or Uncertain Cause with the Functional Reaction Alone Manifest

    Acute brain syndrome of unknown cause

Chronic Brain Disorders

Disorders Due to or Associated with:

Prenatal (Constitutional) Influence

    Chronic brain syndrome associated with congenital cranial anomaly

---

* Many disorders described under this heading and under "Chronic Brain Disorders" have traditionally been subsumed under the heading "organic psychoses" and described specifically as "psychosis associated with (the particular condition supposedly giving rise to it)." The traditional usage has been followed in this book (see especially Chapter 14, Organic Psychoses).

DISORDERS CAUSED BY OR ASSOCIATED WITH IMPAIRMENT OF BRAIN TISSUE FUNCTION (CONTINUED)

Chronic brain syndrome associated with congenital paraplegia

Chronic brain syndrome associated with mongolism

Chronic brain syndrome due to prenatal maternal infectious disease

Infection

Chronic brain syndrome associated with central nervous system syphilis

Meningoencephalitic

Meningovascular

Other central nervous system syphilis

Chronic brain syndrome associated with intracranial infection other than syphilis

Intoxication

Chronic brain syndrome associated with intoxication

Chronic brain syndrome, drug or poison intoxication

Chronic brain syndrome, alcohol intoxication

Trauma

Chronic brain syndrome associated with birth trauma

Chronic brain syndrome associated with brain trauma

Chronic brain syndrome, brain trauma, gross force

Chronic brain syndrome following brain operation

Chronic brain syndrome following electrical brain trauma

Chronic brain syndrome following irradiational trauma

Circulatory Disturbance

Chronic brain syndrome associated with cerebral arteriosclerosis

Chronic brain syndrome associated with circulatory disturbance other than cerebral arteriosclerosis

Disturbances of Innervation or of Psychic Control

Chronic brain syndrome associated with convulsive disorder

Disturbances of Metabolism, Growth, or Nutrition

Chronic brain syndrome associated with senile brain disease

Chronic brain syndrome associated with other disturbances of metabolism, growth, or nutrition (including presenile and glandular disturbances, also disturbances associated with pellagra, and familial amaurosis)

New Growth

Chronic brain syndrome associated with intracranial neoplasm

DISORDERS CAUSED BY OR ASSOCIATED WITH IMPAIRMENT OF BRAIN TISSUE FUNCTION (CONTINUED)

Disorders Due to or Associated with:
Unknown or Uncertain Causes
  Chronic brain syndrome associated with diseases of unknown or
    uncertain cause including:
    Multiple sclerosis
    Huntington's chorea
    Pick's disease
    Other diseases of a familial or hereditary nature
*Unknown or Uncertain Cause with the Functional Reaction Alone
Manifest*
  Chronic brain syndrome of unknown cause

Mental Deficiency

Disorders Due to or Associated with:
*Unknown or Uncertain Cause with the Functional Reaction Alone
Manifest; Hereditary and Familial Diseases of this Nature*
  Mental deficiency (familial or hereditary)
    Mild
    Moderate
    Severe
Undetermined Cause
  Mental deficiency (idiopathic)
    Mild
    Moderate
    Severe

DISORDERS OF PSYCHOGENIC ORIGIN OR WITHOUT CLEARLY DEFINED PHYSICAL CAUSE OR STRUCTURAL CHANGE IN THE BRAIN

Psychotic Disorders

Disorders Due to or Associated with:
*Disturbance of Metabolism, Growth, Nutrition, or Endocrine
Function*

DISORDERS OF PSYCHOGENIC ORIGIN OR WITHOUT CLEARLY DEFINED PHYSICAL CAUSE OR STRUCTURAL CHANGE IN THE BRAIN (CONTINUED)

Involutional psychotic reaction

Psychogenic Origin or without Clearly Defined Tangible Cause or Structural Change

  Affective reactions

    Manic-depressive reaction, manic type

    Manic-depressive reaction, depressive type

    Manic-depressive reaction, other

    Psychotic depressive reaction

  Schizophrenic reactions

    Schizophrenic reaction, simple type

    Schizophrenic reaction, hebephrenic type

    Schizophrenic reaction, catatonic type

    Schizophrenic reaction, paranoid type

    Schizophrenic reaction, acute undifferentiated type

    Schizophrenic reaction, chronic undifferentiated type

    Schizophrenic reaction, schizo-affective type

    Schizophrenic reaction, childhood type

    Schizophrenic reaction, residual type

  Paranoid reactions

    Paranoia

    Paranoid states

  Psychotic reaction without clearly defined structural change, other than above

Psychophysiologic Autonomic and Visceral Disorders

Disorders Due to or Associated with:

Disturbance of Innervation or Psychic Control

  Psychophysiologic skin reaction

  Psychophysiologic musculoskeletal reaction

  Psychophysiologic respiratory reaction

  Psychophysiologic cardiovascular reaction

  Psychophysiologic hemic and lymphatic reaction

  Psychophysiologic gastrointestinal reaction

  Psychophysiologic genitourinary reaction

DISORDERS OF PSYCHOGENIC ORIGIN OR WITHOUT CLEARLY DEFINED PHYSICAL CAUSE OR STRUCTURAL CHANGE IN THE BRAIN (CONTINUED)

Psychophysiologic endocrine reaction
Psychophysiologic nervous system reaction
Psychophysiologic reaction of organs of special sense

Psychoneurotic Disorders

Disorders Due to or Associated with:
Psychogenic Origin or without Clearly Defined Tangible Cause or Structural Change
Psychoneurotic reaction
    Anxiety reaction
    Dissociative reaction
    Conversion reaction
    Phobic reaction
    Obsessive-compulsive reaction
    Depressive reaction
    Psychoneurotic reaction, other

Personality Disorders

Disorders Due to or Associated with:
Psychogenic Origin or without Clearly Defined Tangible Cause or Structural Change
Personality pattern disturbance
    Inadequate personality
    Schizoid personality
    Cyclothymic personality
    Paranoid personality
Personality trait disturbance
    Emotionally unstable personality
    Passive-aggressive personality
    Compulsive personality
Sociopathic personality disturbance
    Antisocial reaction
    Dyssocial reaction
    Sexual deviation

Addiction
  Alcoholism
  Drug addiction
Special symptom reactions
  Learning disturbance
  Speech disturbance
  Enuresis
  Somnambulism
  Other

DISORDERS OF PSYCHOGENIC ORIGIN OR WITHOUT CLEARLY DEFINED PHYSICAL CAUSE OR STRUCTURAL CHANGE IN THE BRAIN (CONTINUED)

Transient Situational Personality Disorders

Disorders Due to or Associated with:
Transient Situational Personality Disturbance
  Gross stress reaction
  Adult situational reaction
  Adjustment reaction of childhood
    Habit disturbance
    Conduct disturbance
    Neurotic traits
  Adjustment reaction of adolescence
  Adjustment reaction of late life

INDEX